PUNK 45

THE SINGLES COVER ART OF PUNK 1975-80

EDITED BY JON SAVAGE & STUART BAKER

SOUL JAZZ BOOKS

First published in 2013 by Soul Jazz Books, a division of Soul Jazz Records Ltd.

Soul Jazz Records

7 Broadwick Street

London W1F 0DA

England

www.souljazzrecords.co.uk

Design and layout by Adrian Self & F'Kuhnt

©Soul Jazz Books ℗Soul Jazz Books, a division of Soul Jazz Records Ltd. ©Soul Jazz Records 2013

Distributed by Thames & Hudson and D.A.P.

ISBN: 978-0-9572600-0-9

Soul Jazz wish to thank: Craig Kallman, Sean Forbes, Roger Gobell, Martin Kelly, John Marchant, Bill Drummond, Marlene Marder, Klaudia Schifferle, Kleenex, Nicky Stephens, Desperate Bicycles, Mike Stone, Edward Ball , Martin Kelly, Bob Stanley, Linder, TV Personalities, Lee Wood, Alice Cowling, Frank Hendler, Judy Nylon, John Crumpton, David García, Garrote Jordi from Wah-Wah RecordsTosh Ryan, Seymour Stein, Peter Saville, Jamie Reid, Richard H Kirk, Glenn Branca, Dennis Morris, Martin Moscrop, Edwin Pouncey, Martin Mills, Dave Robinson, Richard Hell, Gee Vaucher, Bob Last, Marc Zermati, Paul Robinson, Rob Dalloway, Shend, Michael Zodorozny, John Esplen, Chris Ashford, Ralph Records, David Alan Brown, Dan Catsis, Bob Last, Karen Tate, Jon Dennis, Angela Scott, Bridget and Rudy, Pete Reilly, Mark Garland at Thames and Hudson, Todd Bradway at DAP, Newton, Rufus and Clover, Julie Vermeille, Conny Dickgreber, Neal Birnie, Nicole McKenzie, Jim Cronshaw, Karl Shale, Wayne Gilbert, Abi Clarke, Scott Bethell, Dean Atkins, Shelley Latimer, Steve Platt, Jeyda Bicer, Theo Leanse, Jonathon Burnip, Pierce Smith, Ingmar Van Wijnsberg, Boudewijn van Wijk, Anders Sjolin, Lutz Falldorf, Jeffrey Stothers, Maurizio Morozzo, Danilo Durante, Luciano Cantone, Lena Heidema Sylvain Morton, Andre Calman, Jeremiah Lewis, Matt Fischer, Ernie B, Konstantin, Sandro, Maria Calero, David Binette, Lars Borg, Jorgen Angvik, Jose Santos and Luisa Da Silva.

Jon Savage would like to thank: Karen Tate, Martin Kelly, Bob Stanley, Linder, Gee Vaucher

THE SINGLES COVER ART OF PUNK 1975-80
EDITED BY JON SAVAGE
& STUART BAKER

Essays and Interviews

Caption text written by Stuart Baker. Jamie Reid and Gee Vaucher interviews by Jon Savage.
All other interviews by Stuart Baker

INTRODUCTION

Jon Savage

THE DOUBLE NUMBER seems to concentrate minds and hearts. Like 1944 (the year that The Teenager was invented), 1955 (the breakthrough of rock 'n' roll) or 1966 (the high 60s' peak), there was always something mystical about 1977. Always attuned to soundbites, The Clash apotheosised the double seven as a time of extremism, random violence and cultural revolution: 'Danger, stranger: you'd better paint your face / No Elvis, Beatles or Rolling Stones in 1977!'

Even more explicitly, Culture recorded 'Two Sevens Clash', with its mystical invocation of a year when 'past injustices would be avenged'. The key moment would be 7 July 1977, the quadruple seven apocalypse predicted by Marcus Garvey. Early that year, a talkover version was released, 'Prophecy Reveal' by Bo Jangles: 'So you see that Marcus Mosiah Garvey's words must never be despised, and I hope Babylon the wicked will now realise, there will be brimstone and lightning and thunder.'

On the first of January, The Clash played The Roxy club in Covent Garden, central London. Joe Strummer wore an old white shirt with a huge '1977' painted on the front. The countdown was on. This would be the year of punk, with its own notions of revolution and apocalypse. At the end of The Clash song, Strummer counted down the next few years from 1977 ('Sod the Jubilee') right down to the nightmare of 1984: 'Here come the police.' He was half right: there was Orgreave. But no Big Brother, yet.

Punk was from the off a self-starter culture, born out of scarcity and honed with a laser-like focus. It was based on amphetamine logic and encoded an extraordinary acceleration that threw off the uncommitted and allowed it to make an extraordinary impact in a very short time. 'My week beats your year,' Lou Reed had written in the liner notes to Metal Machine Music, and punk's cropped, hostile aesthetic took a while for the music industry to assimilate.

Speed was of the essence, both in musical tempo and the tempo of life. Punk was very good at data-processing and then shredding: a response to the proliferation of the media which, by the last quarter of the 20th century, was already in shape to become the dominant industry. It was also a response to pop history: it was well over 30 years since the beginning of commercialised youth culture, and it was time to put that accumulation of history through the mincer.

Punk was a kind of living collage, both in fashion and music. Except that this collage was not a stylistic game: it was allied to a furious forward motion that, ultimately, was an end in itself. Anything other than the dreadful stasis of consensus politics and trickled-down, sub hippie stylings. But in the short term, it was a catalyst for change, as a new generation of musicians, artists, writers, and designers learned how to do it - not by theory or education, but through praxis: doing it.

It wasn't just doing it, though; it was doing it for yourself. Punk wasn't all

sweetness and light - there was real nastiness among all the speed jive. Punks might well have worn swastikas, but it was a really stupid thing to do. It would take a concerted political action to eradicate any taint of right-wing extremism, any link-up with the National Front - and that particular struggle deserves a separate, carefully researched volume. In the meantime, you won't find any Nazis in this book.

But the idea of independence may well be the movement's most lasting legacy, as it is applicable over time, place and culture. From 1977 on, after the release of the Buzzcocks' seminal 'Spiral Scratch', young people became attuned to the idea that if you wanted to release a record, to write a fanzine, to design a record sleeve, then you could just go ahead and do it. You didn't need to wait for a publisher or a record company - the means of production were, with a bit of saving and a bit of luck, within your grasp.

'It was easy, it was cheap, go and do it,' sang The Desperate Bicycles on both 'Handlebars' and 'The Medium Was Tedium'; their first two EPs (both released in 1977) encapsulated the new DIY ethic. This was supported by the proliferation of fanzines, of which there were hundreds by the end of 1977, inspired by Mark Perry's Sniffin' Glue, and by the consolidation of the independent record shops that would sell these self-produced magazines and records.

Out of this ferment, the perfect form became clear. It was the seven-inch single: seven inches in diameter, housed in a square, usually pictured sleeve: 7" x 7" in 77. Nothing facilitated more easily the insistent impulse to make your statement immediately, before the opportunity disappeared. You've only got two songs and a few hundred quid? Fine. Nothing encapsulated better punk's speed and compression: '1977' lasted only 102 seconds, yet said more than most albums of the day.

Punks eventually made albums, of course, but they were, with a few exceptions (The Damned, The Saints, Sex Pistols, The Adverts), hit and miss: it was hard to sustain that fury over 40 minutes, and it was hard for groups who'd only recently formed to get the variety and the volume of material to make the extended form listenable. Also, the time lag between recording and release could make the eventual LP seem out of date: this pretty much happened to Never Mind The Bollocks.

So it was all down to the mystic sevens. This book celebrates the punk single, the form that most suited the aesthetic, the medium that delivered the message. It begins in the pre-punk era, with the few precursors who were attempting to create a 70s rock music; continues through the build-up of 1976 and the mania of 1977; and passes through to the extraordinary folk-art that proliferated in the years afterwards, when do-it-yourself became a mantra and the mutations were endless.

It ends around 1981, when the mood began shifting again towards a glossy popular music, with a strong dance-floor influence. After this period, the 12-inch single begins to take centre stage, where it will remain for the following decade or so. The seven-inch begins to take a back seat, and will be further eclipsed in the mid-80s by the advent of digital playback technology, the compact disc. Although it has been revived as a boutique item, the seven-inch is basically an obsolete technology.
This book celebrates its last heyday.

The 45rpm single was first launched by RCA in 1949. Pressed on vinyl, it slowly began to replace the more delicate, shellac-based 10-inch 78rpm format during the mid 1950s, and began to really come into its own in the early 60s. The Beatles' breakthrough in 1963 and the advent of the beat boom was fuelled by the availability of comparatively cheap (7/3d) 45s: The peak year for sales was 1964, after which the seven -inch was slowly overtaken by the 12-inch long-play album.

Of the hundreds of millions sold, most singles were housed in generic company sleeves such as Decca, Parlophone, Columbia and Pye. Picture sleeves were reserved for EPs - the Extended Play format, for the occasional export sale or for very special events: like The Beatles' 1967 double A-side 'Penny Lane'/'Strawberry Fields Forever'. By the later 60s, picture sleeves had become a little more common, but by the early 70s, the quick turnover pop economy of glam meant a return to the company sleeve.

The situation wasn't the same on the continent, where every single routinely came in a picture sleeve - either a generic photo or an entirely new design. From the early 70s, these became prized by collectors; they were showcased in London collectors' shops such as Ted Carroll's Rock On in Camden Town, right by the tube station on Kentish Town Road, or on the Rocks Off stall run by Roger Armstrong and Stan Brennan in the old Soho market on Hanway Street, just off the Tottenham Court Road.

In these shops and their like, crowded with fans and obsessives flicking through the racks and listening obsessively, there is one grassroots origin of punk. As Armstrong remembers: 'We were selling a fair amount of rockabilly, and the blues, of course - the blues punter goes on forever. A bit of 60s soul, there was still a bit of a mod thing around. One of the biggest things was The New York Dolls, Flamin' Groovies, Iggy and the Stooges. Also 60s garage and Small Faces records.'

This pattern was repeated in Paris, where Marc Zermati's Open Market shop in Les Halles sold records by The New York Dolls, The Flamin' Groovies and Kim Fowley. During 1972, Zermati started to release records on his Skydog label: first a couple of bootlegs by Jimi Hendrix and The Velvet Underground; then in 1974, two EPs by street-rock faces The Flamin' Groovies, 'Grease' and 'More Grease' - the latter with a ferocious version of 'Jumping Jack Flash' and an eye-catching picture sleeve.

Quite apart from the discovery of the actual music - a whole range of forgotten, gnostic material from the 1950s ('Brand New Cadillac') right through the mid 60s ('Psychotic Reaction') to the cut-out 1970s (Raw Power), the records that you'd find in these shops were an education in themselves. Often they were foreign pressings, with picture sleeves, and they were a complete statement - a total fusion of image and sound, a world unto itself on 45.

This is displayed in a classic Ray Stevenson pic from the Sex Pistols' first organised session in April 1976. A decidedly young Johnny Rotten - smirking like a naughty schoolboy - is painstakingly applying chewing-gum to deface an image of The Beatles on a seven-inch French EP in a Soho record shop window. Also displayed are an array of Rolling Stones picture sleeves. It's an ambiguous snapshot: to hate, you must once have loved. Punk would adapt what it despised to its own ends.

Around the same time, the first products of the fan/activist economy were coming to fruition. Formed out of Rock On and Rocks Off, Chiswick Records released their first seven-inch in late 1975: The Count Bishops' 'Speedball'. As an EP, this automatically had a picture sleeve; but it was the label's third release that pointed the way forward - The 101'ers 'Keys To Your Heart'. Released in June 1976, this posthumous 45 housed a couple of terrific songs within a sleeve that displayed an image of a blank brick wall.

In the first few months of 1976, there was a trickle of pre-punk/pub rock/street rock 45s with picture sleeves or specially-designed labels. Copies of The Flamin' Groovies' 'You Tore Me Down' began to filter through; this wonderful 45 had been released in late 1974 by Greg Shaw, whose Who Put The Bomp magazine was a must-read during this period. It was followed in June 1976 by a new album, Shake Some Action, on which the Groovies harked back to the pop mania of the mid 1960s.

Island Records released a quick three 45s by young, aggressive pub rockers Eddie and the Hot Rods. 'Wooly Bully', the second, featured a striking picture sleeve with a young man holding a gun to his head. The third was the 'Live At The Marquee' EP, released in August, which featured sped up versions of ? and the Mysterians' garage classic, '96 Tears', 'Gloria' and '(I Can't Get No) Satisfaction', with a cool picture sleeve. It made the top 50.

During the summer of 1976, the pace began to quicken. The release of the first Ramones album in April transformed British rock music; if there is one

single influence on the sound of British Punk, this is it. Sire released the opening track, 'Blitzkreig Bop', as a 45 in June. It came with a picture sleeve, designed by John Holmstrom of Punk magazine, that took live photos of the group and treated the lyrics - an exhortation to movement and action - as a comic strip narrative.

Chiswick's innovations - derived from their intimate knowledge of the fan market - were quickly imitated by another new independent label, Stiff Records, formed in mid 1976 by Dave Robinson and Jake Riviera. Their first single, Nick Lowe's 'So It Goes', was housed in a detailed generic bag - designed by the wonderful Barney Bubbles - that was covered in slogans: 'TODAY'S SOUND TODAY', 'IF IT MEANS EVERYTHING TO EVERYONE … IT MUST BE A STIFF'.

Three months later, Stiff released the first single to come out of British punk: the Damned's 'New Rose'. Naturally, it came with a picture sleeve - a grainy black and white picture of the group. It was followed by the first Sex Pistols 45, 'Anarchy In the UK', early copies of which came in a stark, pure black sleeve designed by Jamie Reid. A few weeks later came the first UK release of the Saints' primal 'I'm Stranded', again with a black and white photo of the group looking suitably threatening.

As punk exploded in the mass media - thanks to the Bill Grundy incident - the format of choice and the graphic style was becoming set; the 45rpm single, accompanied by grainy black and white imagery. Punk presented itself as a stark choice. It was flagrantly divisive and dismissive of the uncommitted: 'I wanna destroy the passer-by'. It was an aesthetic that stripped everything back to the basics; minimal choice of colours - binary black and white - and elemental, accelerated music.

January 1977 saw the issue of Buzzcocks' 'Spiral Scratch', the first truly independent punk seven inch. As guitarist and writer Pete Shelley recalls, 'we had to borrow the money. It was £500 - my dad got a couple of hundred from the Friendly Society, and some friends of Richard (Boon) and Howard (Devoto) and we had this artefact. We didn't think anything else would happen, it was fun doing it. It was a memento. It was early days, there was no record company interest or anything like that.

We had a thousand done, and we checked each and every one of them for scratches and stuff. We rejected about 25. The day they arrived we bought two bottles of Spanish red wine, and drank a toast to it, and the toast was that we'd sell half of them, so we'd get the money back. With a few phone calls to Rough Trade, in four days, we got all of them off our hands.'

As manager Richard Boon remembers, 'the Buzzcocks phenomenon was desperately unskilled with no industry experience at all, and no resources, no way of dealing with the industry, no-one was really sure that this was going to become a career base, it just seemed worth documenting the activity, perhaps as the end result, perhaps the only result. There was also a feeling amongst the group and myself that this could illustrate part of the do-it-yourself, xerox/cultural polemic that had been generated'. Boon designed the EP's picture sleeve - a snapshot of the four Buzzcocks in Manchester's Piccadilly Gardens - which would prove almost as influential as the music inside. 'I took the picture with a polaroid, which was a joke. A very Walter Benjamin, art-in-the-age-of-mechanical-reproduction sort of joke. Because any kind of material has to go through the same stages of printed reproduction, but it was also a joke on the fact that it was done, it was instant replay.'

In the early part of 1977, Punk or its facsimile was attracting serious record company interest. Early singles by the Stranglers ('Grip', January 1977), Elvis Costello ('Alison', March) and the Boys (the immortal 'I Don't Care', April) were released with grainy b/w picture portraits. The process was carried further by Barney Bubbles with the Adverts' first single, 'One Chord Wonders', which featured a close-up of bassist Gaye Advert blown up to the point where the image was fragmenting into dots.

One of the most influential early punk 45's was the Clash's first single: 'White Riot' (March). It came in a colour sleeve, in primary colours - with the group logo picked out in day-glo pink - and was packed with information; the words stencilled and painted on the clothes in the group shot by Caroline Coon – 'heavy manners', 'Sten Guns In Knightsbridge', '1977' - and the collage on the back, which featured tower blocks, policemen, and a quote from the 1964 pulp paperback Generation X.

In late May 1977, the Sex Pistols finally released their anti-Jubilee anthem, 'God Save The Queen', after a whole tangle of obstacles. First the CBS pressing plant refused to press the vinyl record, because of its content. Secondly, the platemakers refused to print the sleeve designed by Jamie Reid. This took an old Cecil Beaton photo of the Queen and tore out the image around the eyes and the mouth. In the gap read the legend, in ransom-note lettering: GOD SAVE THE QUEEN SEX PISTOLS.

Despite a cross-media campaign that included 3,000 streamers and 6,000 stickers, 'God Save The Queen' was very difficult to promote. It was effectively banned right across the BBC - although John Peel played it twice - and all commercial media, including TV and radio. It was also banned from sale in Woolworth's, Boots and W.H.Smith - all key record outlets during that period. It still made number two in the charts, and - thanks to music industry connivance - was kept off the top spot.

The banning of 'God Save The Queen' sealed Punk's outlaw status at the same time as its success illustrated its commercial viability. The Sex Pistols were an international news phenomenon, the kind of publicity you could not buy. It also highlighted the importance of the youth media - the four weekly music papers, who gave the record and the Sex Pistols blanket coverage - and also the country-wide network of independent record shops, which were all-too-often the only place you could buy the record.

With much of the media closed off to the Sex Pistols, their record sleeves became all-important, as a way of disseminating an attitude. Reid's design for 'God Save The Queen' is simple but complex, transmitting a whole range of ideas in an immediately accessible form. Are we not all held to ransom by the Royal Family? In the lack of any video - one was filmed but, again, banned right across the board - the sleeve took up the slack. No band picture, no celebrity image, but instead an idea.

Even as it became the latest youth cult fad, punk in general was also shut out from much of the mainstream media. There were no pop pages in the broadsheets, almost no pop videos, and the tabloids were stuck in their shock horror mode. So in the lack of going to a concert or reading the music press, you got your information about a punk group from the seven-inch by seven-inch record sleeve - which by now, had become an integral part of the package.

After 'God Save The Queen' it was open season. Any punk group that moved was signed. The basic templates of punk design thus far - ransom note lettering, torn paper, Xerox culture, urbanist scenes, and photomontage among others - were enthusiastically taken up by the major labels. Many of these products were marked by a certain glossiness - thanks to increased budgets - and also a reliance on what John Cooper Clarke pungently called 'Gimmix'; limited editions, deliberate mistakes etc.

Stiff Records had paved the way earlier in the year, with the release of the first Damned album. The first few hundred copies of Damned, Damned ,Damned featured a picture of Eddie and the Hot Rods - all assuming 'Rat' postures in honour of drummer Rat Scabies - placed where a photo of the Damned should have been. An 'erratum' slip apologised for the 'inconvenience caused' and promised that 'the correct picture will be substituted on future copies'.

When EMI subsidiary Harvest Records issued the Saints' 'This Perfect Day' - a thundering juggernaut of nihilism - in July 1977, the 12-inch version had a similar notice: 'due to an administrative error, this limited pressing of the Saints' 'This Perfect Day' contains a third, additional title not available on the normal 7-inch pressing. The additional title, 'Do The Robot', has consequently been withdrawn from future release consideration and will now only be available on this 12-inch pressing'.

The fan/ activist culture that had nurtured punk's beginnings now informed a feeding frenzy of consumer inducements - free singles, deliberate mis-pressings etc. As Roger Armstrong explains, 'With the 60s garage period, there were certain records that fetched high money 'cos they were on red vinyl or spotted vinyl or whatever. Punk took that to extremes, records coming out in five different colours, and collectors would buy every single one. It was the first really instant collectors' scene'.

From the summer of 1977, coloured vinyl and multi-edition sleeves augmented the limited edition ploy. Knowing trickery became part of the sales pitch. A very good example can be seen in the first Jet Bronx and the Forbidden seven-inch, which slid into the Top 50 at the end of 1977. A warning on the front of the sleeve proclaimed, 'if you are not among the first 15,000 purchasers of this record you will have to be content with crummy black vinyl instead of terrific red vinyl'.

Major label punk releases tended to follow a tried and tested format. Punk had become a genre, and the signifiers of that genre were: surly band photos, usually in black and white, alternating with live shots (the Saints' '1-2-3-4!'); urban backdrops, whether streets (the Rude Kids' 'Raggare Is A Bunch of Motherfuckers'), brick walls (Tom Robinson Band 'Up Against The Wall' EP), derelict sites (the flip of the Adverts' 'One Chord Wonders') or high rise blocks (the Boys 'The First Time').

At the same time, the volume of product allowed for a lot of creativity. Record companies were throwing punk singles at the wall, and it didn't really matter what went on the cover as long as it was eye-catching. Many young designers got a start during this period. Thanks to punk's origins in fan culture, there was a lot of experimentation and even humour - largely thanks to Stiff's influence, best seen in the 'paper bag' cover to the Damned's immortal 'Neat Neat Neat'.

So there were a lot of primary colours and games played with the artwork process itself. A good example is the cover for 999's 'Emergency' - their best single, from January 1978 - a good band photo is printed in pink and solarised green, then covered with the group logo (which featured on all their releases), and then black strips featuring the song titles and the name of each musician picked out in punch-out typography. Like most of their other 45s, their sleeve was designed by George Snow.

The Adverts' 'Gary Gilmore's Eyes' was a big punk hit in late summer 1977, and the sleeve offers another classic piece of high punk design. Here the band's name and song title are picked out in decayed, distressed Letraset, while repeated images of the group - their eyes blacked out like unidentifiable criminals or FBI fugitives - are printed in light green, pink and orange. On the top are overlaid cut snippets of press about the subject of the song, the recently executed murderer Gary Gilmore.

The punk brand leaders were, of course, the Sex Pistols, and they had a distinct visual identity courtesy of Jamie Reid - an art student in the late sixties who was thoroughly steeped both in the radical politics of the era and the possibilities of cheap, do-it-yourself printing. Since the summer of 1976, he had taken over responsibility for the group's visuals - cementing the ransom note graphic as their logo in August 1976 - and developing a series of handbills and concert posters.

After 'God Save The Queen', Reid's sleeves for 'Pretty Vacant' and 'Holidays In The Sun' turned pro-Situ art into mass-market artefacts. On the reverse of the smashed glass frame for 'Pretty Vacant', the design for 'No Fun' included a couple of San Franciscan buses with the words 'boredom' and 'nowhere' in the destination boards. This image was detourned from a 1972 San Franciscan situationist pamphlet about, inter alia, transit problems in the city, 'Point Blank'.

For 'Holidays In The Sun', Reid took a pamphlet from the Belgian travel service and overlaid it with his own captions, taken from the provocative lyric: 'I don't want a holiday in the sun, I wanna go to the new Belsen', or, 'a cheap holiday in other peoples misery'. For the flip, Reid dusted off an old image from the early seventies - an advertising photo of a 'normal' family sitting down for a meal, with overlaid captions that said 'nice image', 'nice people', 'nice gesture'.

In this way the best sleeves contained a perceptual challenge that matched the ferocity of the music within. A perfect fusion was achieved in Buzzcocks' 'Orgasm Addict' (November 1977). This fast furious and witty song - concerning what might be called today 'sex addiction' - was matched by a sleeve that showcased Linder Sterling's brilliant 'iron head' lady montage with a clean but striking yellow backdrop from Malcolm Garrett. It remains the most striking design of the era.

It was also highly influential - see the Vibrators' 'Automatic Lover' (February 1978) for a cheap, cheerful and effective knock-off. Linder remembers 'the pure pleasure of photomontage. It was a moment of glorious liberation to work purely with a blade, glass and glue. Almost a scientific methodology. Sitting in a dark room in Salford, performing cultural post-mortems and then reassembling the corpses badly, like a Mary Shelley trying to breathe life into the monster'.

'For a short period I'd found a perfect mode of articulation. Punk was cutting out the question, 'Can I do this?' I'd always loved magazines and I had two separate piles. One you might call women's magazines, fashion, romance, then a pile of men's mags - cars, DIY, pornography, which again was women, but another side. I wanted to mate the G-Plan kitchens with the pornography, see what strange breed came out. I did it all on a sheet of glass with a scalpel, very clean, like doing a jigsaw. Rising above it all.'

The second single by Ultravox!, 'Young Savage' (May 1977) had a striking montage sleeve. Designed by singer John Foxx and credited to his given name Dennis Leigh, it was composed of finely calibrated paper tears - into an image that was anatomically impossible but that radiated speed, angst and glee. Their subsequent single, 'Rockwrok' (October 1977) pursued the same approach, but with greater sophistication - the two montaged faces dissolving into a disturbing dehumanisation. Another key element was adapting the past avant-garde. One of the most influential sleeves in this regard - cited by both Malcolm Garrett and Peter Savile, who would explore these avenues in the future - was Barney Bubbles' artwork for Generation X's 'Your Generation' (September 1977). This was inspired by the geometric shapes and the bright colours of the

Constructivists, a group of artists and designers who embodied the brief period of possibility and freedom after the Russian Revolution.

The group's co-manager, John Ingham, remembers that 'Stewart Joseph, Gen X's co-manager, arranged for us to go and see an art professor friend of his, Michael Collins, with a view to getting information/inspiration on where to look for creative ideas. Malcolm had Dada and the ripped aesthetic, The Clash had the Pollock thing - what could we do? Michael suggested the Constructivists - specifically El Lissitsky. The name was enough for me and fortunately the images were fantastic'.

'I loved the graphic strength, which struck me as important for a band to get noticed. We borrowed some books and the more we looked the more we liked. A few days later I was talking to my girlfriend Susanne Spiro, who was Jake Riviera's personal assistant, telling her about the visit. She repeated what I was saying, and Barney overheard her. He came barrelling out asking who the hell was talking about El Lissitsky. He got on the phone and it turned out the Constructivists were a big influence'.

'I'd always liked Barney's work so I pitched for him to design our single cover. I went around to Stiff a few days later and we sat outside on the stoop talking about various Constructivist images and ideas. He came up with a cover of the four in an X-shaped headshot Ray Stevenson had taken in black and white, with the band's name - in red - repeated four times in an X shape across the cover. The clever part was that whichever way you held it, the band's name was the right way up'.

'We had agreed that one of the things to steal from El Lissitsky was to use just black, white, and red. Hence the black and white photo. The band rejected it because they felt it looked too much like a typical band cover but loved the back cover. That was heaven to Barney - a band that didn't want to be typical. Pretty quickly he suggested making the back into the front so that both sides were essentially the same. He loved the idea that it would 'read' essentially the same on both sides. We all agreed.'

For the Clash's 'White Man In Hammersmith Palais', the anonymous artist - probably member(s) of the group with CBS designer Jules Balme - took the Lichtenstein-style gun image from an obscure San Francisco Surrealist magazine. In the same way, the Malcolm Garrett designed sleeve for Magazine's first single, 'Shot by Both Sides', (January 1978) reproduced, at the suggestion of leader Howard Devoto, Odilon Redon's 1886 drawing 'La Chimere regard avec effort toutes choses'.

It wasn't enough, in the majority of cases, just to have a moody pic of the group on the front of the sleeve. Punk had originated in a kind of living fashion collage, with clothes from the 1940s through to the 1960s ripped up and put together (often with safety-pins). Several sleeves ripped up the image ('God Save The Queen', 'Gary Gilmore's Eyes', 'Clash City Rockers'), although the safety-pin became an instant cliché - used only by cash-ins like Plastique Bertrand ('Ca Plane Pour Moi').

Thanks to the fanzine, exploring the limits of Xerox and printing technology became an important theme. Having set the tone with 'One Chord Wonders' and 'Your Generation', Barney Bubbles' design for Generation X's 'Wild Youth' featured shots of the band, taken from Peter Kodick's contact sheets, with the frames visible. The four members were hand coloured in, and then the image was distressed with scalpel marks: on the flip was a constructivist '45' logo.

The sleeve for 'Identity' by X-Ray Spex (July 1978) took the 'One Chord Wonders' idea further, setting a grainy picture of Polystyrene - almost a mug shot - underneath a fake Identity card that showed the rest of the group in colour. The flip printed some of the lyrics, concentrating attention on what was a powerful, if not actively frightening account of fame and breakdown. The idea of an identity card, of course, tapped into Punk paranoia, which was never far from the surface.

The group's previous record, 'The Day The World Turned Day-Glo' was a perfectly integrated and thought through design. To showcase a song about man's disconnection from nature in a consumer society, Falcon Stuart and Polystyrene placed a hand coloured globe on front of a shockingly bright green pantone - an effect enhanced by the sickly orange colour of the vinyl inside, a colour that reflected the song's title on the front of the sleeve.

Another popular approach was the idea of the grid, partially suggested by the shape of the tower block that loomed so large in Punk iconography. The effective design for Sham 69's 'There's Gonna Be A Borstal Breakout' (February 1978, by Jimmy Pursey and Jill Mumford) features the group exploding from the parallel lines of a large, wooden warehouse door. From the same month, Wire's 'I Am The Fly' is showcased in a simple, repetitive nine by nine grid design, with randomly inserted images.

The major label funding for punk gave designers the opportunity to build a visual identity for the group concerned - and then to play with that identity. Taken together, the serial 45 sleeves for the Sex Pistols (Jamie Reid), the Clash (Bernard Rhodes, Paul Simonon and Jules Balme), Buzzcocks (Malcolm Garrett), Elvis Costello (Barney Bubbles) X-Ray Spex (Polystyrene and Falcon Stuart), and Wire (Graham Lewis and Bruce Gilbert) among others add up to astonishing achievement, a true burst of popular art.

However for every mass-produced masterpiece there were dozens of truly terrible, identikit major label punk sleeves. They might be divertingly kitsch today, but back then they were just depressing - a sign that the lifeblood of punk was being sapped by cash-ins and no-hopers (even if they did make entertaining records).

It had been the idea of punk, to be new. But things were happening so fast that punk wasn't new, anymore. 1978 was rough. The demands for purity - the campaign for 'real punk' - and continuing novelty created conflict between competing genres old and new - punk, power pop, Rock Against Racism, electronics, industrial music et al - and the clashing youth tribes itemised on the scratched out sleeve for Sham 69's 'If The Kids Are United': 'Punks, Skinheads, Hippies, Rastas, Teds …'

During the first few months of 1978, much of the creative slack in sleeve design would be taken up by the independent sector - which was expanding in leaps and bounds. Buzzcocks' 'Spiral Scratch' had pioneered the idea, which was taken up by the Desperate Bicycles, whose first two EPs gave a strong boost and a theoretical underpinning to the idea of independence - in thought, aesthetic, and means of production.

Released in April 1977, the Desperate Bicycles' 'Smokescreen' had enshrined a shambling ethos, while July's 'The Medium Was Tedium'/'Don't Back the Front' had an explicit DIY manifesto on the back sleeve: 'It was easy, it was cheap, go and do it (the complete cost of 'Smokescreen' was £153) The medium may very well have been tedium but it's changing fast. So if you can understand, go and join and band. Now it's your turn ...'

Back in November 1976, in the fifth issue of Sniffin' Glue, Mark Perry had issued a similar call, 'All you kids out there who read 'SG' don't be satisfied with what we write. Go out and start your own fanzines or send reviews to the established papers. Let's really get on their nerves, flood the market with punk-writing!' Within a few months, there were dozens of self-produced magazines, ranging from the sacred to the profane, the transcendent to the stupid - each with their own individual design.

Whether fanzines or DIY 45s, the idea was the same. Without the commercial pressures of major labels and large publishing combines, you could play what you want, write what you want, design what you want, say what you want. You didn't have to rely on the established way of doing things, you could maintain the original momentum of punk, namely that everything should be new. The interval between thinking and acting was eliminated. Just go and do it.

In early 1978, the fourth issue of Don't Flex elided the gap between the fanzine and the seven inch. A 'silent single', it was printed like a 45, with an outside sleeve and the bulk of the fanzine - four larger size images on each side of two inserts - folded inside. As well as interviews with Penetration and the briefly notorious Moors Murderers, it featured a memorable anti-fascist graphic and a pro-Red Brigade slogan: 'to-day Aldo Moro, to-morrow Callaghan'. Many of the early indies came out of retail outlets, like Chiswick (Rock On), Beggars Banquet and Small Wonder. Many 1977 sleeves reproduced the basic major label punk aesthetic with a little less polish and a little more verité, like the design for the Lurkers' 'Shadow' (August) - a monster tune that encapsulated the 'anyone-can-do-it' spirit: a candid street shot of four non-smart punk types outside their local boozer. One of them - Arturo Bassick - was even wearing straight-leg trousers, but it didn't matter.

There were many crossover bands, who caught the spirit if not the fashion sense. Examples include Venus and the Razorblades ('Punk-A-Rama', September 1977) who were promoted by svengali Kim Fowley;

the Twinkeyz, a shit hot neo-psych band from Sacramento ('Aliens In Our Midst', late 1977); the Count Bishops, whose Mike Spencer had been among the candidates for Sex Pistols' singer in 1975 ('Baby You're Wrong', May 1977).

The Rings' 'I Wanna Be Free' (June 1977) showed four young and not-so-young men - in leathers, shades and skinny ties - doing the 'Beatle' leap in front of the Rock On store in Camden Town. The group included former Tomorrow and Pink Fairies drummer Twink. Patrik Fitzgerald's 'Safety-Pin Stuck In My Heart' EP (January 1978) took from the same template as the Saints' 'I'm Stranded' -the artist posing in the middle of dereliction, with the title graffitied on an empty wall.

Some designs were simply amateurish, and not necessarily in a good way. The Killjoys' 'Johnny Won't Get To Heaven' (November 1977, on Raw Records, a Cambridge label and shop) featured an ugly surrealist drawing on the 'live fast die young' theme, with a razor, some pills, brick walls, and an underground sign. Others, like O Level on their first EP, 'East Sheen' (May 1978) turned this into a virtue, the sleeve's artlessness complementing the sketchy directness of the music within.

In general, as a person's eyes are a window to the soul, the sleeve tended to reflect the music within. Subway Sect's monolithic March 1978 two-sider, 'Nobody's Scared' and 'Don't Split It' was housed in a black and white sleeve that featured a montage of Piccadilly Circus station (and an incoming 1938 stock train) with a posed shot of the band having a cup of tea. The platform has turned into the street grid of Hiroshima. On the flip, the destination board says 'Oslo, Morden, Leningrad, Liverpool …'

Early 1978 saw the onset of experimental analogue electronica, and two sleeves - both from May - summed up the mood. Throbbing Gristle's United had a high gloss montage of urban blocks and naked limbs. It was designed - as was all the group's output - by group member Peter Christopherson, who also worked at Hipgnosis. (They were responsible for the memorable image on the Cortinas' 'Defiant Pose' (February 1978), as a young man pukes up behind his mother and father).

The Normal's 'Warm Leatherette' uses a crash test photo to illustrate the song inside, a musical extrapolation from J.G.Ballard's 'Crash'. On the flip there are a couple of stylised images from advertising - such as Malcolm Garrett would use on Buzzcocks' sleeves. The Human League's 'Being Boiled' (June 1978) featured a similar approach, an idealised ad image of a dancing couple superimposed over a diagram of New York's skyscrapers.

Many independent designs continued classic punk themes. There was a lot of urbanism, for example the Now's 'Development Corporations' (November 1977) - well, the city was the topic of the tune. Otherwise see the grid-like high rise montage sleeve for John Cooper Clarke's

'Innocents' EP (on Tosh Ryan's Rabid Records, November 1977), or the tower-blocks on Metal Urbain's first 45 (Cobra Records late 1977), which also features contact sheets and 35-mm film strips.

There were many simple band pictures, whether posed (Tubeway Army's 'Bombers' EP, June 1978) or live (Radio Birdman, 'Burn My Eye' EP, Australia 1977). Slaughter and the Dogs' early indie 45, 'Cranked Up Really High' (May 1977) featured the group in full horror rock style, with ghoulish lettering and cheap red print. The Only Ones' first 45, 'Lovers of Today' (Vengeance Records, June 1977), featured a rather disturbing black and white portrait of the defiantly non-teenage musicians.

There are liberal doses of black humour: Alberto Y Lost Trios Paranoias' parody punk 'Snuff Rock' EP (September 1977, also 'Heads Down No Nonsense Boogie', September 1978), or the cartoon sleeve to Black Randy and the Metrosquad's 'Trouble At The Cup' (Dangerhouse, Los Angeles, December 1977 - designed by David Brown and K.K. Barrett), a tender ode to the joys or otherwise of male hustling – 'schools and factories make me sick, I'd rather stand here and sell my dick'.

The media was a constant presence, being a perennial punk fascination. Had not the movement received its single biggest boost from a fabricated scandal? Quite apart from band names - Television, the Adverts, Magazine, TV Personalities - televisions made an appearance on several single sleeves: Alternative TV's 'How Much Longer' (November 1977), the Monochrome Set's 'Alphaville' (January 1979) and the Pack's 'Heathen' (April 1979).

Then there were the mass media parodies. The Snivelling Shits' 'Terminal Stupid' (September 1977, designed by Dave Fudger from Sounds music paper) used the picture of an ecstatic punk fan that had appeared in the Daily Mirror - which made the point nicely. Public Image Limited's first single, 'Public Image' (October 1978) came with an added free newspaper, a fake tabloid - designed by Dennis Morris - that folded out to offer humorous stories about the group.

During 1978, independent labels began to develop their own identity. In Los Angeles, Dangerhouse Records (designers David Brown and Pat Garrett) favoured strong, simple black and white design with clear typography (the Weirdos, the Bags, the Avengers). Andrew Lauders' Radar - an indie tied into Warner Brothers - had Barney Bubbles as house designer, weaving his magic on covers for Elvis Costello, Nick Lowe, Richard Hell and the Voidoids, the Yachts, Iggy Pop and many others.

Rough Trade covers like those for Cabaret Voltaire's 'Extended Play' EP (November 1978) and File Under Pop's 'Heathrow' (February 1979) were functional and monochrome yet allusive in sympathy with the analog electronica inside. In February 1979 Rough Trade issued the first ever single by legendary Cleveland avant-punk way before the event group the Electric Eels. Recorded in 1975, 'Agitated' was housed in a sleeve by John Morton that took amateurism into Fauvist territory.

Bob Last's Fast Records, based in Edinburgh, featured a run of sophisticated covers - for the Mekons, 2:3 and the Human League - that built a visual brand for the label at the same as they show a fascination with advertising and disposability. Last would indeed produce two issues of a fanzine called 'the quality of life', some copies included decaying orange peel. During 1979 Fast Records also issued three multi-group samplers, Earcoms 1-3, which included Middle Class, the Prats and Joy Division.

October 1978 saw the release of two classic independent 45s. The first EP by Gang of Four came in a sleeve that included the Fast Records logo, as well as a statement on the front that this was 'the sleeve for a Gang of Four recording'. On the back was a press cutting that the group intended to comment on, situ-style, but instead of a speech bubble there was a letter stating what the anonymous designer wanted to happen. Inside was a sticker, a negative photo of the group in a supermarket.

Scritti Politti's first EP, released on their own St Pancras label, had a complex fold out sleeve. On the front were exercises in Xeroxology, with basic black and red printing and images of the group and record manufacturing. On the flip was a montage of group shots with detailed breakdowns of how much it cost to record, master and press up 2,500 copies of the EP. In keeping with this aesthetic, the cut '28/7/78' was an aural record of that day - if you want to hear what 1978 felt like, play it.

Aided by a strong idea, powerful music press support and some big sellers - most notably the first Stiff Little Fingers album and Joy Division's Unknown Pleasures - the independent sector exploded in 1979 and 1980. Quite apart from the cassette tape ecology - a topic outside the remit of this book - there were two main strands. The first was the construction of label identities, a kind of taking on the majors at their own game, as well as piecing together a story in which every record was part of the whole.

Factory Records began with posters for the Factory Club in Hulme, designed by Peter Saville. These were at once striking and minimal, in tune with the industrial aesthetic of the time. 'A Factory Sample' was issued in January 1979, with two EPs housed in a beautiful silver sleeve - encased in soft plastic, like records were in the far East - that featured an industrial worker wearing a hard hat and ear plugs. Inside were four stickers, including the Situationist graphic, 'The Return of the Durutti Column'.

Boosted by the success of Joy Division's 'Unknown Pleasures' (May 1979), Factory Records became a leading independent and Saville's designs - both sophisticated and easily graspable - became an integral part of the Factory identity. His posters, label notepaper and badges were given catalogue numbers alongside actual records. For instance early Factory gig posters were Fac 1, Fac 3 and Fac 4. His sleeves graced records by Section 25, Durutti Column and A Certain Ratio.

Joy Division became more and more popular during 1979 and, after the death of Ian Curtis in May 1980, their next single 'Love Will Tear Us Apart' made the top 20. The simple but striking design - prepared before Curtis'

JET BRONX & THE FORBIDDEN
AIN'T DOIN' NOTHIN'
c/w I CAN'T STAND IT

ATTENTION!
IF YOU ARE NOT AMONG THE FIRST 15,000 PURCHASERS OF THIS RECORD YOU WILL HAVE TO BE CONTENT WITH CRUMMY BLACK VINYL INSTEAD OF TERRIFIC RED VINYL.

suicide by Peter Savile and Trevor Key - had the title and the catalogue number stamped into oxidised metal. Inside, the record label had an 'f' hole logo, designed by Martyn Atkins, that denoted not Factory Records but Fractured Music, Joy Division's publishing company.

Beginning in May 1979 with 'Reality Asylum', Crass set a new standard for design with the releases on their own label. With fold out sleeves, beautifully printed on thick paper, that featured a circular grid on the front, on the circumference of which was stencilled the name of the artist and the song title. Inside there was usually a collage - by designer Gee Vaucher - and information about the song. For instance, Nagasaki Nighmare (Crass, 1980) included a long essay about the nuclear holocaust.

Honey Bane's 'You Could Be You' (December 1979) has the price, 'no more than 65p', and 'a big piss off to the musick-biz!' in ransom note lettering on the front. Others feature sprayed stencilling, a result of Crass' long-standing graffiti campaign, which was part of their program - to counter-act the idea that there was no future by offering a broad-based and inclusive politics that included feminist ideas, anarchism, commune living and the Campaign for Nuclear Disarmament.

From late 1978, slogans like 'Fight War Not Wars' and 'Stuff Your Sexist Shit' were sprayed on posters all over London. As Gee Vaucher remembers, 'Stencil graffiti was very much inspired by New York 'cos it used to be on the pavements, which was great. Every time you'd cross the road, there was something to read. When we came over, we plastered it everywhere, on the walls, on the street, all this cut-out stuff and put it on the pavements'.

The records were part of Crass' agitprop aesthetic and they were, amongst many other things, responsible for the rebirth of grassroots anarchism in the early 1980s, which were given power and depth by Gee Vaucher's designs. These were contained, not only in record sleeves, but posters, handbills and magazines like the International Anthem - the second edition of which has one of the period's most memorable image, the montage of the Queen and the Pope on top of the Sex Pistols' bodies.

Vaucher had worked as a professional designer and her experience gave her montages sophistication and power. She remembers that Crass were trying to cover 'the whole gamut of senses, as much as possible. People look, but they don't see. We were trying to throw people into another way of seeing. We tried to use images that everybody could recognise, but because of the way they were put together, maybe it threw a new light on something'.

This was the seven-inch as a total artwork - a complete fusion of art, music, ideas, politics and packaging. Art was indivisible from life. All available for under a pound. This generous spirit wasn't always shared, but like skiffle or the early days of punk - a genre that, apart from some great records by the Ruts and the Members, was beginning to subside

into Oi - the new indies offered a chance for young musicians to start from scratch, to say what they would.

Amateurism was a big part of this explosion. By necessity as well as choice. Records as diverse as the 'Last Thoughts' EP by Beyond the Implode (September 1979), the Urinals 'Sex' (1980) and the Raincoats' 'No-One's Little Girl' (July 1982) all had hand-drawn sleeves in varying degrees of artfulness. Other examples include the Epileptics' '1970s' EP (November 1979), Bok Bok's 'Come Back To Me' and Thin Yoghurts' 'Girl On A Bus' (both 1980).

Hand tinting was a big feature of the first few singles released on Alan Horne's Postcard Records out of Glasgow. Orange Juice's 'Blueboy' and Josef K's 'Radio Drill Time' had individually coloured in sleeves that, together with the child-like drawings, conveyed an atmosphere of innocence and freshness. Horne went on to a strong regional identity on the sleeves for later records like Orange Juice's 'Poor Old Soul' (1981), which came with the tag The Sound of Young Scotland.

The Xerox aesthetic was important for the same reasons. Robert Rental's 'Paralysis' (September 1978) combined the grid with industrial unpleasantness - a picture of a monkey undergoing medical experiments - and a trace of hand colouring. Records by the Urinals (their first EP, 1978) and Red Alert (their first EP, 1980) made a virtue out of primitive copiers, accentuating the image's disappearance. Tony Sinden's 'Magificent Cactus Trees' (1979) distressed the already blurry cover photo.

With so many seven-inch squares to fill, the past was heavily plundered. Apart from famous film images (like the homoerotic gun/ penis still from Jean Genet's 'Chant D'Amour' used by the Offs on 'Johnny Too Bad', 1978), there was plentiful use of 1950s stock imagery - the young boy throwing paper plates on the B-52's 'Rock Lobster' (April 1978) or the golfing design on Devo's 'Be Stiff' (May 1978). Devo in particular had a fine line in disturbing retro or fake retro graphics.

The Sixties were plundered as well. The Avengers' 'We Are The One' EP (December 1977) sported a target sleeve, while the Sleepers' 'Seventh World' EP (Summer 1978) had a belched out shot of the group posed, Haight Ashbury style, in a field of flowers. Cabaret Voltaire's 'Extended Play' EP (October 1978) and 'Nag Nag Nag' (June 1979) featured blurred black and white live shots of the group with back projections, Velvet Underground style.

In among the ever-present black and white band portraits, there was a good run on death and horror. The Boys' 'Terminal Love' (February 1980) featured an agency photo of a corpse. The Users' 'Kicks In Style' (December 1978) and the Police's 'Can't Stand Losing You' (August 1978) featured images of young men at the end of a rope. The Drones' 'Bone Idol' (September 1977) and the Specials' infamous 'Ghost Town' (June 1981) used the image of a skeleton.

THE SOUND OF THE SUBURBS

THE MEMBERS

Urban settings continued to predominate. One of the most fascinating sleeves was for the Panik's first EP 'It Won't Sell' (November 1977). Managed by Rob Gretton, the band placed a picture of Manchester's gay hustlers on their front cover. Chelsea's 'High Rise Living' (December 1977) featured a drawing of a tower block, while the UK Subs' storming 'CID' (October 1978) had the band, as if imprisoned behind a set of railings, with the song titles marked out in graffiti.

Suburbia was another topic. Released in autumn 1978, the Middle Class' 'Out of Vogue' showed two young girls deep in a Californian suburban tract - one looks at the camera while the other holds a gun. The Members' 'Sound of the Suburbs' (January 1979) - a major label record, I know, but it's a great sleeve, designed by Malcolm Garrett - had a television on the front, opening into a montage of suburban houses topped by a British Airways Tristar plane, which you could see through the clear vinyl record.

Riot and war became an increasingly popular trope. The path had been set by Sham 69's sleeve for the 'I Don't Wanna' EP (September 1977), which showed Jimmy Pursey being carted off by several police officers. Records by Stiff Little Fingers (the famous 'Alternative Ulster', October 1978), the Chords ('Maybe Tomorrow', January 1980) and the split EP between X-Cells/ Schizoid (1980) all featured images of urban riot. In the case of 'Alternative Ulster', it was a British soldier with a rifle.

In the early 1980s, the escalation in the cold war - prompted by the Russian invasion of Afghanistan - accelerated the paranoia of punks and post-punks, already fairly acute. Killing Joke's 'Wardance' (March 1980) had the image of a tuxedo clad man waltzing through the killing fields of Flanders, while 'Follow the Leaders' (May 1981) had an insert about military conscription. Vital Disorders' 'Wargames' (1982) showed a picture of an urban guerilla and on the other side an injured baby.

Angst was a powerful theme, reflecting the despair felt by a generation just coming to terms with unemployment and the prospect of war. The Last Gang's 'Spirit of Youth' (November 1979) combines urbanism - a deserted alleyway - with a downbeat punk etched out in red, slumped in a doorway. Demob's 'No Room For You' (November 1981) has a powerful picture of a tired punk. The first and infamous Minor Threat EP (June 1981), shows an exhausted skinhead, head in arms.

There was a tribal/ exotic influence, clustering around the Pop Group and the Slits, that signified the adoption of funk and/or African rhythms. You can see it in the sleeves for 'She Is Beyond Good and Evil' (March 1979), and 'Typical Girls' (September 1979), 'Man Next Door' (June 1980) and 'Earthbeat' (October 1981). Another good example is to be found on the Bush Tetras' sole release on Fetish Records, 'Things That Go BOOM in the Night' (1981) - by upcoming designer Neville Brody.

Agitprop was important, as the DIY imperative had implications beyond releasing records. It was part of a progressive and active politics. Apart from Crass Records - which released dozens of singles during the early 1980s - there were also provocative designs by the Pop Group. The cover of 'We Are Prostitutes' (November 1979) stated, 'Department stores are our new cathedrals, our cars are martyrs to the cause'. At the bottom they state, 'At this moment despair ends and tactics begin.'

In the early days women singers, writers and musicians had been a natural part of the punk upsurge - Siouxsie and the Banshees, the Slits, X-Ray Spex, The Adverts. As the music industry came to define punk in terms of Four Man Rock 'n' Roll bands, this instinctive radicalism was cut short by the major labels. In the progressive political atmosphere of the period, several groups pursued the original ideas into active feminism, and their record sleeves reflected these ideas.

The Au Pairs' first EP (September 1979) featured a song called 'Kerb Crawler', the sleeve showing a scene of male on female violence. The first single by Girls At Our Best, 'Getting Nowhere Fast' (April 1980), had an illustration of three women standing and peeing at a urinal. The 1981 single by Ludus, the group formed by artist Linder Sterling, was 'Mother's Hour'/ 'Patient'. She designed the sleeve, which showcases a pair of pristine bandaged hands, on the flip the blood seeps through.

These kind of singles and sleeves revelled in the freedom brought by independence, and its survival as a viable market for difference and dissonance. In 1981/2, this began to change. The idea of Pop was back among those who had been through punk and its possibilities. Gary Numan had shown the way in 1979, with the huge success of 'Are Friends Electric?' and 'Cars'. At his first post-fame shows in the autumn, girls were screaming. His peers took note.

During 1980, Adam and the Ants had huge hits with 'Dog Eat Dog' and 'Antmusic'. The next year, the Human League and Soft Cell had number ones with 'Don't You Want Me' and 'Tainted Love' respectively. In the return to pop, the focus shifted back to gloss and accessibility, and major label control. The period of anything goes experimentation and easy access to the means of production had become just another fad, ready to be discarded. The handmade sleeves began to yellow and collect dust.

Thirty years on, the seven years between 1977 and 1980 seem like one golden age of youth culture. The energy of punk enabled groups all over the country to put out a record, even if was in a tiny edition and only distributed locally. These records and their often anonymous sleeves add up to an extraordinary period of folk art, a time when teenagers could say what was on their minds - even if it was trivial, amateurish, or unpalatable. It didn't matter, this was the Teenage News.

PUNK 45s

This is a book about the cover art of punk and includes artwork from America, Britain, France, Japan, Italy, Sweden, Australia, Spain and more. The book covers the period 1976-1980 and also includes select sleeves from 1969 onwards which we would describe as punk before punk.

Johnny Rotten's description of the Sex Pistols as 'a bunch of cunts'* helpfully defines punk. Outsider music fuelled by negative energy flipped back into creativity. Whilst music in the UK can simply be described as before and after the Sex Pistols and all their bollocks, there's a clear musical line of punk back to 1960s American garage punk. This path is made by the group themselves - from The Stooges to The Trashmen, and even includes the bubblegum rock of The Monkees' Stepping Stone, honoured as one of the Pistols favourite cover versions.

In New York we begin with Television or The Ramones - somewhat dependent on your point of view of guitar solos. Patti Smith's Piss Factory, self-released on her own label in 1974 is the start of punk's DIY culture (a variant on the path of poets self-publishing their work on private presses). But step back a couple of years, honey, and you're with the trash of the New York Dolls and their take on the Velvet Underground, Stooges and MC5.

Johnny Rotten's embracing into the fold of his friend Sid Vicious was an attempt to keep the intelligencia out of defining punk – for the group to remain 'a bunch of cunts'. Equally stooopid (once again an identity so cultivated that they could have been an art project) The Ramones remind us to do the same whilst they created a new sound out of a love for garage, bubblegum and even doo-wop.

Punk's 1960s garage roots were partly instilled by the small shops and labels that promoted this music in the UK in the mid 1970s - as Velvets and Stooges bootlegs, collectors' edition promos and coloured vinyl passed into young hands. And hence the seven-inch (picture sleeve of course) became the natural medium to send out aural messages of truth from the inner city to the suburbs (or, truth told, sometimes the suburbs to the suburbs).

It is also from these small beginnings that the independent UK music industry begins with early starters Chiswick and Stiff Records soon joined by the likes of Factory, Rough Trade and Beggars Banquet.

Even earlier still was Mark Zermati's Skydog Records, originally based in France but well connected in both the USA and UK. Chiswick and Stiff's first releases were distributed in the UK by Zermati and partner Larry Debay's Bizarre distribution service. The pair also distributed select 'special products' from major label artists and for this privilege encouraged the larger record companies to start making picture sleeves for these releases.

My own youthful suburban experience of the record sleeve was asking the apparently hip guy in HMV Catford in south London if the new Magazine seven-inch (Shot By Both Sides) came in a picture sleeve to which he replied, 'Yes, but don't you find the paper gets stuck in the needle when it goes round?' Now I'm not one to bare a grudge but 35 years on I'd like to say 'fuck off, you cunt', an artful riposte that my meagre 13-old wit was in no way capable of at the time. Much friendlier by far was my local Bonaparte record shop in Bromley – my introduction to the world of punk on vinyl. Thanks!

Punk soon became a sophisticated game of cat and mouse between the majors and the indies as authencity was soon replicated. First rule of economics – if it sells, copy it. The first-wave bands seemed to co-opt themselves into this game. How could rebellion be signed to CBS (The Clash), UA (The Stranglers and The Buzzcocks) or Harvest (Wire)? Only the Sex Pistols abuse of EMI seemed in any way anarchic and sets the group apart from others.

Following in the wake of The Pistols chaos came an avalanche of British urban and suburban invective courtesy of 1000s of bands that were punk, post-punk, nearly-punk (like pub rock but still going) and not-really-punk-at-all (power pop, bubblegum and worst of all musos - bleauch!) but who were all around at the right time. As long as you were on speed when you recorded it, there was a good chance it would sell.

And with these 1000s of new bands came 1000s of new labels as the means of production became affordable. Through the cypher of John Peel, NME, Sounds and Melody Maker (sort of), you could shift 10,000 of your own or your mate's band's new seven-inch. Following in the wake of the Pistols' nihilism and first-wave punk came Rough Trade, distributing and releasing in a kind of somewhat hippyish everything's cool, sort of co-operative style groove, everything from electronic experimentalism (Cabaret Voltaire, Metal Urbain) and art-school punk (Swell Maps, Scritti Pollitti) to want-to-be pop releases by The Raincoats, Mark Belly and more. Stiff Records continually walked a fine line between genius and stupidity as pub rock, bubblegum, punk, pop, comedy, cabaret and well anything really were given a platform. In Manchester, Factory Records showed us the link between style and experimentalism.

Across the Atlantic punk had soon spread across the USA as bands and labels sprang up in Cleveland, Los Angeles, San Francisco, Akron and elsewhere. In New York the early success of The Ramones, Television and Blondie meant that they soon evacuated the city leaving a void that no wave, possibly fuelled on an even more extreme form of punk's musical nihilism, would soon fill.

99% of punk singles have sleeves, and thus was born a generation of designers - all touched by a healthy disdain for the mainstream. Jamie Reid's work was an equal to the Pistols' anarchy, Barney Bubbles captured the humour of Stiff, Peter Saville the intensity of Joy Division. But this is just the tip of the iceberg with Malcolm Garrett, Gee Vaucher, Dennis Morris, Savage Pencil, Bazooka, Linder Sterling, Neville Brody and hundreds of others all providing startlingly creative work.

*'You must be fucking mad, coming to see a bunch of cunts like us.'
Rotten on the mic at the Village, Newport 23 Dec '77.
And then again (now as John Lydon) at the Guitar Hero 3 computer game press conference held in London on 7 Nov 2007:
'My respect goes back to say, 'Thank you Sex Pistols' regardless of what a bunch of cunts that band are.'

MC5

Kick Out The Jams b/w Motor City is Burning

ELEKTRA RECORDS USA 1969

Robin Tyner Vocals
Wayne Kramer Guitar
Fred 'Sonic' Smith Guitar
Michael Davis Bass
Dennis Thompson Drums

Guidance John Sinclair
Spiritual Advisor Brother JC Crawford
Recorded live at the Grande Ballroom in Detroit
Produced by Bruce Botnick, Jac Holzman
Artwork by Robert L. Heimall, William S. Harvey
Cover photograph by Joel Brodsky
*French-only picture sleeve. Legendary confrontational proto-punk
garage band. MC5 formed in Lincoln Park, Michigan in 1964.*

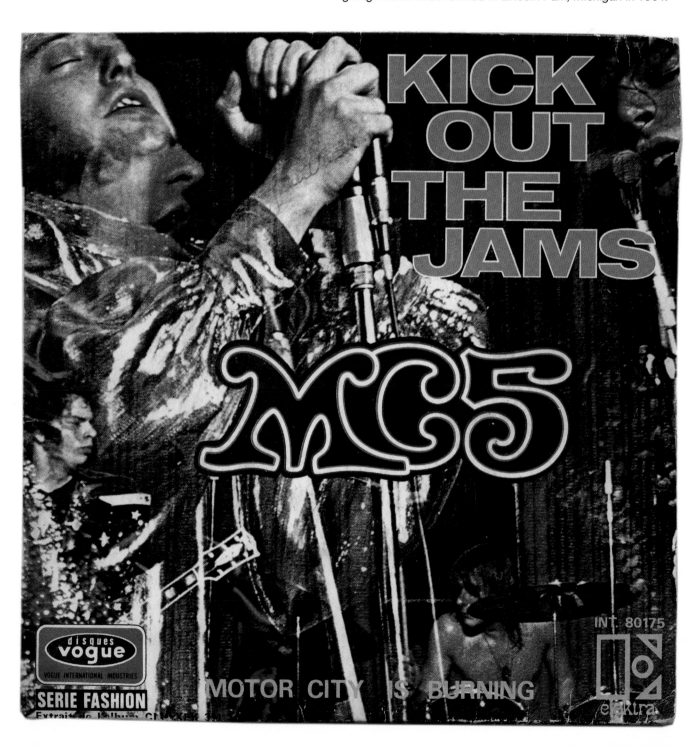

THE STOOGES
1969 b/w Real Cool Time
ELEKTRA RECORDS USA 1969

Iggy Stooge Vocals
Ron Asheton Guitar
Scott Asheton Drums
Dave Alexander Bass

Produced by John Cale

French-only picture sleeve release, the second ever single by The Stooges.

NEW YORK DOLLS

Trash b/w Personality Crisis
MERCURY USA 1973

Arthur Harold Kane Bass
Jerry Nolan Drums
Sylvain Sylvain Guitar, Piano, Vocals
Johnny Thunders Guitar, Vocals
David Jo Hansen Vocals, Harmonica, Gong
The Fantastic Buddy Bowser Saxophone

Produced by Todd Rundgren **Photography by** Toshi **Cover by** Album Graphics Inc.
Hair by Shin **Makeup by** Dave O'Grady

Spanish-only picture sleeve edition of the debut single by the New York Dolls

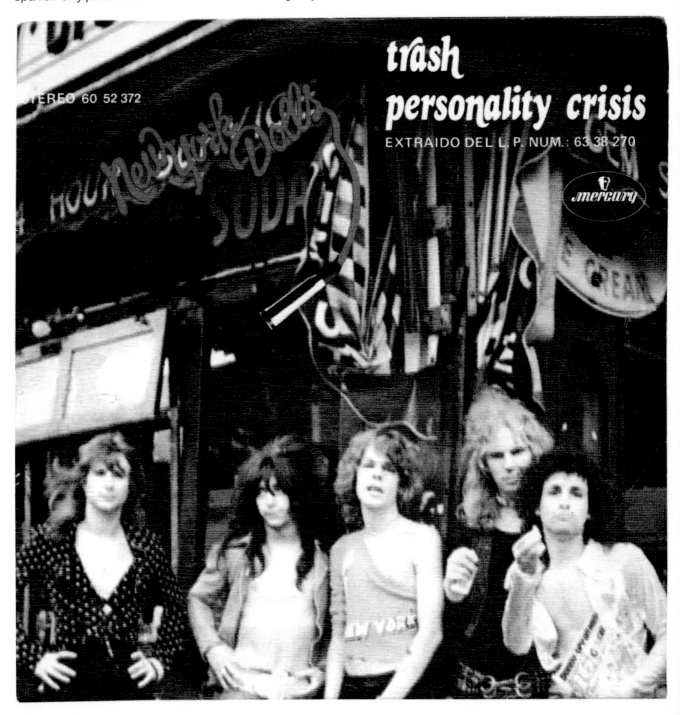

THE FLAMIN' GROOVIES

Grease EP
Let Me Rock/Dog Meat/Sweet Little Rock/Slow Death
SKYDOG USA 1973

Cyril Jordan Guitar, Vocals

Chris Wilson Guitar, Vocals

George Alexander Bass, Harmonica, Vocals

Tim Lynch Guitar, Harmonica, Vocals

Danny Mihm Drums

Sleeve Design by Vidal.

Unreleased tracks from psych rock band Flamin' Groovies recorded at Cyril Jordan's garage in Mangel's Street in San Francisco and released by French independent label Skydog.

THE NEON BOYS

That's All I Know Right Now/Love Comes in Spurts
SHAKE RECORDS USA 1980

Richard Hell Vocals, Bass
Tom Verlaine Guitars
Billy Ficca Drums

*Tom Verlaine and Richard Hell's pre-Television group, The Neon Boys.
These 1973 Neon Boys recordings did not surface until 1980 on Shake
Records with two tracks by Richard Hell and The Voidoids on the other side
('Time' and 'Don't Die')*

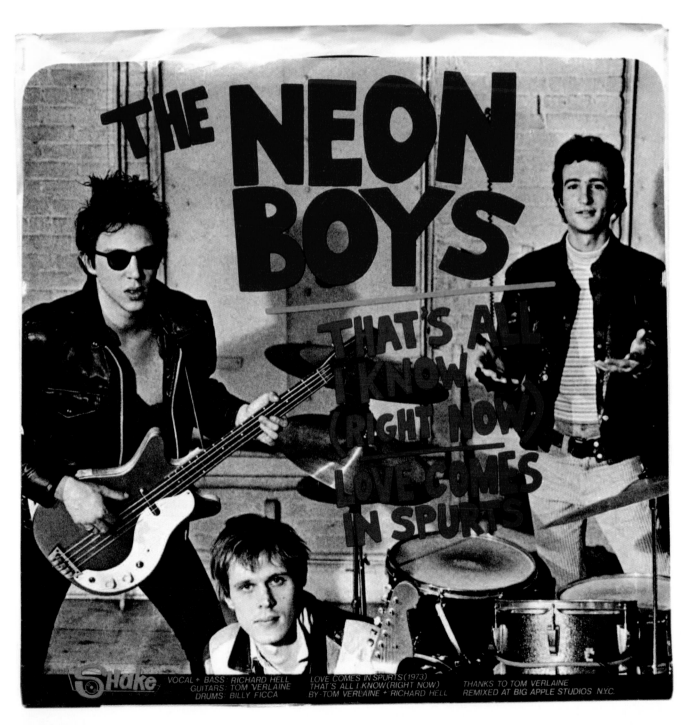

PATTI SMITH
Hey Joe b/w Piss Factory
SIRE RECORDS USA 1977

Patti Smith Vocals
Jay Dee Daugherty Drums
Tom Verlaine Lead Guitar
Lenny Kaye Guitar
Richard Sohl Piano

Recorded June 5, 1974 at Electric Ladyland, New York City
Produced by Lenny Kaye

Originally self-published by Patti Smith in 1974 and released on MER Records (see above left) Released on Sire in 1977. This is the Italian-only picture sleeve.

PERE UBU

30 Seconds Over Tokyo b/w Heart of Darkness
HEARTHAN RECORDS Cleveland, Ohio USA

Crocus Behemoth (David Thomas)
Lead Vocals, Radio, Cpt. of Palcontents
Peter Laughner Guitar, Cat Piano, Bass, Whisper
Thom Herman Guitar, Spinal Guitar, Bass, Whisper
Tim Wright Phynancial Guitar, Bass, Whisper
Scott Krauss Drums
Allen Ravenstine Synthesizer, Modulation

Recorded Sept. 28 - Oct. 1, 1975, at
Audio Recording
Produced by P. Ubu and Bill Cavanaugh
Cover Art Jon Luoma
Package Design Crocus Behemoth

Band formed by David Thomas and Peter Laughner in Cleveland, Ohio, 1975 out of the ashes of proto-punk Rocket From The Tomb. Hearthan, later Hearpan, was owned and run by David Thomas.

CROCUS BEHEMOTH and the sound of C-Town
An interview with David Thomas of Pere Ubu

DAVID THOMAS is one of the founding members of the short-lived but highly influential proto-punk band Rocket From The Tombs, which formed in Cleveland, Ohio and existed between 1974 and 1975. Members of the group went in to help form Television (Richard Lloyd) and The Dead Boys (Cheetah Chrome). In 1975 Thomas formed the group Pere Ubu and began releasing the group's music (and related others) on his own Hearthan record label. Hearthan's Pere Ubu sleeves were illustrated by Crocus Behemoth, a pseudonym of Thomas.

Why Cleveland? What was going on in socially and economically Cleveland in the 1970s and how was this reflected in the music that came out of it in which you were involved?
This is just the sort of question I hate dealing with. 'Why?' 'WHY?!' Who the hell knows? Why? Because.

Whatever I say you cannot understand. I was there. You and most of the planet were not. We did what we were supposed to do. Other people elsewhere and also in Cleveland weren't paying attention. And now WE (or rather I) have to be interrogated about it. We did the right thing. Why are we being punished? Interrogate all those others who weren't doing the right thing and who weren't paying attention.

Rocket From The Tombs is 'before punk'. What was the lineage of the music you were playing? What historical line of music were you following (if any)? Garage bands? Avant-garde? Rock and roll?
We listened to everything we could get our hands on. We were fortunate to have great record stores in town and many of us worked in record stores. If the store you worked in, or shopped in, didn't have the latest Popul Vuh album then you better not show your face around. If you hadn't been over to Jimmy's to utterly consume and digest the split channel Beatles tapes then you were a flatworm. If you hadn't listened to 'Summertime Blues' full blast on Tim's VOT speakers then you may as well live in Omaha. If you hadn't snuck into La Cave to hear the VU in '68 then you'd better have heard the bootlegs from those who did.

Did you feel a part of punk with Pere Ubu – clearly different to guitar band punk but somehow connected artistically?
No, we never felt part of punk or anything else. First, we're American and have no use for your punk music, gringo. Second, we were on our own - we knew there was somebody out there called The Residents doing cool stuff, and some band from Indiana, and this group and that group and we paid attention, determined that nobody nowhere was going to get the drop on us. But, being part of something - no way. Certainly nothing that a bunch of sad sack foreigners was doing, i.e. punk.

Is there an artistic connection between Paris at the end of the 19th century and America (or Cleveland?) in the mid-70s?
We learned two things from the French: Absurdism/Surreality is a useful tool with which to analyze the modern world, and French radicals created something in the film world they described as the New Wave. That also sounded like a useful perspectual tool.

Did the actual manufacture of Hearthan Records mean anything separate to the music? Is this different now that you distribute music digitally?
No, not really. At least nothing more than is obvious. Not different now.

Could you talk a little about the imagery on the sleeves of the first Hearthan releases?
It's pictures. Pictures are supposed to go on a record sleeve so you look around for something to slap on it. It's best if whatever you do isn't embarrassing or stupid, and doesn't detract from the music or mislead about the music.

TELEVISION

Little Johnny Jewel (Parts 1 and 2)
ORK New York, USA 1975

Tom Verlaine Guitar, Vocals
Billy Ficca Drums
Richard Lloyd Guitar
Fred Smith Bass

*Their debut single, recorded on 4-track on 14 August, 1975.
Ork Records was owned by Terry Ork, Television's manager at
the time, and Charles Ball.*

PARIS IS BURNING ...
An interview with Marc Zermati, Skydog Records.

Skydog Records was created in 1972 by Marc Zermati, who ran the Open Market record shop in Paris. The independent Skydog was ahead of its time, predating Stiff, Chiswick and the British labels that grew up with punk by a good few years.

Skydog made a name for itself releasing rare or unreleased material from The Velvet Underground, MC5, The Flamin' Groovies and - most successfully - Iggy and The Stooges (Metallic KO). Skydog's output became a guidebook for young punk's history lessons.

In 1973, Zermati linked up with another Frenchman, Larry Debay, who ran a record shop in west London. Together they set up the Bizarre record distribution network in the UK. This was how the first British labels (Stiff and Chiswick) got their records to the listeners and became the template for Rough Trade's 1980s distribution network.

In 1976 Zermati organised the first of two European punk festivals in Mont-de-Marsan, featuring The Damned, who were playing only their fifth concert. The second one, in Paris, featured the Sex Pistols. To put this into context, both these events occurred before The 100 Club's Punk Rock Festival in London on 21 September of that year.

As well as American proto-punk, British pub rock and punk (The Damned, Sean Tyla, Ducks Deluxe and the Gorillas), Skydog also released some of the first French punk records (Asphalt Jungle, 84 Flesh) and their artwork often featured the work of Bazooka, the French artists' collective whose work influenced a number of British artists.

How did Skydog Records start?
Skydog started in Amsterdam with my friend Peter Meulenbrok. Amsterdam was the right place at the time as many people from the underground and the free press were living there.

Did you have the Open Market record store at this time? Yes, Open Market started in early 1972.

Can you talk a bit about Larry Debay, the Bizarre shop and distribution? Back in 1973, Larry wrote me a note and I went to see him in London. We became friends and partners shortly after.

Would you describe the music of The Flamin' Groovies as punk, or pre-punk, or garage? Punk garage - they were dandy rockers.

How did you come to release The Flamin' Groovies?
In February 1973, we went to San Francisco to see Cyril Jordan, a founding member of the group, who I had met the year before in France. Cyril gave me some taped demos that he recorded with the band in his garage in Mangels Avenue in San Francisco.

Skydog is an important link between US garage, British pub rock and pre-punk and punk in the USA, isn't it? For me, the connection between punk, American garage rock and English pub rock was obvious. Take for example Eddie and the Hot Rods, who to me are real punk. Of course, the punk scene starts in America, and we were also very well connected with the New York punk rock scene - at the time Paris and New York were on the same artistic line. London came after. Also, most of the London scene came to Paris very often, including Malcolm McLaren and a lot of rock press - people like Nick Kent, Jon Savage and Giovanni Dadamo.

Skydog was the first independent punk label – three years before Stiff, one year before Bomp! in the USA. Can you talk about this? We had decided to fight for rock 'n' roll, and things that were real, so we created the label for fans back in 1972. We were connected with Greg Shaw from Bomp! and other American people from the press underground, like Lester Bangs and Lenny Kaye - all of whom supported us in our bid to change the music business situation.

How did the Bizarre distribution start? We started distribution in the UK at the end of 1973. We started to distribute all the underground and small labels at the time; from the USA like Bomp! Records, Red Star (Suicide etc), and from the UK, Stiff and Chiswick at their beginning. Also those first punk singles from New York, like Patti Smith's 'Piss Factory', Television's first single, The Saints' first single. We sponsored Sniffin' Glue, the first punk fanzine in the UK. We also distributed all the special products from bands on the major labels who asked to go through our

outfit - like Graham Parker and the Rumour, Eddie and the Hot Rods, The Heartbreakers and more.

Who did the sleeves for Skydog? The Flamin' Groovies' 'Grease' was done by Vidal Angels (RIP) who had worked many years ago for Walt Disney. He was a good friend of mine from the 60s underground. Then it was the Bazooka team of Loulou Picasso, Olivia Clavel, Kiki Picasso and Lulu.

What is the connection between US garage and punk? Do you see it as a continuation of the same thing - or was punk something new? No, punk was nothing new, but Malcolm succeeded in manipulating the press and media using situationism. At the time Malcolm and I were very close. He wanted to call the movement 'new wave', but we pushed that the name should be punk as the only way to call this music. Of course, MC5, The Velvets and all those bands were punk garage. Maybe Elvis was the first punk, as rock 'n' roll was the first teenage music, and full of rebellion.

Do you think the French (and European) idea of picture sleeves influenced the fact that British punk singles had sleeves? Yes, very much so. And also the artists we had in France, like Bazooka - Oliva Clavel, Loulou, Lulu and Kiki Picasso - influenced even Jamie Reid, who I met with Malcolm at the time. Barney [Bubbles] was also impressed with the work of these artists. Also we pushed major record companies into doing special products such as picture sleeves that then went through our distribution service.

How did you know Nico? She was living in Paris with a friend of mine, Philippe Garel, an underground film-maker. We met in 1974 and were very close - she often came up to the Open Market, where I lived in a loft. She liked to cook for people there – she introduced me to both Jim [Iggy Pop] and Lou [Lou Reed].

How did you know Johnny Thunders? I met The Heartbreakers in Boston in 1973. They were playing in a club called The Donkeys and they were fantastic. They was the kind of band I was looking for. We really thought they were going to be big. Then they came to Paris. Everybody was there – Malcolm [McLaren], Vivienne Westwood, Castelbajac, Jean-Pierre Kalfon, Octavio, Yves Adrien. It was a famous dinner at the Coupole in Paris. Then I took them to parties and there was a riot at Bataclan – they sold out three concerts in a week.

How did you hook up with Iggy Pop and Kim Fowley? Iggy, it was easy – I had a lot of friends very close to him, like Nico. It was Cyril Jordan in San Francisco in 1973 who actually gave me the tapes of Kim Fowley's 'Animal God of the Street'. Then I decided to put the album out after talking with Kim. I liked him being so different from other people, and I'm proud of this album that never sold!

How did you come in contact with Roger Armstrong or Dave Robinson in the UK? We worked closely with Chiswick and Stiff. Dave Robinson introduced me to Sean Tyla at the Hope and Anchor [in Islington, north London]. I was actually closer with Jake Riviera, as he was tour-managing a French band called Variation. He had just got sacked from managing Dr Feelgood, and we had a meeting in a pub with Nick Lowe - who put in £500 - and we supported and pushed him to start Stiff. And we, Bizarre distribution, would distribute the label.

We sold Skydog releases to Roger and Ted at Rock On and became friends. A quick story: Joe Strummer wanted to be on Skydog, but I was already taking care of The Flamin' Groovies - so I turned down The 101'ers! But myself, Ted and Roger went to see a showcase for them at the Virgin shop and they decided to sign the band to Chiswick!

Iggy Pop's Metallic KO seems to coincide with the explosion of punk. Do you think this was an important release for punk, making a link with the past for new punk bands? We put out Metallic KO in August 1976 and the first copies were sold at the Mont de Marsan 1976 punk festival. The US release was number one in Punk magazine for months, and in the UK Johnny Rotten was so impressed with Iggy's talking between songs that he could recite the whole album.

Can you talk a bit about the French punk festivals? Actually my first pub rock/punk festival was in 1975 in Le Havre, which had Little Bob Story, The Dogs, Tyla Gang and The Snakes. In 1976 the French media were saying that we were a bunch of neo-nazis when we did the Palais des Glaces punk festival.

Who were 84 Flesh? My friend Henri Flesh was the leader of the band 84 who later became Angel Face. They were a bit older than others in the punk scene and were also part of the fashion scene. Kind of designer arty punks.

ORIGINAL RECORDING A 333
PRODUCED BY TOTAL ENERGY MUSIC
THE BAND : FRED SMITH . ROB TYNER . WAYNE KRAMER . MICHAEL DAVIS
DENIS THOMPSON
PHOTOS: CLAUDE GASSIAN
COVER : BRUNO CARUSO
A SKYDOG RECORDS PRODUCTIONS 1977

MC5

Borderline b/w Looking At You

SKYDOG RECORDS France 1977

Dennis Thompson Drums
Michael Davis Bass
Fred Smith Guitar
Wayne Kramer Lead Guitar
Rob Tyner Lead Vocals

Produced by John Sinclair
Photography by Claude Gassian **Cover by** Bruno Caruso

Originally released on A-Square Records in Ann Arbor, Michigan in 1968 and then later issued by Skydog in France in 1977.

PUB ROCK and the roots of British punk rock

An interview with Roger Armstrong of Chiswick Records

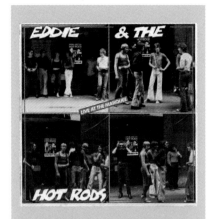

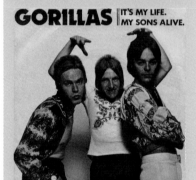

Pre-punk pub rock 45s

Roger Armstrong and Ted Carroll created Chiswick Records in 1975. Both had managed Irish rock bands in the early 1970s – Armstrong worked with The Chieftains, Carroll with Thin Lizzy. Carroll had opened the Rock On record stall on Golborne Road, west London, in 1971 and a second record shop/shack situated in a market in a disused car-park in Chinatown in London's Soho while the land awaited redevelopment, where Armstrong first came to work with his partner.

By 1975, both were keenly aware of something in the air, a collective zeitgeist of like-minded attitudes yet to be given a name. The same faces were turning up at the same gigs in London – be it Dr Feelgood, Brinsley Schwartz, Eddie and the Hot Rods or the Flamin' Groovies, who had temporarily relocated from San Francisco.

'Pub rock' had first emerged at the start of the 1970s, when the American group Eggs Over Easy moved to London. As an unknown band they had little access to traditional rock venues and instead began playing live gigs in … well, maybe you can guess. By the mid-1970s, Dr Feelgood were the crème de la crème of this pub rock scene, searing adrenalin-charged rhythm and blues that came complete with vocalist Lee Brilleaux's menacing glare and guitarist Wilko Johnson's equally disturbing but slightly more disturbed stare, and angular movements of both body and guitar. A year or two later John Lydon took this attitude to a logical conclusion, removing the pub rock while the stare remained the same (to badly paraphrase some rock dinosaurs).

The Rock On stall catered to the growing thirst for knowledge that a (still unnamed in the UK) generation of young music fans were avidly searching out - Iggy and the Stooges, MC5, the Nuggets 60s psychedelic rock compilation, rock and roll and Motown 45s. When Marc Zermati and Larry Dubay at Skydog Records began distributing their Velvet Underground, Stooges

and Flamin' Groovies releases, they gave Carroll and Armstrong the idea that they could do something similar themselves.

A cursory view of the back pages of British music papers at the time would have shown a phalanx of energetic bands filling watering holes across London. So this is exactly what the two entrepreneurs did – took a cursory view of these same music papers and put a drawing pin on the ad of one group. This turned out to be Chrome, who you may not have heard of (they soon changed their name to The Count Bishops, who you hopefully have heard of). They went to the gig and asked if the band wanted to make a record.

Not such a strange thing, you might say, but the only people who had done this before were … erm, no one. That's right, Carroll and Armstrong's newly formed Chiswick Records, is the first small independent record label in Britain. You had your technically independent but actually very big one person-led labels such as RAK or Island and there were also independent UK labels within reggae music, but Chiswick gave birth to the British independent music industry.

But it was not until the manipulation of the major record companies by arch svengalis Malcolm McLaren and Bernie Rhodes, that punk really became an industry. While the movement already existed, it was not until 1976 that punk in the UK was born - and not from the collective spirit of a million DIY labels (as you may have expected or hoped), but from the signings of the Sex Pistols to EMI, The Clash to CBS and the Buzzcocks and The Stranglers to United Artists. (Actually, the first UK punk record was The Damned's New Rose, released by Stiff on 22 October 1976. But you get the point.)

Armstrong says every month of 1976 felt like a year, because everything was moving so fast. He recalls standing in the crowd, waiting for his new signings The 101ers to play, when Joe Strummer walks up to him before the show saying, 'Roger, have I done the right thing?'

'Have you done the right thing what, Joe,' replies Roger.

'I've just left the band and formed a new one with that guy at the bar.' That guy was Mick Jones. Strummer had left to form The Clash before The 101ers' first record had even come out.

Similarly, a week's holiday for Armstrong after a Damned gig meant that Chiswick missed out on signing them to what would become their first competitors – Stiff Records.

Marvel also that on the day Chiswick were supposed to be signing another then-unknown group, The Jam, they were informed the band had instead just signed to Polydor. The story was that on that same day The Clash's manager, Bernie Rhodes, had switched his deal at the last minute from Polydor to CBS - and so Polydor had a hole to fill very quickly if they were to catch any of the breakers of the punk wave.

Signing (well nearly) The Jam had made perfect sense to Armstrong. Chiswick Records saw the bigger picture of punk, before the manufactured creation of punk. Punk, pub rock, power pop, new mod – it was all the same thing to Chiswick – and it was this wider view of music that enabled them to grow quickly, and makes them a fitting template to the most successful independent labels of today in the UK – Beggars Banquet, XL, Domino, Warp.

Chiswick records were manufactured by Lyntone, an independent company that specialised in flexi-discs and novelty items - an important aspect of punk singles that fed to the collectors market of young fans. Coloured vinyl was a relatively inexpensive gimmick. But how about The Count Bishops' 'I Want Candy' on six-inch vinyl, or competitor Beggars Banquet's release of The Lurkers' Fulham Fallout Forty Free, where a limited-edition (of course) gold vinyl flexi-disc falls out of the sleeve when you held the cover up? The major record companies learnt fast from these tools – the white-vinyl 'Tits' EP (yes, how wrong is that?), which came free with The Stranglers' Black and White album, was limited … to the first 75,000 copies. Nowadays that would seem like a record company's arch copywriter's joke.

Similarly, the humble picture-sleeve became a defining characteristic of punk. Prior to punk, the only singles that came with picture sleeves were EPs, European singles and a few Beatles releases.

Chiswick Records came out of Rock On record stall. How did the Rock On record store start?
Ted Carroll had a weekend market stall down in Goldborne Road, west London, called Rock On. Ted was known as the guy to go to for rock and roll 45s. This was 1971, so at this time bands like The Stooges and the MC5 were still current acts.

I began working on Ted's new stall in Soho, London, around 1974. It was a parking lot in Chinatown and they had these temporary units up for years, and we were like a proper record shop. Around 1975, very much inspired by Chess and Atlantic and all those guys, we started a label. I mean, not that we were anything like them, but they gave us the idea that you can start a record label, that it's not impossible.

There were no independent record companies at that time. Island was regarded well, but was a big operation. They were not street level, there was no culture of 'let's record a band you find in a pub and take it from there'.

So you thought you could do that?
Yes, that was our idea. Melody Maker used to be full of pages of gigs – and we found a band playing at the Lord Nelson pub in London called Chrome. I said, well, that looks like a good rock and roll name. It was as dumb as that.

We'd been to the Lord Nelson before to see Dr Feelgood play and they were the big signature band at the time in London. They were the band you went to see every time you could. They ruled the roost.

What was different about Dr Feelgood?
Well, they were just slightly younger than say Brinsley Schwarz or Bees Make Honey. Eggs Over Easy were an American band that came to London and are always regarded as the founders of pub rock – they started playing in pubs rather than rock venues. But they had more of a country, American edge. Then the Feelgoods came along with this sharp image, that was both threatening and tough.

They're the first British pre-punk band, essentially?
Well, yes. The audience could make a comparison with the

MC5 or the Stooges, as these guys were also making tough, uncompromising rock and roll, but in a different way. Their first couple of albums - they don't sound like it now - but in that climate it was tough, hard-nosed rock and roll. Essentially, that was what was carrying us out of the 1960s and through, into the 1970s, in that period before punk came along.

How did it change?
One of the things pub rock had done was open the pubs up, so suddenly it went from not just being Brinsley Schwartz gigs - we had the Gorillas on the scene, and that was kind of the dawn of punk. Punks used to come along to see the Gorillas, because Jesse [Hector] would be hanging from the ceiling with his toes, playing his guitar with his teeth; he was so over-the-top. The other thing about the early punk days is they didn't have much of an act going. I mean the Pistols used to just stand there and just sing in a mic. And then they all went to see Jesse, he'd be lying on the floor with his feet over his shoulders, still playing guitar - you know, he put an act on.

So you wanted to find a band?
Yes, we found Chrome and said, 'Right, we'd like to make a record with you.' They weren't terribly impressed, but agreed to it. Shortly after they became The Count Bishops and they were great, they just hit that moment - they were really tough.

It always seemed like The Count Bishops had come out of pub rock, but had the attitude of punk before it existed ...
Oh yes, absolutely. I mean, we made their first record in August 1975. The Ramones come over a year later, so the American scene had just about started to take off then. But with the American scene - I mean, the Ramones were undoubtedly punk - but it appeared to us that Blondie, Talking Heads and Richard Hell had more of an arty edge to them.

The Ramones
We sold some glam stuff on the stall - the more edgy side of it, like Sweet and T-Rex stuff. In 1976, when the Ramones played the Roundhouse and Dingwalls, I opened the stall after having gone to see them the night before. It was 10am and four guys in leather jackets wander up to the market stall. Joey doesn't talk, but one of them says, 'Hey, Joey wants to know, have you got any Sweet records?' So I pull a box of Sweet records out. Joey pulls out three 50p singles, and buys them and goes 'Great! Different b-sides to the American ones!' He was very pleased.

One of the points of this story is that there was a collector mentality kicking in which was new. You'd had it with jazz and pre-war 78s and stuff, but by the time we got going in 1974 people were collecting singles, making their own links with the past.

Did you see punk as connected to the New York Dolls, or connected to MC5 or something else?
No, I think, that the New York Dolls and the MC5 and The Stooges were like autodidacts, in a sense - they just invented it. And even though they did rock and roll covers, they were kind of mangling them up. I think Blondie felt like they'd slightly studied the 1960s and were doing something with it. I think the Ramones were more original, in a certain sense, but the British punk thing I always thought was a bit different.

I mean, when I first saw the Sex Pistols, they were a 1960s covers band. You know, they did Small Faces, Dave Berry's 'Don't Gimme No Lip

Child', The Monkees' '(I'm Not Your) Stepping Stone'. But that was a brief period, and then they became something that was quite unique - it definitely had roots, but it wasn't a studied look at the past and doing something with it, you know.

So, I think the British thing was a bit more 'street' in a way than in America. There's caveats in all of this, but as a general drift, I think, there's a bit of a difference there. But the Ramones were terribly inspiring to people. They were just such a breath of fresh air and just such a blast. To see the Ramones live at Dingwalls was just awe-inspiring. The set was over in 32 minutes and they'd played, like, 40 songs. I mean, it was like, 'Wow, what was that?'

How do you press a six-inch record?
Lyntone's pressing plant made flexi-discs - that's where they made their money. But they also did normal vinyl and were actually also quite flexible as a company. I mean, when we wanted to do a 10-inch record, they'd say, fine. We also did a six-inch at one point for The Count Bishops. They had a machine that made smaller records for little kids' record players.

Early on we realised that punk fed into this collectors market of record-buying. The first record was distributed out of the back of Ted's car; he just drove round and sold records to people.

So that's how Chiswick started?
Yes, we started with the Bishops, produced an EP in a day and stuck it out, and we did quite well. It was rock and roll. This is where the 'McLarenista' view of punk - that Malcolm McLaren woke up one morning and invented punk rock - is such bollocks. Malcolm didn't really know what he was doing. At one stage, we were at a Bishops gig, just before we put out their single, and Malcolm was going on at me, 'Hey! The lead singer of the Bishops is the guy I need for my band!' And I was, like, 'Fuck off Malcolm, I haven't even put the bloody record out and you try to nick the singer!'

Everybody knew something was happening. You know, when something's happening, but you don't know what it is. It was sort of strange ... the scene was very 60s oriented, everybody was doing covers, but it was coming from a new angle. Mick Jones, with The Clash his big influences were Mott the Hoople. I mean, we were actually quite pivotal in this with our market stall, because that's where these 60s records were bought. I mean even before punk, people were coming to buy Stooges records.

So punk was an extension of 60s garage?
Yes. One of the records that we sold was the Nuggets compilation. And Nuggets was big. Everybody had Nuggets - that's where they learnt about American, more obscure garage stuff. Every generation that comes along invents the music of the past for themselves. In the mid 60s, when I was buying Beatles records, you didn't know about obscure garage bands - you didn't know about The Sonics or The 13th Floor Elevators. So at the time, you thought you knew your music - and then the next generation comes along and all this other stuff gets thrown up or reissued. And, suddenly, that's what they see the 60s as.

So for punk, there was definitely a new generation coming up, born out of the garage or the glam things. It's the big brother syndrome, isn't it? Your big brother liked prog rock, so you hate it, and you like this glam stuff that's, kind of, a bit outrageous and outlandish, you know.

That was the thing about punk. And in the words of The Desperate Bicycles: it was easy, it was cheap, go and do it. We were the beginnings of that. Ok, we were guys who'd been in the business, we knew how to do things. But still, we were, pretty much, coming out of a couple of market stalls, you know, and just putting records out.

When is the first punk release on Chiswick?

We didn't really do a punk record, per se, until The Radiators' 'Television Screen', which was in fact the 10th single we'd put out. The truth of it was that the first punk bands surfaced quickly and there was no way that we could sign most of them. Malcolm wasn't going to sign the Sex Pistols to us. I mean, Malcolm wanted EMI from day one. Bernie Rhodes was out chasing after all the majors. Andrew Lauder was hip enough at UA to grab The Stranglers and the Buzzcocks quickly. So that was that. And then all the other punks were kids who were doing it themselves. So there wasn't much left you could sign, funnily enough.

There was a mixed thing in the record business at the time. Half the record business was horrified at punk, in the same way as in 1955 half the business was horrified at rock and roll when RCA had the good sense to sign Elvis. And the other half of the business were going, 'We need to be in on this, this is the next big thing.'

It's the opposite of DIY?

Oh, absolutely. There was a DIY element in it, for sure, and there were bands inspired by that. But they were slightly later, the second wave of bands. When I say second wave of bands, we're talking about months, you understand! We're not saying three years later, you know.

That was May!

Exactly! 'That was May! Hey, man, that was so May, you know! We're now in July, you know, and it's like a different ballgame!' That's what it was like.

I mean, it was twofold. You had your Radio Stars, Police, Stranglers, Elvis Costello, Nick Lowe - these people had already been around before punk - they didn't come off the street. They saw what was happening and I wouldn't say they jumped on board, but they kind of realised they needed to put a bit of an edge in their music - crank the speed up a bit, make it a bit more intense, make it a little less produced, a little more homegrown sound. And that was that.

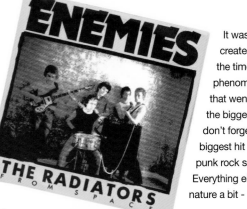

It was a funny thing. Punk rock created more around it than it sold at the time. It was a strange little phenomenon, but it was like a bomb that went off - its repercussions were the biggest thing that it achieved. I mean, don't forget the Feelgoods had their biggest hit after punk. So it wasn't as if punk rock stopped everything, you know. Everything else kept going - changed its nature a bit - but kept going.

How did Eddie and the Hot Rods compare with Dr Feelgood?

The Rods were a bit more fun than Dr Feelgood. The Feelgoods were pre-punk - they had the look, and were more threatening than any punks ever were. A Dr Feelgood gig could be a terrifying thing to go to. Lee Brilleaux used to wear this white suit and he just wore it throughout a tour, he looked like he'd slept in it. At the time, everybody knew each other. The Rods were a bit more inclined to power pop than other groups, but you know, The Damned and the Hot Rods were great mates.

What about the Pistols?

The Pistols were always a bit aloof. John Lydon was a bit aloof. You'd always see Glen [Matlock] at gigs, he liked it all. Steve [Jones] and Paul [Cook] as well to an extent. But Lydon was always a bit outside. You'd be more likely to see Phil Lynott and Lemmy [from Motorhead] at The Roxy. They weren't about to become punk rock, but they liked it. There was the Greedy Bastards gig at the Electric Ballroom, with Rat [Scabies] on drums and Phil [Lynott] on bass and vocals. Steve from the Pistols played - they did fun things like that. It was a brilliant year.

I always said that by the end of 1977, punk was over. It was finished. That was it. There was a glorious period starting in 1976 where it just started to build. I mean, let's see, February 1976, the 101ers single came out, and Joe Strummer tells me he's just left the band, and I'm thinking, 'No problem., we'd already made a record by the Gorillas, and we were looking at other bands. The next thing, Bernie [Rhodes] got in touch that summer and invited us up to the rehearsal for the sort of press debut of the new band. My press release for The 101ers finishes by saying, 'PS. Since making the record The 101ers have broken up and Joe Strummer's gone on to form a new band called The Heartdrops. They were briefly The Outsiders earlier this summer, and then they became The Clash.'

1976 PUNK 45s

THE RAMONES
Blitzkrieg Bop b/w Havana Affair
SIRE RECORDS New York USA April 1976

Joey Ramone Vocals
Dee Dee Ramone Bass
Johnny Ramone Guitar
Tommy Ramone Drums

Produced by Craig Leon
Photography by Roberta Bayley

The debut single. Two minutes and twelve seconds long.
UK-only pressing with picture sleeve.

NEW YORK and the birth of punk rock in NYC
An interview with Seymour Stein of Sire Records

Seymour Stein is a central figure in the rapid transformation of New York punk in the mid-70s into a worldwide phenomenon. Stein is a music institution, having learnt his craft with legendary music men such as George Goldner at Roulette and Syd Nathan at King Records (where he toured on the road with James Brown). In the late 1960s and early 1970s he had great success signing a slew of British and European progressive rock groups, including Renaissance, the Climax Blues Band and Focus to Sire Records.

Then in the middle of the 1970s he caught the New York punk scene in its ascendancy signing The Ramones, Talking Heads, Richard Hell and The Voidoids, The Dead Boys and others.

He also signed many UK bands for release in America including The Undertones, Madness, The Pretenders and The Smiths. In 1982 he then signed Madonna. Here he talks to us about the birth of the punk scene in New York.

When did you first see the Ramones?
I first heard about the Ramones from Danny Fields. When I finally had an opportunity to see them, I flew home from England - but got the flu, so my then-wife Linda went to see them instead of me. She was a schoolteacher in the Bronx, but always loved music. She came back raving about them. The next day I took them into a rehearsal studio and rented it for an hour. They played for about 15 or 20 minutes; they must have done 18 songs in that amount of time. I said, 'I want to sign you!' We spent the rest of the 45-or-so minutes discussing terms and who would produce the record.

So it was as quick as that?
Yes. Well, I told them they had to go to a lawyer, and they didn't want to at first, but I said you must. 'I won't sign you unless you see a lawyer!'

Did they have a manager?
Tommy [Erdyli] was sort of acting as manager. Very smart guy. Then right after that they appointed Danny Fields, and my then wife. She fell in love with the Ramones. And so that's how it all started.

Was anyone else trying to sign them?
No. Can you believe that?

What about Talking Heads?
I'd been wanting to see Talking Heads. By this time my wife was co-managing the Ramones and the band knew my every move. I came in to New York on a Sunday and the phone rang 15 minutes after, and it was Johnny [Ramone]. He said, 'Seymour, we've got some new songs - you've got to hear them.' I said, 'Great, I can't wait. I just got back from London – which of course he knew – so let me check my diary.' He said, 'We know you've got no plans for Wednesday night, so we booked ourselves into CBGB.'

It was in mid-November, but it was a really mild night. This was before global warming, but it was a beautiful night. I'm standing out front of CBGBs. All of a sudden I hear this music, and I actually feel myself being sucked into the room by the music.

I'm walking into the room, going, 'Where are The Shirts? I thought they were the support?' And Hilly Crystal, the owner of CBGBs and The Shirts' manager, says, 'Oh - they had a paying gig in Brooklyn so the Ramones thought you'd want to see Talking Heads instead. Didn't they tell you?'

So that's how that happened. I just couldn't believe what I was seeing. It was only a three-piece then but I was like a little child, like a teenager, I ran up after they'd finished and I started helping Tina down with her equipment and I said, 'Look, I'm Seymour Stein from Sire Records ...' and she said to me, 'Oh, we know who you are.' I said, 'I've got to have you on my label!' Then David Byrne said to me, 'This is where we live. Come round tomorrow.'

And I did. They were living in a loft very close to CBGB, and I made them an offer - but they couldn't make up their minds. It took almost 12 months. I signed them on November 1st of the following year. Eleven and a half months later! I can't tell you how crazy I was. You wouldn't have wanted to have been around me. I was sure somebody would sign them, one of the majors with a lot of money, and I

really became a nervous wreck. But they signed it and I was in heaven.

It took the Ramones 45 minutes to sign and Talking Heads a year?
Exactly. But I've had a lot of luck with signing bands on the night I saw them. Echo and the Bunnymen. Depeche Mode. I read a headline in the Melody Maker saying, 'Daniel Miller signs real band'. I had put out his first two records - The Silicon Teens and The Normal's TVOD - and I thought this man's got such great taste, this band must be something. I grabbed my passport, ran out to the airport. I had a small office in London and I said, 'Please meet me - we're going to go to a town called Basildon, so get the directions.' And we saw them, and I signed them that night.

One time Geoff Travis called me about The Smiths. He said, 'Seymour, I've just seen a band, and I'm crazy about them. I signed them - I need a partner in the United States. I'll tell you, honestly, as much as I love them, I know your taste. You'll love them even more!' So I said, 'When are they playing? I'd like to see them.' And I went. I might even have signed them without even hearing them, because he was so over the top.

You don't like the term punk?
I don't like any terms. I'll tell you the terms I like: pop, country and western, rhythm and blues, jazz, classical. I like them.

I considered what the Ramones were doing, back in the mid 70s, to be new music. And that's what it was. And, of course, people like to put labels on things. What's bad about labels is that it marginalises it. To me - you might think I'm crazy - but when I heard the Ramones, I heard pop songs.

They can sound a bit like 60s bubblegum ...
It was sort of bubblegum, but it was also Abba, it was also the Beach Boys - and I worked with Brian Wilson.

I was also very friendly with Jeff Barry and Ellie Greenwich. Great writers. I adore Carole King and Jerry Goffin, Barry Mann and Cynthia Weil, Howie Greenfield and Neil Sedaka. And to me, the Ramones were songwriters of the same calibre.

So punk was just new music?
It was music I liked. Why put a label on it? There are two labels: good and bad. Throw away the bad and then how good is good? That's how I've run my career.

Were there any other bands in New York coming out at the same time as Taking Heads and Ramones, that you'd wanted to sign if you could have?
I tried to sign Television. I liked their music quite a lot, but they decided to sign with Karen Berg over at Elektra Records. And, of course, I loved Blondie.

Did you try and sign them?
Richard Goettherer was interested in them. He was my partner at Sire until this point, but we had just split up our partnership, but it was friendly. Well, I wouldn't say friendly - our wives hated each other and it was really terrible. His wife was from a small town in southern Illinois, hated the music business - and my wife was over the top, and they just didn't get on. He was a great partner, he's still my best friend in the world after so many years. He wanted to try to save his marriage, but he didn't.

But he found Blondie around the same time that I found Talking Heads and the Ramones. So he not only found them and signed them, he produced their first records. He signed them to a little label, Private Stock, owned by Larry Utal. The guys from Chrysalis Records were in love with the band and waved a huge cheque in front of Larry's face, and he sold the band to Chrysalis.

So music labels stink. Not record labels - I worship the old Chess and Atlantic and King. I mean, I can't tell you the numbers on Sire Records, but I could tell you that Honky Tonk by Bill Doggett was King 4950. And I could tell you that James Brown's Try Me was Federal 12337.

Would you have liked to sign The Stooges?
I'd have loved to have signed The Stooges!

Or MC5?
Are you kidding me? I'd have loved to have signed them too.

Were the Ramones a hard band to deal with?
They were the easiest. First of all, only one member was really into drugs - Dee Dee. And Tommy was the commander in chief. I mean they weren't easy to deal with, but they didn't give me any trouble because we both were on the same course - we wanted them to make it. And they would do anything to do it. We suggested they go to the UK and they were all in favour of it. The only thing they were very much against was that they didn't want to go on the tour with the Sex Pistols and the Clash, because

SEYMOUR STEIN SIRE

said, Ok but it will hurt your career.' I mean, these guys took three baths or showers a day they were so clean. They were good kids from Queens.

Did you feel a connection, being from New York yourself, with the music you were signing at this time?

Yes, and the Ramones were definitely a part of New York music heritage. And Johnny, in particular, loved doo wop - in fact, they all did, which was very much an east coast thing. Although having said, that some of the best doo wop came out of Chicago and LA. The Moonglows and The Flamingos were mid-west and the Penguins were a west coast group.

Do you think your time as a journalist at Billboard made you realise it was important to sign bands fast, because trends move on fast in music?

No, I signed bands fast because I had no money, and I figured if I didn't sign them fast a major label would come along.

Why did you sell Sire?

Well, Sire was distributed by Warners and I was very happy to be there. Eventually I sold them first half and then the other half of Sire, because I felt if they had ownership they would do more for my artists. And I don't want to say I didn't want to be rich and successful, but the main thing I wanted to do was have hits. I knew I had two acts that were amazing and I knew that I could sign so many more if they helped bankroll me. I was so hot. And I'm not saying we were making a lot of money for the company, but we were giving them a fucking great image. The final sale took place in 1980. And then two years later I signed Madonna. But, hey, I've no regrets.

What was your involvement in the UK punk scene?

Malcolm [McLaren] hated me, because it was my idea for the Ramones not to do the Pistols' Anarchy Tour. I came to see The Clash - whom I fucking adored – to try and sign them. I flew in from New York and I had to go all the way out to Cleethorpes to see them. I never even knew there was a place called Cleethorpes! I had to take two trains and then a coach.

I had a lot of time for [The Clash's manager] Bernie Rhodes. Bernie had given me a phone number to call him when I arrived, but Malcolm answered the phone. I said, 'Bernie Rhodes, please.' He said, 'This is Malcolm. Bernie's not around.' I said, 'This is Seymour Stein.' And he said, 'What are you doing here?' And I said, 'I'm here to see the Clash.' I said, 'Malcolm, Bernie was going to make sure that I got in - do you know if it has been taken care of? I've come a long way.' He said, 'I'll take care of it, I'll just put down that there's a middle-aged man coming down tonight.' Bernie was two years older than me! That fucking Malcolm McLaren. I just didn't like him.

Malcolm just wasn't in it for the music. Please, don't ever believe he was in it for the music. He was in it for the glorification of Malcolm McLaren. And then he said to me once, 'You're Jewish, right?' I said, 'What difference does it make?' He said, 'No difference.' And he was Jewish himself, or part-Jewish. I didn't know that - I don't care what people are.

So you would have signed the Pistols and The Clash if you could have?

I would have signed them both.

So could you get to speak to the Sex Pistols, even?

Of course I did. I spent a Christmas with them right at the time when they threw Glen [Matlock, bassist] out of the band. I was with Caroline Coon and Vivien Goldman. I spent Christmas with all of them in this one house. I had the most wonderful Christmas ever with all of those people - partly because I did so many drugs I almost killed myself.

I was thinking, 'Oh my God, they're throwing Glen out. He writes all the songs! Because, to me, songs are everything, and he writes all the fucking songs! What are they doing? But I must say that Sid Vicious, Glen's replacement, was very good looking, he looked like he was right out of Central Casting - a star. I understood that, and I had no problem with him.

THE SAINTS

(I'm) Stranded b/w No Time

FATAL RECORDS AUSTRALIA August 1976

Chris Bailey Vocals
Kym Bradshaw Bass
Ivor Hay Drums
Ed Kuepper Guitar

Produced by Mark Moffatt

Formed in Brisbane, Australia in 1974 inspired by proto-punk bands such as MC5 and The Stooges. This single was released in the UK on Power Exchange Records (with this picture sleeve) in Sep 1976 - before the Sex Pistols, The Buzzcocks, The Damned and The Clash had all released their debut records. (I'm) Stranded is one of the best records ever (acknowledged fact).

THE DAMNED

New Rose b/w Help

STIFF RECORDS London, UK 22 Oct 1976

Dave Vanian Vocals
Captain Sensible Bass
Brian James Guitar
Rat Scabies Drums

Recorded at Pathway Studios, London **Produced by** Nick Lowe **Mastered by** Bilbo

Formed in London in 1976. The Damned were made up of Brian James who had played in the earlier group Bastard and the infamous London SS (to which Rat Scabies failed an audition), alongside Dave Vanian, Rat Scabies and Captain Sensible, all three of whom had previously been in Masters of the Backside (along with Chrissie Hynde before The Pretenders). Supported the Sex Pistols at the 100 Club on 6 July 1976.

SEX PISTOLS
Anarchy In The U.K. b/w Wanna Be Me
EMI RECORDS UK 26th November 1976

Johnny Rotten (Lydon) Vocals
Steve Jones Guitar
Paul Cook Drums
Glen Matlock Bass

Produced by Chris Thomas **Design by** Jamie Reid

Recorded at Wessex Studios 17th October 1976.Originally issued in plain black sleeve then reissued in a plain EMI sleeve before being withdrawn by the record company after the Sex Pistols' appearance on the Today show with Bill Grundy. In January 1977 the band were also dropped by EMI.

KILLER KANE BAND

Mr. Cool b/w Longhaired Woman/Don't Need You
WHIPLASH Naugatuck, Conneticut, USA 1976

Arthur Kane Bass, Vocals
Blackie Goozeman Guitar, Lead Vocals
Andy Jay Lead Guitar, Vocals
Jimi Image Drums, Vocals

Arthur 'Killer' Kane was the bass player in The New York Dolls and had formed The Killer Kane Band in San Francisco after leaving the Dolls. Whiplash Records first release was The Brats 'Keep On Doin' released in late 1975.

Killer Kane Band

Side I   Side 2
I. Mr. Cool   I. Longhaired Woman
             2. Don't Need You

The Killer Kane Band is:

Arthur Kane — Bass, Vocals

Blackie Goozeman — Guitar, Lead Vocals

Andy Jay — Lead Guitar, Vocals

Jimi Image — Drums, Vocals

Color Coated in 4X   33⅓ EP

THE NERVES

Hanging On The Telephone/When You Find Out/
Give Me Some Time/Working Too Hard

THE NERVES RECORDS Los Angeles, California
USA 1976

Jack Lee Guitar
Paul Collins Drums
Peter Case Bass

Self-released single distributed by Bomp! Records. Despite writing one of the catchiest songs in pop history this San Francisco-relocated-to-LA band had already disbanded by 1978 morphing into new bands The Breakaways, The Plimsouls and The Beat. It would be left to Blondie to give the song the exposure it deserved, with their cover of Hanging On The Telephone.

Inset text:

HANGING ON THE TELEPHONE

WHEN YOU FIND OUT

GIVE ME SOME TIME

WORKING TOO HARD

Cover photo (left to right)

Jack Lee, Paul Collins and Peter Case

THE NERVES RECORD CO.
7188 Sunset Blvd. Suite 204
Hollywood, Calif. 90046

CRIME

Hot Wire My Heart b/w Baby You're So Repulsive
CRIME MUSIC San Francisco, California USA 1976

Frankie Fix Guitars and Vocals
Johnny Strike Guitars and Vocals
Ron The Ripper Bass
Ricky Tractor Drums

Sleeve by James Stark

First ever west coast USA independently released punk record from San Francisco group formed in 1976.

BLONDIE
X Offender b/w In The Sun
PRIVATE STOCK New York, USA 1976

Debbie Harry Vocals
Chris Stein Guitar
Gary Valentine Bass
Clem Burke Drums
Jimmy Destri Keyboards

Produced by Richard Gottehrer and Craig Leon

Debut single by Blondie released on Larry Uttal's Private Stock label before the band switched to Chrysalis. Gottehrer was a Brill Building songwriter and producer since the 1960s and had recently split from his partnership with Seymour Stein at Sire Records.

RICHARD HELL
Another World b/w Blank Generation/You Gotta Lose
ORK RECORDS New York, USA 1976

Richard Hell Vocals, Bass
Marc Bell Drums
Ivan Julian Guitar, Backing Vocals
Robert Quine Guitar, Backing Vocals

Produced by Craig Leon and Richard Hell
Photography by Roberta Bayley **Design by** S.W. Taylor

First generation punk, formed in New York in early 1976. In 1972 Hell and Tom Verlaine starting rehearsing as the Neon Boys (for which Hell wrote "Blank Generation"), but never appeared in public. When they finally found a second guitarist in late 1973, they re-named themselves Television.

TWO SINGLES and their sleeves
by Richard Hell

MY BANDS didn't release very many singles, maybe six or eight in the ten or eleven years I was active in music. Only a couple of those came from major labels; the others were independent 'do-it-yourself' efforts in tiny printings, like these two. The Ork record is my first release ever (1976), while the 1980 Shake Records 'Neon Boys' EP preserves my first 'studio' recording, made on a four-track set up in a guy's basement in Queens, NY in 1973.

The performances on the Ork EP are a bit of an embarrassment because the band hadn't been playing together long enough to have its style really going. The music plods, though I actually prefer the Ork rendition of the funky 'Another World' track to the version on the 'Blank Generation' album the following year. I see that the group, the Voidoids, isn't named on the sleeve. I must not have settled on the name yet. The picture is from the first photo session we did, shot by Roberta Bayley in my apartment in the East Village. I like the way we look, even though it's grim (you can't see that Marc's shirt -which was really mine - is bright red, and that Ivan's is satin). We appear threatening, kind of alien, but also various enough that we look like we really could be a group of neighborhood pals. The slum Musketeers. Nobody is conforming to an existing style, and that's true of every aspect of the artifact. It's a nice item for the way it's true to its moment. As I say, the music leaves something to be desired, but I like the overall package.

The 1980 Shake EP comprises material that's archival rather than originally intended for release. One side is the 1973 Neon Boys tracks, which were made just to preserve a record of our exertions as the band was dissolving for lack of a second

guitar player, and the other side sports two demos of new songs recorded by me with the Voidoids (plus a bassist) in 1979. Those 1979 demos were financed by Stiff Records' Jake Riviera in anticipation of recording a new Voidoids album for his subsequent Radar Records label.

As it worked out I wasn't prepared - to put it kindly - to make a whole new album and that idea was scrapped. The EP is meant as a double A-side—neither side emphasized over the other. There's a recent headshot of me on the side of the sleeve for the '79 tracks, while the Neon Boys picture comes from late 1973 or early '74. It's actually a very early (pre-public appearance) Television photo taken at our rehearsal space in Terry Ork's loft.

Richard Lloyd is simply cropped from the shot. 'Television' is what we renamed the stalled three-piece Neon Boys when Lloyd was added to the group. Tom Verlaine plays both guitars on the Neon Boys tracks. I'm fond of this record. The Neon Boys material is my earliest singing and lyric-writing and a rare example of the frantic style of the original Television, while the '79 Voidoids side features the first appearance of a version of a favorite song of mine, 'Time', including gorgeous soloing by Robert Quine. The photos and design complement the music in a traditional way: classic picture sleeves endearingly representing visually a kind of confrontational, quasi-poetic pop.

THE RUNAWAYS
Cherry Bomb b/w Blackmail
MERCURY RECORDS USA 1976

Cherie Currie Vocals, Piano
Jackie Fox Bass, Vocals
Sandy West Drums, Vocals
Lita Ford Lead Guitar
Joan Jett Rhythm Guitar, Vocals

Orchestrated by Rodney Bingenheimer
Produced by Kim Fowley

The all-female Runaways created by Kim Fowley in Los Angeles in 1975.
Japanese-only picture sleeve of their debut single.

THE RESIDENTS

I Can't Get No Satisfaction b/w Loser=Weed

RALPH RECORDS

San Francisco, California USA Sep 1976

Line-up: Unknown

Produced by Residents Uninc. **Artwork by** Porno/Graphics

Art/music collective formed in Shreveport, Louisiana, sometime in the 1960s. Buried somewhere in here is the Rolling Stones original. Insane and excellent! This is the 1978 re-issue of the 1976 original hand-screen sleeve. Yellow vinyl.

PASTICHE

Flash Of The Moment b/w Derelict Boulevard

EUPHORIA Boston, Massachusetts USA 1976

R.A. La Centra Vocals, Drums, Percussion
Mener Sheene Lethal / Lewd / Lead Guitar
Kim Preston Vocals, Organ, Electric Piano, Guitars
Mr. Curt Vocals, Guitars
Dave Godbey Bass and Vocal

Recorded August/September 1976 at Euphoria Sound Studio, Boston, MA
Produced by Mr Curt **Layout by** Karen Jones Lipman.

First of three singles by this Boston group.

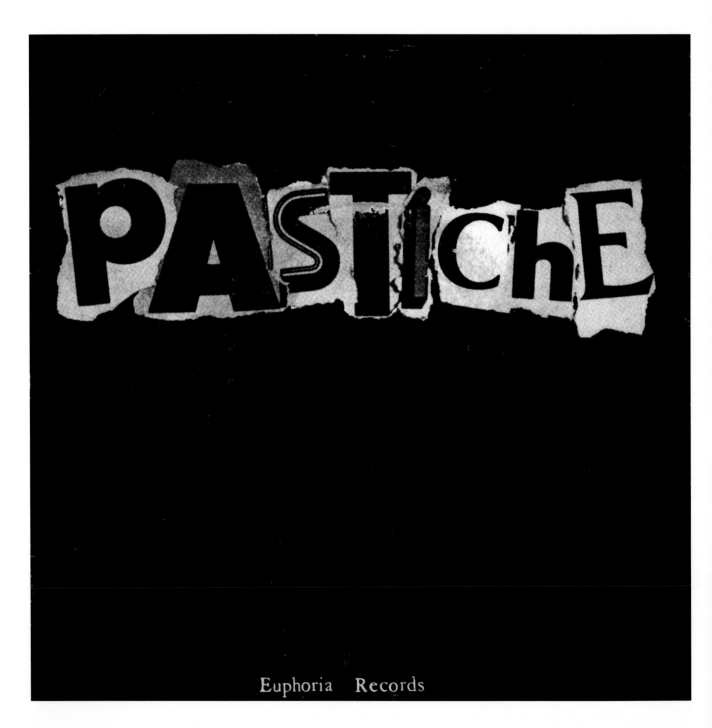

CHRIS SPEDDING AND THE VIBRATORS

Pogo Dancing b/w The Pose

RAK RECORDS London, UK 1976

Chris Spedding Vocals, Guitar
'Knox' Carnochan Vocalist/Guitarist
Collier Bass
Ellis Guitar
Eddie Drums

Produced by Mickie Most

The Vibrators had formed in South London, Feb 1976. The band played at the 100 Club Punk Rock festival in London twice – once on their own and once as guitarist Chris Spedding's backing band. Spedding then got them signed briefly to Mickie Most's RAK Records before moving to Epic. This was one of the first 'punk' records in the UK in that it features The Vibrators and that Spedding's song is about pogoing but is really power pop.

006-98449

IF IT AIN'T STIFF it ain't worth a fuck ...

Stiff Records and the artwork of Barney Bubbles. An interview with Dave Robinson.

Stiff Records was started by Dave Robinson and Jake Rivera in London in 1976. Stiff's eclectic roster of artists included Ian Dury, Elvis Costello, The Damned, Wreckless Eric and Nick Lowe, whose records were all packaged in the striking, creative and humorous artwork of designer Barney Bubbles. Slogans adorned records, badges and house bags, frequently mocking the seriousness of the mainstream music industry. These included:

'If it ain't Stiff, it ain't worth a fuck'
'Undertakers to the industry'
'When you kill time, you murder success'
'Round records for square people'
'Even our socks smell of success'
'Pre-planned deletions'
'The world's most flexible record label'
'If they're dead – we'll sign 'em'
'We came, we saw, we left'
'Reversing into tomorrow'

These ingredients, along with a knack for off-the-wall marketing and a fast-responsive attitude to music trends, made Stiff one of the most important independent labels. It was rewarded with number one hits for Ian Dury (Hit Me With Your Rhythm Stick) and Madness (House of Fun), but went bankrupt after releasing The Pogues' second album Rum, Sodomy and the Lash, and was sold first to Island and then ZTT Records.

Stiff's origins were in the London pub-rock scene, and its early roster included bands such as Roogalator, Tyla Gang and Lew Lewis. But Stiff was quick to adapt, and caught punk in its ascendancy.

The Damned's 'New Rose' on Stiff Records is the first British punk record – beating the Sex Pistols' 'Anarchy in the UK' by two months. How do you feel about this?
We were always working a little faster than other people and getting the first punk single and also the first punk album [Damned, Damned, Damned] out was definitely something we worked on. Because, you know, punk was certainly very quick and sharp, but Malcolm McLaren was actually fairly slow and quite considered in what he was doing. Brian James [of The Damned] is a great writer, and I think the song stands up to this day.

Did you know that 'New Rose' was something new?
Yes, it was quite extraordinary. And also Nick Lowe, who produced it, will tell you it was also very, very quickly made. We recorded it in a small eight-track studio [Pathway in Islington, north London]. Captain Sensible tells the story of how Nick Sellotaped a biro pen across the faders so he could push the drums up every time there was a break in the music - very primitive, but effective.

Did punk follow on directly from pub rock?
Yes. But I don't suppose the punks would want to hear that they were a direct link. Pub rock bands set up a live circuit in the pubs, and as these bands got successful and moved on, punk rockers were then able to play in these venues. Landlords just want people at the bar, so they weren't too concerned what the music was. A few people spitting or whatever didn't bother them - as long as they were spitting pints they'd bought!

The simplest part of three-chord rock and roll is the fact that it's quite easy to play. From this, I think a lot of future punks were thinking, 'I can buy a guitar and learn to play in a day or two. I can certainly learn three chords.' You've got to remember that pub rock was a British version of rhythm and blues from New Orleans, which had a kind of punk element of its own. It was all three-minute songs, or shorter, and that was part of the reason for its existence. Because before this, you had prog rock, where people were jamming for a day-and-a-half on the chord of E, and it was very, very boring.

Stiff signed Ian Dury, Elvis Costello, The Damned and Nick Lowe. Was your plan to have the best songwriters signed to Stiff?
Yes. The fact that these songwriters were not oil paintings, or the accepted type of artist that the major record companies seemed to want, did not bother me. The music industry thought you had to look a certain way to be a 'star'. My attitude was that a good song and some decent promotion could get you almost anywhere.

Stiff started before punk. Did you adapt the label to punk as it came along?
Yes. We were a record company recording what was current, and punk was around. So it was quite natural.

Early on, Stiff released Richard Hell's 'Love Comes in Spurts' single. What was your link or connection with America?
Hell had met my partner Jake Riviera in New York. Jake was there as tour manager for Dr Feelgood, and Hell had been at the gig. When we got the record label going we were rooting around for material to release, and trying to be a bit notorious at the start. And The Voidoids' 'Love Comes in Spurts' was a great track, which caused a lot of controversy at the time.

You released quite a lot of material from the town of Akron, Ohio – Devo, Jane Aire and the Belvederes and Rachel Sweet. What was Stiff Records' connection with Akron?

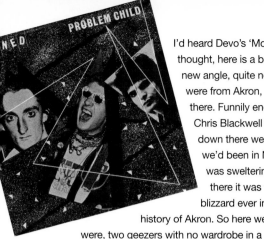

I'd heard Devo's 'Mongoloid', and I thought, here is a band with a brand-new angle, quite novel. I knew they were from Akron, so I hurried over there. Funnily enough I played it to Chris Blackwell and we both went down there wearing only T-shirts – we'd been in New York, which was sweltering. When we got there it was the biggest blizzard ever in the history of Akron. So here we were, two geezers with no wardrobe in a motel, and word got around, and groups started walking across the snow to this motel with their tapes.

Akron was very weird. It was the end of the town's rubber-tyre business and it had become a wasteland, essentially a town disappearing off the map - all the industry had gone and there was always the smell of rubber in the air.

I thought about this and later I talked to a few of our manufacturers, who told me they could make a cover smell of rubber. So when we made the Akron compilation [of Akron bands such as Jane Aire, Tin Huey, Bizarros and The Waitresses] it was a scratch-and-sniff record – you scratched the cover and it smelt of rubber.

It wasn't really very expensive, but we had a warehouse where the smell kind of percolated out of the covers, so you went into our warehouse and it had a very unpleasant smell of burnt rubber, because it seeped out by itself - it didn't need scratching.

How important was the artwork of Barney Bubbles to Stiff Records?
Barney was a phenomenal graphic designer, a remarkable guy. I had first used him for Brinsley Schwartz back in 1970. Subsequently he did a lot of Hawkwind sleeves. He did a lot of sleeves at Stiff. Eventually, for whatever reason, he seemed to get himself into financial pressure. He seemed to not be billing for his work to other companies, and he got into an income tax situation, and the whole thing depressed him. Art was very important to him, and he felt he was getting behind, so eventually he committed suicide.

Did you encourage the humour in the artwork?
He was a very witty guy, and a genius. He took a lot of acid and worked all night. He'd work for days, wouldn't sleep. When you see the Ian Dury covers, especially the singles or the Blockheads logo, they were phenomenal artworks.

Barney Bubbles also did artwork for Chiswick. Did you mind this?
Chiswick were friends of ours and we didn't own Barney. I mean, he had a studio for a while in Stiff and did all the work in there. But subsequently when I split up with my partner Jake Riviera, Barney then went freelance and did work for us as well as Chiswick and even a couple of majors. He did some great corporate work. He did some corporate logos - there is work in his catalogue that was really straight,

proper, commercial stuff. And of course, in those days you didn't have the computer, so you have to remember it was all done by hand, essentially.

Were you in competition with Chiswick?
No. We did the Stiff and Chiswick challenge, where we went around the country having a gig every now and then and asking local bands to pitch up and perform. Both Stiff and Chiswick signed various people from that tour.

I would have liked to sign The 101'ers. Chiswick beat us there, because I really thought Strummer's band was very punky, they were a very angst kind of band, and it would've been something I would've loved to have signed.

How was Stiff different from the major record companies?
Having been in management before I ran a record company, and having had to deal with major record companies as a manager, I realised that they really didn't know what they had, and they didn't really know what real marketing was. They didn't have the attitude of feeling something in your chest saying, 'Wow, we've signed a phenomenal band here and we're going to do a marketing campaign.' They didn't seem to understand that. They thought the band touring live was what the band did and if they got lucky, then the record company were able to take advantage of that. And the record company guys would talk to each other and tell you how much money they had spent on the deal, more than the music that they had made.

So I never liked major record companies. As a manager, I thought they were simply twats. And so Stiff was set up to show them what a real record company could do, with an attitude, and where the music was real - we were signing things straight off the street, so to speak. This stuff was way down the feeding chain for the majors to be interested in.

All those A&R guys who came to the pubs to see all these bands, none of them signed any of them. They couldn't see it, because it wasn't colourful enough for them. They couldn't see that the music was an entity in itself, and they kept looking for more - that attitude of major record labels, always talking about stars, 'He's a star, he's a star.' I came up with the expression, 'A star is a person that nobody tells the truth to.'

1977 PUNK 45s

BUZZCOCKS
Breakdown/Time's Up/Boredom/Friend's Of Mine
New Hormones Manchester, UK 29 Jan 1977

Howard Devoto Vocals
Steve Diggle Bass
John Maher Drums
Pete Shelley Guitar

All recorded 'live' at Indigo Sound Studio in Manchester, England on Dec 28 1976. **Produced by** Martin Zero **Polaroid photography by** Richard Boon. Later editions of the sleeve state 'with Howard Devoto'.

This is the third UK punk record released in the UK (after The Damned's New Rose and The Sex Pistols Anarchy in the UK) and the first self-released punk record in the UK. Martin Zero was Martin Hannett, photographer Richard Boon was the band's manager. Singer Devoto left the band just before the release of the single, shortly after forming Magazine, leaving Pete Shelley to become the Buzzcock's singer.

X-RAY SPEX

Oh Bondage Up Yours! b/w I Am A Cliché
VIRGIN UK September 1977

Poly Styrene Vocals
Jak Airport Guitar
Paul Dean Bass
Paul 'BP' Hurding Drums
Lora Logic Saxophone

Produced by Falcon Stuart

Formed in London, 1976.

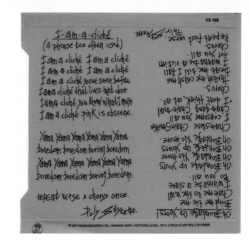

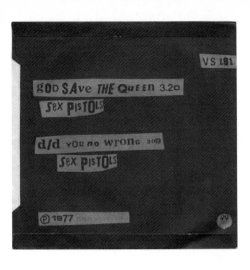

SEX PISTOLS
God Save The Queen b/w Did You No Wrong
VIRGIN London, UK May 1977

Johnny Rotten Vocals
Steve Jones Guitar
Paul Cook Drums
Glen Matlock Bass

Recorded at Wessex Sound Studios, London
Produced by Chris Thomas
Artwork by Jamie Reid

ANARCHISTS IN THE UK

An interview with Jamie Reid by Jon Savage.

Jamie Reid's artwork for the Sex Pistols, featuring re-appropriation of imagery and letters cut from newspaper headlines in the style of a ransom note, was a fitting visual representation of the iconic band's anarchism and came close to defining the image of punk rock, particularly in the UK, while its impact was worldwide.
Reid attended Croydon art college with Malcolm McLaren, and in 1970 Reid founded Suburban Press, an anarchist publishing house. As was the case with McLaren, Reid's anarchic principles led to chaos – including copyright issues from his appropriation of imagery.
His best known works include the Sex Pistols album Never Mind the Bollocks (whose cover and title led to an obscenity case in the British courts); 'God Save the Queen' (based on a Cecil Beaton photograph of the Queen, with an added safety pin through her nose and swastikas in her eyes); and Holidays in the Sun (where appropriation of imagery by a Belgium travel company led to a further court case).

How long did it take for you to develop a style that you were happy with, as far as the Pistols were concerned? A lot of the images came from stuff done in the early 70s. This was to do with what was at hand at Suburban Press - Xerox and cheap printing, rips and blackmail lettering.

Did you ever discuss with Malcolm and the band what should be in the images? I kept very quiet, because everyone wanted to be the star in that situation. I knew there'd be too much flak. Initially I had arguments with Malcolm, who originally wanted them to be a Sex band [after McLaren and Vivienne Westwood's shop Sex on London's Kings Road], and milked that Bay City Rollers phenomenon.

Right from the start Malcolm and Vivienne were not happy with making the band so overtly political - from the Anarchy flag, even up to God Save the Queen. But I just used to keep quiet and get the designs in to the fucking printers. I used to talk to John a lot, probably more then Malcolm. Malcolm and I knew each other's heads, so we didn't have to blag a lot. We'd criticise. I used to talk to John about Suburban Press, about Situationism.

The Sex Pistols seemed the perfect vehicle to communicate ideas that had been formulated, and to get them across very directly to people who weren't getting the message from left-wing politics. They were totally untouched. How did the group respond to that? It was a merry-go-round. It was just assumed that it was right. There was surprisingly little talk about the words that John had written, what the tunes of the band were, what my graphics were, what angles Malcolm was taking. We didn't ask, why we were sacked by EMI, what we should do with the anarchy flag or why John put a line in a song. It was just right for the time, and it was very exciting, very enjoyable.

When did it become a deliberate thing to keep the band off the graphics? Pictures of the band? I didn't see the need. What's the point, when you're on the front page of The Sun and The Mirror anyway? And they were ugly! Not really! I wanted the graphics to articulate what the song was about, and what the attitude of the whole band was.

Did they mind not having their faces all over the place? I think Steve did, a bit. But then it was Steve who came up with the title Never Mind the Bollocks.

Did you feel something coming up musically or culturally during 1976? There was such an obvious hole to be filled, but we had to do a lot of it off our own backs, we had to create it. I think that is ultimately why the Pistols went too far out on a limb. We were alone more than people think.

They'll hate this up in Manchester and Liverpool - but it was very much what we were doing in London at that time, around Louise's [an infamous private lesbian club in Soho, London, popular with punks]. It was associates of Malcolm, and it spun out from there.

One of the things we were aware of was never to go stagnant, never to remain still. By the time three or four records had come out, you had created a typical sort of fan. A typical punk fan, who identified the way fans always do. I'm not putting any blame on them for that, but it's a fact of life. And when you made moves that they didn't understand, in the end it was our fault that we didn't articulate our ideas well enough. Sacking Rotten from the Pistols and putting Ronnie Biggs in was a classic. It seemed like a really good move, but it didn't communicate to the fans.

It had to be teenage musicians on stage in a classic rock-band format. Which is what the Pistols were, an average heavy metal band, really. But as soon as you put a middle-aged guy like Biggs in, it throws that whole thing out the window. I think our best product from my point of view was the [Great Rock 'n' Roll] Swindle album, not the film. There was a tremendous amount of humour to it.

Swindle was trying to show how such a lot of showbusiness is hype, 90% hype. I think it was brutally honest, which from Glitterbest's (Malcolm Maclaren's company) end, we were. Going back to the EMI sacking, I don't think it was the outrageousness or the Grundy interview that upset them. It was the fact that Malcolm publicly exposed deals. As you know, you can get a banner headline in the daily newspapers saying, 'Pistols sacked again for £75,000' – but it's peanuts. They didn't like having that made public, the ins and outs of their business. That's what freaked the high-ups at EMI.

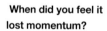

The EMI company were investing money in a new brain-scanner at the time with the Thorn link-up, and people putting big money in didn't like that association with the Sex Pistols. To a company like EMI, pop music is just a trivial little thing, but they didn't like the associations. Up to the point of actually getting product out, and perhaps two or three months afterwards was when we were most powerful, because people didn't know about Malcolm's background and my background and Sid's background. They didn't know which direction we were coming from.

In the same week we would be accused, quite seriously, of being National Front, and in the next breath you were mad communists and anarchists. It's pertinent to English politics. They like to label you really fast, and anything that can't be labelled is a bit dangerous.

Throughout the punk period you had the emergence of Rock Against Racism and this, that and the other, which at the time we felt was a very bad thing. You could see the journalists taking over, becoming establishment. Rock Against Racism happened - if it wasn't meant to have happened then it wouldn't have, but it ends up with something as sickening as Band Aid, which reeks to me of all the pomposity of early

colonialism and imperialism. Trying to impose ourselves in other countries.

The years of Thatcher have had an effect, particularly on the generation of journalists who have come up under Thatcher. Cynicism is flavour of the month. And being very negative.

Do you feel partly responsible for that?
It has a lot to do with the way it was interpreted. There was a lot more fun to the Pistols than most people would believe.
I don't think pop music's as important as you do, Jon. I think Thatcherism was more important than the Sex Pistols. Only history is going to tell, but the impression she's made on us is quite phenomenal. The things that the Pistols were on about, the dole queues and everything, have got worse and worse and worse ever since then.

When did you feel it lost momentum?
The week we got arrested, Jubilee week [in June 1977], I thought really as a pop format, there wasn't much further the idea could be taken. It should have been the end of the band. But we carried on, tried to fill out the ideas, and that's when we started to lose control, because it had got so much bigger. Malcolm was around less. This was when he was spending time in America.

METAL URBAIN

Panik b/w Lady Coca Cola **COBRA** Paris, France 1977

Eric Debris Vocals, Programming
Clode Panik Vocals
Hermann Schwartz Guitar
Pat Luger Guitar

Artwork by Gal, Daugu and Peronne

Debut single by Métal Urbain, one of the first French punk groups, formed in 1976 in Paris. The band's use of experimental instrumentation including synthesizers and drum machines, endeared them to Rough Trade and the group's Paris Maquis became the first single on the fledgling label. The band broke up in 1979 (reunited 2003).

JOHNNY AND THE SELF-ABUSERS
Saints and Sinners b/w Dead Vandals
CHISWICK RECORDS London, UK 11 Nov 1977

Jim Kerr Vocals
John Milarky Vocals, Guitar, Saxophone
Charlie Burchill Guitar
Alan McNeil Guitar
Brian McGee Drums
Tony Donald Bass

Produced by Johnny And The Self Abusers

Founded in Glasgow in 1977. Split-up on day of release of this their only single. Milarky and McNeil formed The Cuban Heels, rest of the group became Simple Minds.

BUZZCOCKS

Orgasm Addict b/w What Ever Happened To?
UNITED ARTISTS UK 28 Oct 1977

Pete Shelley Guitar, Vocals
Steve Diggle Guitar, Backing Vocals
Garth Smith Bass
John Maher Drums

Produced by Martin Rushent
Collage Linder
Photography Kevin Cummins
Design by Malcolm Garrett

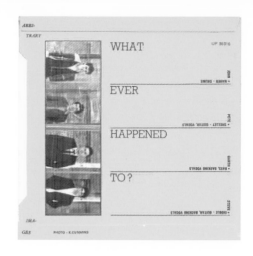

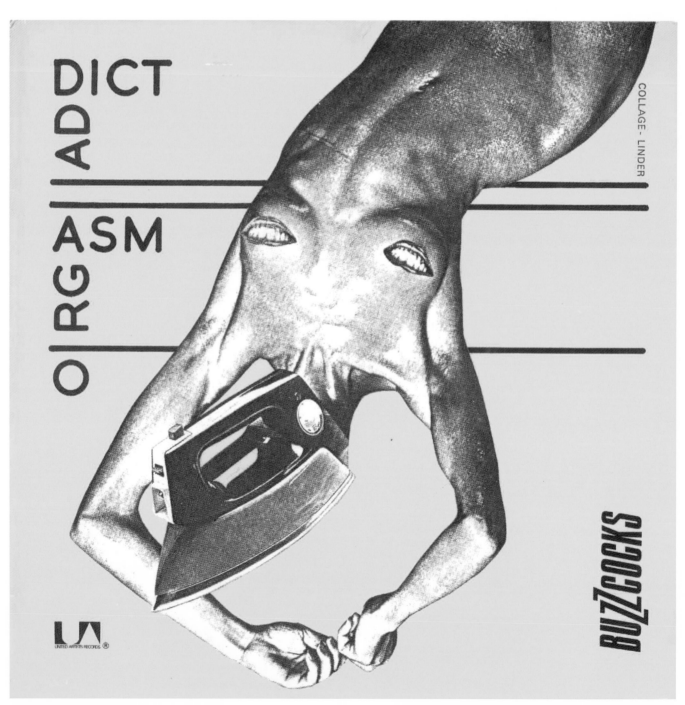

THE CLASH
White Riot b/w 1977
CBS RECORDS UK 18 Mar 1977

Joe Strummer Guitar Vocals
Mick Jones Guitar Vocals
Paul Simonon Bass
Tory Crimes Drums

Produced by Micky Foote
Photography Caroline Coon

SLAUGHTER AND THE DOGS
Cranked Up Really High b/w The Bitch
RABID RECORDS Manchester, UK June 1977

Wayne Barrett Vocals
Mike Rossi Guitar
Zip Bates Bass
The Mad Muffet Drums
Produced by Martin Zero

Formed in Wythenshawe, Manchester in 1975. One of the first punk bands in the north-east who supported the Sex Pistols at their now legendary gig at the Manchester Lesser Free Trade Hall on 20 July 1976. Rabid Records was owned by Tosh Ryan and John Crumpton. Producer Martin Zero (Martin Hannett) shortly afterwards began working with the newly formed Factory Records.

THE ADVERTS
One Chord Wonder b/w Quickstep
STIFF RECORDS London, UK April 1977

T.V. Smith Vocals, Guitar
Gaye Advert Bass
Howard Pickup Guitar
Laurie Driver Drums
Produced by Larry Wallace

Artwork by Barney Bubbles

TALKING HEADS

Love Goes To Building On Fire b/w New Feeling

SIRE RECORDS New York, USA 1977

David Byrne Vocals, Guitar, Bells
Chris Frantz Drums, Tambourine
Martina Weymouth Bass

Associate Producer Tommy Erdeyli
Produced by Tony Bongiovi
Photography by Jimmy DeSana

Debut single from Talking Heads as a three-piece group before Jerry Harrison joined. Associate producer is Tommy Erdeyli from The Ramones.

USA 1977

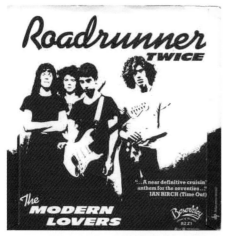

THE MODERN LOVERS
Roadrunner Once b/w Roadrunner Twice
BESERKLEY RECORDS USA 1977

Jonathan Richman recorded various versions of this song. The song was first recorded in 1972 and first released on UA in the UK in 1975. This 1977 UK release has his 1974 recording backed by the Greg Kihn Band on the A side, and on the B side is his John Cale produced 1972 version - very fitting as the song is inspired by The Velvet Underground's 'Sister Ray'. Johnny Rotten said Roadrunner was his favourite song.

SNATCH

I.R.T. b/w Stanley

BOMP! RECORDS

Los Angeles, California USA Feb 1977

Judy Nylon Vocals
Patti Palladin Vocals
Captain Sensible Guitar

Judy Nylon and Patti Palladin moved from New York to London in the early 1970s. These tracks were recorded in Patti's flat in Maida Vale, London.

I.R.T. & STANLEY

THE CLASH
Remote Control b/w London's Burning (live)
CBS RECORDS UK 13 May 1977

Joe Strummer Vocals, Guitar
Mick Jones Guitar, Vocals
Paul Simonon Bass, Vocals
Nicky 'Topper' Headon Drums

Produced by Micky Foote

THE DEAD BOYS

Sonic Reducer b/w Down In Flames

SIRE RECORDS New York USA Nov 1977

Stiv Bators Lead Vocals
Cheetah Chrome Lead Guitar
Jimmy Zero Rhythm Guitar
Jeff Magnum Bass
Johnny Blitz Drums

Produced by Genya Ravan
Photography by Glenn Brown

Formed in Cleveland 1976 after Rocket From The Tomb split-up. Shortly after forming The Dead Boys relocated to New York and signed to Sire alongside The Ramones and Talking Heads.

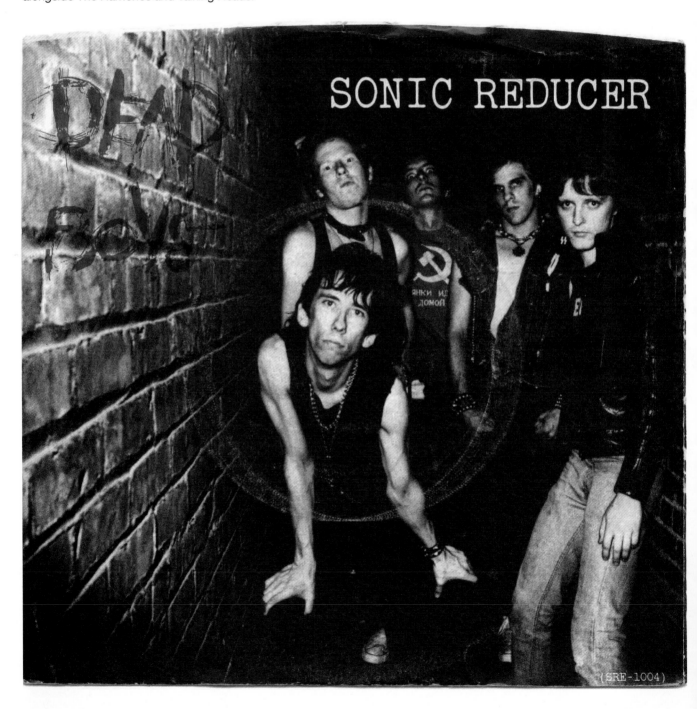

PERE UBU
Heaven b/w The Modern Dance
HEARTHAN RECORDS
Cleveland, Ohio USA August 1977

David Thomas Vocals
Tom Herman Guitar
Tony Maimone Bass
Scott Krauss Drums
Allen Ravenstine Keyboards
Tony Maimone Keyboards

Produced by Pere Ubu and Ken Hamann

Photo: Steve Kornajcik

THE ONLY ONES

Lovers of Today b/w Peter And The Pets

VENGEANCE RECORDS London, UK June 1977

Peter Perrett Guitar, Vocals
John Perry Guitar
Alan Mair Bass
Mike Kellie Drums

Formed in South London in 1976 by Peter Perrett. This is their debut release on their own Vengeance Records. Split in 1982, recently reformed.

THE ONLY ONES

LOVERS OF TODAY

b/w

PETER AND THE PETS

BLITZKRIEG BOP

Let's Go/9 'Til/Bugger Off

MORTONSOUND Newcastle, *UK* 14 July 1977

Blank Frank Vocals and Keyboards
Mick Sick Bass
Nicky Knoxx Drums
Gloria Guitars
Telly Sett Guitars

Recorded at New Barn Studios, Norton, UK
Produced by Alan Cornsforth.

Band from north-east of England released just two singles. 500 copies pressed in picture sleeve. Cost £275 to produce (less than what it now costs to buy one!).

THE SNIVELLING SHITS
Terminal Stupid b/w I Can't Come!
GHETTO ROCKERS UK Aug 1977

Giovanni Dadomo Vocals
Pete Makowski Guitar
Dave Fudger Bass
Steve Nicol Drums

Producer by Ed Hollis
Front cover photography Brian Randle

Front cover photo originally appeared in The Sunday Mirror newspaper, June 12th 1977 - girl fan watching The Stranglers in Manchester with headline 'Punk Rock Jubilee Shocker'. Ghetto Rockers is actually EMI but hiding their name. The band was made up of journalists from British weekly music paper Sounds (rival to the NME). The group had split by 1978. End refrain is the rather eerie repetition of the words "You're a damp squib."

THE KILLJOYS

Johnny Won't Get To Heaven b/w Naive

RAW RECORDS Birmingham, UK 27 July 1977

Kevin Rowland Vocals
Ghislaine 'Gil' Weston Bass
Mark Phillips Guitar
Heather Tonge Backing Vocals
Joe 45 (Lee Burton) Drums

Produced by Lee Wood

Band formed in Birmingham in 1976, released one single. Rowland would later form Dexy's Midnight Runners and Ghislaine 'Gil' Weston joined Girlschool. This was the third release on Lee Wood's Raw Records based in Cambridge.

AVENGERS

We Are The One/ I Believe In Me/Car Crash

DANGERHOUSE RECORDS

Los Angeles, California, USA Dec 1977

Penelope Houston Vocals
James Calvin Wilsey Bass, Vocals
Danny Furious Drums, Vocals
Greg Westermark Guitar, Vocals

Recorded in Hollywood, October 1977. **Produced by** Rand McNally
Formed in San Francisco in 1977 and supported The Sex Pistols on their final show in the city. This is the second edition of the sleeve.

RADIO BIRDMAN

Burnt My Eye EP Smith And Wesson Blues/Snake/I-94/Burned My Eye
TRAFALGAR RECORDS Australia Jan 1977

Chris Masuak Guitar
Deniz Tek Guitar
Pip Hoyle Keyboards
Rob Younger Vocals
Ron Keeley Drums
Warwick Gilbert Bass

Recorded at Trafalgar Studios, Sydney Australia. **Produced by** Charles Fisher and John Sayers
Cover Photography by Brian Bolton. **Layout by** W. Lord

Early Australian proto-punk band who formed in Sydney in 1974.

METAL URBAIN

Paris Maquis b/w Cle De Contact
ROUGH TRADE *UK* 1977

Clode Panik Vocals, Guitar, Drum Machine
Hermann Schwartz Bass
Pat Luger Guitar
Eric Debris Synthesizer

Recorded at Pebble Beach Studios
Produced by Metal Urbain and Ross Crighton

First ever release by Rough Trade

DO-IT-YOURSELF

An interview with Geoff Travis of Rough Trade.

Rough Trade was one of the most important post-punk record labels in the UK. The label came out of a record shop and distribution company of the same name, all of which were spearheaded by Geoff Travis. The Rough Trade shop opened its doors just months before punk and was to prove a pivotal to the movement's evolution in Britain.

How did the Rough Trade record shop start? I studied English at college - Blake, Melville and Joyce. I loved reading, and I still do. I became a teacher, but wasn't really enjoying it, and decided to go on holiday to Chicago in 1975. Later we hitchhiked down to San Francisco. When we arrived in San Francisco I realised I'd bought a load of records - being a record addict - all along the way from Salvation Army charity stores. Parliament records, Funkadelic records, Stooges records, Tim Buckley records - all kinds of records that I'd got really cheap. And this guy said, 'What are you going to do with these?' and I really didn't know. He said, 'Well, they're too heavy to carry home, why don't you ship them back to London and start a record shop?'

I'd primarily gone to San Francisco to see the City Lights bookshop. I was a big fan of the beat writers and knew it was Lawrence Ferlinghetti's bookshop and that he was still there. I visited lots of record shops in America, but didn't feel they had a community feel – whereas City Lights did, because that was the whole point of it. There was a noticeboard with cards asking 'Do you need help?', or food, or medication, or this and that. And there was a basement in the shop with tattered old armchairs where you could sit down and read all day long and drink coffee and no one would throw you out.

And I just loved that fact that here was a place that was full of culture and amazing things, and knowledge and wisdom, and books and strange people, and that they would allow anyone to walk in off the street and just participate in this.

So I took this idea back with me to do a shop in London that would be the same but with music instead of books. Our first shop location wasn't right. Eventually we found 202 Kensington Park Road, and something about a Wagon Wheel sign outside attracted us. We found out it had been an old head shop from the 1960s. When we first opened it was empty for months and months, but it was nice because we could just play records in the shop. At this time we were just living in different squats around London.

So it wasn't really a business? It was meant to be a business - but

really it was a place where we could just play music, not do 'work' work. That was 99% of the idea.

I was always a big music fanatic. I was born in 1952, so I was 13 when the Beatles and Stones started, and I loved all that stuff. My sister took me to the Empire Pool, Wembley, and we saw the last Beatles concert in the UK - you couldn't hear a thing from all the screaming. The Kinks played, The Rolling Stones and then The Beatles. We were seated on what felt like the back row - about eight miles away - but we were there, and it was amazing. And growing up in London, I used to go out all the time, places like the Marquee where I saw The Who after school one night.

The Rough Trade record shop opened in 1976, So had punk started by this time? No, it was a good six months before punk, it was the tail end of pub rock – you had Dr Feelgood, bands like Kilburn and the High Roads, Chilli Willi and the Red Hot Peppers. But it felt like something was definitely about to happen. The 101-ers had started and there was also this legacy of The Pink Fairies and Twink. All this mutated into punk in a weird way.

So there was a musical line from pub rock to punk? I think so. I mean, obviously, year one was the Pistols. I mean, it was seeing the Pistols that persuaded Joe Strummer to leave The 101-ers.

Who were your customers? When the shop opened, it was pre-punk, but punk quickly started happening and then we quickly got to know people like Joe and Mick from The Clash. I was living in a flat with Vivian Goldman and she was writing for Sounds – she'd been the first person to interview the Wailers and many other reggae artists, so we often had half the Jamaican music community in our flat. We'd have Niney and others staying with us. It was amazing. We sold reggae pre-releases in the shop - that was an important thing to us because we were in Ladbroke Grove and we wanted to serve the local community.

We'd go up to the reggae warehouses in Harlesden and buy records there. I'd say I learnt a lot of my A&R skills there because when someone buys pre's in record shops, you stand behind the counter, put the first 10 seconds and they have to decide. And it's the same thing when you go to buy it from the distributor, you get 10 seconds and then - do you want it or not? And of course being like a dumb white person, they think right let's get rid of all the crap, and they'd play you a load of crap and you'd have to decide quick. It's a good way of learning. I think it's a good education – if you buy the wrong record, no one's going to buy it from you!

What was the shop like at the start?
Well, at the beginning no one came in. Then eventually people started trickling in, and then word got out. We started tracking down fanzines, and that became a big part of the shop. Even before punk started we would sell Let it Rock, west coast fanzines, Scottish fanzines, then Search and Destroy, ZigZag, New York Rocker. People would often come especially to buy these magazines.

And then people started making their own records. The whole do-it-yourself thing started with the Desperate Bicycles. There was also Larry Debay up in Baker Street in a little grotty office that was called Sky Dog, who was importing a lot of records from France – brilliant records like the Flamin' Groovies' Sneakers 10-inch album, Iggy Pop's Metallic KO, a fantastic Velvet Underground bootleg … We'd buy truckloads from them and sell them in the shop.

To make the shop special we'd have records that other people didn't have. So we would write to Ork Records when they put out Little Johnny Jewel, Television's first single; or when Blondie released X-Offender, before they signed their deal with a major. We'd write and get 50 copies at a time to sell in the store. We'd also write to this guy on a farm in Cleveland called Crocus Behemoth who turned out to be David Thomas of Pere Ubu.

This is the era when the music was mutating into punk. It was bands on the periphery, not in mainstream rock 'n' roll, that were interesting to us. Like The Residents, or Devo's first records, all these things. Anything that was interesting that we could track down, we would get and import, like Alex Chilton' s Bangkok – an amazing single. Sstuff like this.

So when the Sex Pistols started, you probably don't connect them straight away with the records you were selling?
That's right. They were like a local phenomenon. We didn't think, 'I'm going to get their records.' We just thought it was exciting. So I went to see them at Screen on the Green, saw the punk festivals at the 100 Club.

Did you sell the first Ramones records? Yes, of course. We would have been the shop in London selling the most Ramones albums at that point. We also sold the first Talking Heads single, Love Goes to Building

on Fire – we had that before anyone else and we just literally sold a hundred of them. Our first two in-store concerts in the early days were Talking Heads and the Ramones. When Talking Heads came there was no one in the shop – no one turned up! And we were going, 'Erm, do you want a cup of tea?' So they had a cup of tea and a chat, and they were really nice.

And then by the time the Ramones played live it was just massive - the shop had got so busy by then. We had these two giant reggae sound-system speakers pumping out great music all day long – you couldn't even get in the door some days. Saturdays, it was like mayhem, people had to shout to buy records. It was really, really exciting.

By this time our customers were changing to punk, coming in with bondage gear that they've bought or that they'd made themselves. It was a mixture of normal people, straight people and absolute punks.

The bands would come in, people like Billy Idol. David Bowie came in once. He didn't actually speak to us when he came in, he got his minder to buy him a record – but that was very exciting! Everybody came. Patti Smith came in, asked me where she could score, and I said 'I'm not really into drugs,' but pointed her in the right direction.

And the fanzines were such a great part of it too. Mark Perry would come in and literally be stapling his magazines together.

So it became a community – like City Lights? Yes, I think so. People felt comfortable coming in. We distributed all Crass records, so Penny Rimbaud and John Loder would come in with a van and we'd load up thousands of Crass records that we'd buy off them and we'd make about two pence a record, because they were selling them so cheap – but we didn't care. We also had a similar relationship with Throbbing Gristle - Genesis [P Orridge] would often come in. We distributed their first single and then we asked if we could do a record with them, and this became 20 Jazz Funk Greats.

So is this when Rough Trade set up distribution? Yes. And that was an important step that was a lot to do with Richard Scott who came to work with us. Richard had really good taste, and his idea was to start mail order, because we had records that no one else had. We thought, why don't we set up a network around the country so that other people can get them? People had been contacting us in different shops around the country trying to get these records.

So that's what we did, and we set up a distribution network with shops like Fast in Edinburgh, Small Wonder in Walthamstow, which eventually became Cartel. At first it was just a group of friends round the country - about six or seven. We'd source some records and then sell them onto them, and they'd sell them to their customers.

Were these shops similar to Rough Trade?
Yes, but everybody started doing their own thing, and it created a feeling of humanity around the country - a feeling that we're building something here, which also meant that we could sell lots of records. This in turn meant that bands no longer had to sign to a major for their records to be a success. And eventually we started distributing massive hit records by Joy Division, Depeche Mode, Bomb the Bass, M/A/R/R/S, and many others.

Then you started the Rough Trade record label? Yes, in 1977. There was a French group that we really liked called Metal Urbain. We wrote to them and bought 50 copies of their first single, Panic, and they were so amazed that anyone would buy their record. One day they all turned up in London asking if we would you listen to a tape of their new single, and would we help them release it? We said yes, we'd help them with the pressing - and that's how the label started.

I didn't have a grand plan to be like the Sam Phillips of west London. But we knew Stiff Records were just up the road – we'd go there to buy records. We'd also go to Virgin nearby to buy records - just the titles we wanted, like XTC, Devo or the Pistols. Chiswick had also started, and these companies were all definitely an inspiration. All these people were putting out records, and we thought we could also do that. We thought they were good, but they didn't know more about music than us. You know, we were sort of semi-arrogant. We thought, if they can do it, and we've met them and they're human beings, we can do it too. These labels broke the myth that the music industry was something where you had to be in a high-rise office with thick carpets to be a part of it.

And the Desperate Bicycles did their own DIY single, and came in with that. This was also an important factor in us realising we could start a label.

Do you call the music on Rough Trade punk, or post-punk - or something else? We were really post-punk. DIY post-punk - we were too young to get involved with the first set of great punk groups.

Would you have wanted to?
Yes, of course. I mean, had we started two years earlier, and had our distribution up and running then, we may have been in a position to say to Bernie Rhodes (The Clash manager) why don't you work with us?

Roger Armstrong at Chiswick says that one minute punk didn't exist and then it did. So when Malcolm and Bernie Rhodes arrived, it was already sewn up, and they only wanted to deal with the majors. That's all they wanted to do, yes. Because they were very old-school, and also I think they were really into money. You know, we weren't into money - I think that's a big difference. And also I think they were into the idea of messing around with the big labels - they thought that was fun, whereas we just thought it was a waste of time.

So was this DIY culture punk?
It started with punk. I mean, Metal Urbain were a punk band. I mean it was a reaction to punk, it was an empowerment by punk, but it wasn't a slavish copy of punk. It wasn't like Eater or Chelsea, it wasn't any of that, although obviously they were independent records, some of those.

I mean, Miles Copeland started Faulty Products because of punk, really, which released ATV, Chelsea, Squeeze, and The Police. These were all bands reacting to the breaking down of the barriers, of the idea that you had to sign with 'proper' companies to get something done, And that empowered a lot of people to do things. I would say this idea was led by the Stiffs and the Chiswicks, really.

And would you say you were a DIY label? Yes. It was more about the artists and what they wanted to do than others, like, say, Virgin, where it was about 'Let's build an empire of our own.' I think that was the crucial difference. Virgin had had some great records, obviously, and they did do some good things, but they had a different mentality I think.

And was that to do with you keeping hold of the City Lights community ideas?
I think so, yes. A mixture of community feeling and socialist ideals about society and wealth distribution.

How did that affect your attitude to artists? Well, we felt were working for them. We didn't feel, like, 'You are lucky, Son, that we want to put your record out.' It was more like *we* are lucky you want to put your record out with us. That's how we felt. We still feel like that.

And how does that attitude affect, say, the record sleeves? Our record covers never had a house style, like, say, Factory did. But we felt we didn't want to say to an artist, 'This is the sleeve you're going to have.' We wanted them to say what they wanted to have, as long as it was good. I mean, we'd say if it was rubbish, you know.

BLACK RANDY & METROSQUAD

Trouble At The Cup/Loner With A Boner/
Sperm Bank Baby

DANGERHOUSE RECORDS

Los Angeles, California, USA Dec 1977

Black Randy (John Morris) Vocals
David Brown Keyboards
Pat Garrett Guitar

*Black Randy and The Metrosquad formed in Los Angeles in 1977. They
made three singles and one album - Pass the Dust, I Think I'm Bowie.
David Brown and Pat Garrett also ran Dangerhouse Records. LA punk
legend Black Randy died in 1988.*

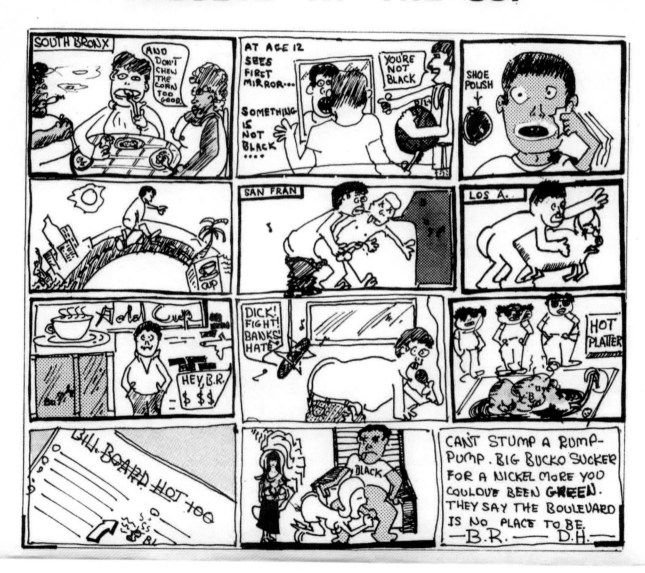

THE WASPS

Teenage Treats b/w She Made Magic

4 PLAY RECORDS London, UK 25 Nov 1977

Jesse Lynn-Dean Vocals
Steve Wollaston Bass
Johnny Rich Drums
Gary Wellman Guitar

Formed in Feb 1976. Back cover: 'One day soon an exciting New Wave quartet will explode out of nowhere like Walthamstow with high-energy music which is hard, smart, dynamic & tuneful, but until they do, you'll have to settle for The Wasps.' A mix of punk energy and power-pop – very out of kilter with the times. Consequently sank without a trace and split-up soon after. Sounds good now!

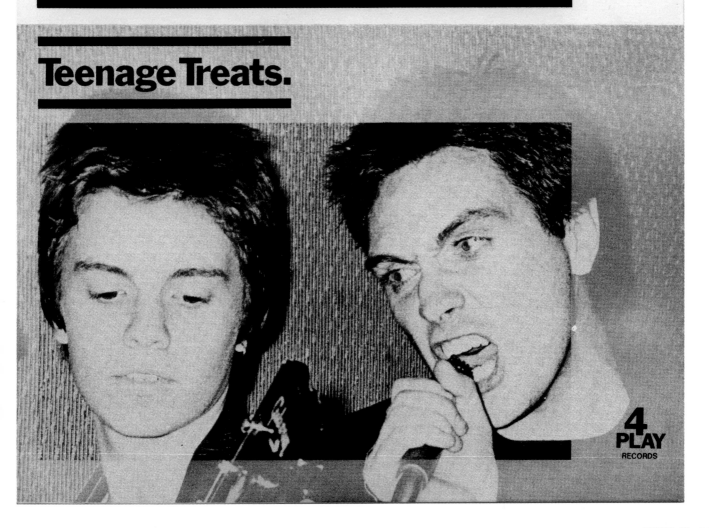

CHERRY VANILLA
The Punk/Foxy Bitch
RCA RECORDS UK 2 Sep 1977

Cherry Vanilla Vocals
Louis Lepore Guitar
Howie Finkel Bass
Michael (Manny) Mancuso Drums

Produced by Stratten Hoy

Ex-Bowie/Mainman publicist and Warhol actress. Her first group Cherry Vanilla and her Staten Island Band appeared on Max's Kansas City album. She then relocated to London in 1976. This was her first single - sort of post-New York Dolls revisited after The Ramones and Blondie have arrived. Sort of wrong-y right. After two albums the group split-up and Vanilla returned to the US.

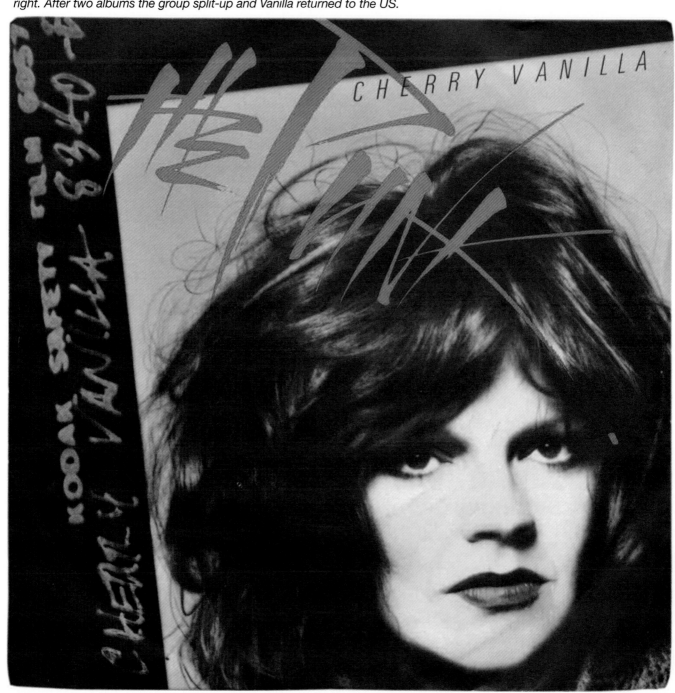

THE NOW
Development Corporations b/w Why?
THE ULTIMATE RECORD LABEL
Peterborough, UK 1977

Mike McGuire Vocals
Paul Farrar Bass
Joe MacColl Drums
Steve Rolls Guitar

Peterborough's first punk rock band, formed late in 1976.
Founded by Mike McGuire and Steve Rolls. Followed up this
single with just one more a year later.

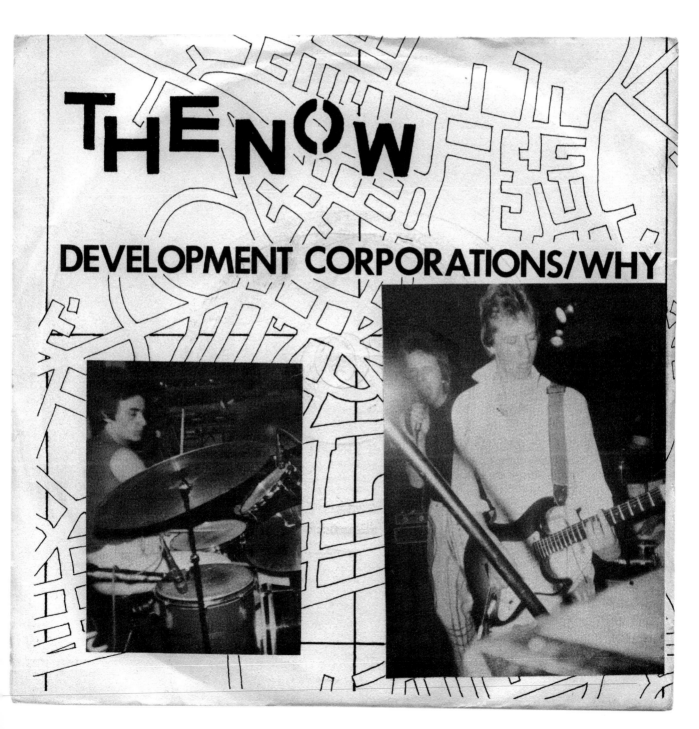

STINKY TOYS

Boozy Creed b/w Driver Blues

POLYDOR Paris, France 1977

Albin Deriat Bass Guitar
Elli Medeiros Vocals
Bruno Carone Guitar
Jacno Guitar
Hervé Zenouda Drums

*French punk band formed in Paris, 1976. The band was dropped from
Polydor after one album (which was only released in France), signed to
Disques Vogue for one more release and then split-up in 1979.*

THE NASAL BOYS
Hot Love b/w Die Wüste Lebt!
Periphery Perfume Switzerland 1977

Leo Remmel Vocals
Konrad Sauber Bass
Päde Schletzer Drums
Heinrich Wüstenhagen Guitars
Rudolph Dietrich Guitars

Recorded at Studio Bottmingen, Switzerland, October 1977
Artwork by P. Mattioli

Swiss Punk band formed in December 1976 and disbanded in 1978.
This is their only single – the first-ever Swiss punk record. Bad tune!

THE RAMONES

Sheena Is A Punk Rocker b/w I Don't Care

SIRE RECORDS New York, USA July 1977

Joey Ramone Vocals
Dee Dee Ramone Bass
Johnny Ramone Guitar
Tommy Ramone Drums

Produced by Tommy Erdyli and Tony Bogiovi
Photography by Roberta Bayley

GENERATION X

Your Generation b/w Day By Day

CHRYSALIS *UK* 1977

Tony James Bass
Billy Idol Vocals
Mark Laff Drums
Derwood Guitar

Design by Barney Bubbles

Formed by ex-Chelsea members Billy Idol, Tony James And John Towe in 1976. Split in 1981 after three albums when Idol went solo. James formed Sigue Sigue Sputnik.

THE HEARTBREAKERS
Chinese Rocks b/w Born To Lose
TRACK RECORD London, UK 20 May 1977

Johnny Thunders Guitar, Vocals
Billy Rath Bass
Jerry Nolan Drums
Walter Lure Guitar,Vocals

Produced by Chris Stamp and Speedy Keen **Art and photography by** Micheal Beal

The Heartbreakers formed in New York in May 1975 by two ex-New York Dolls (Johnny Thunders and Jerry Nolan) and one ex-Television (Richard Hell). Hell left the following year to form The Voidoids and was replaced by Billy Rath. Chinese Rocks is a song about heroin co-written by Dee Dee Ramone (The Ramones did not want to perform the song, but later did). In 1976 The Heartbreakers turned up in London where they briefly signed to Kit Lambert and Chris (brother of Terrance) Stamp's Track Records.

Side One
Neat Neat Neat
Side Two
Stab Yor Back
Singalonga Scabies

32 Alexander Street London W2
Today's Sound Today

THE DAMNED
Neat Neat Neat/Stab Your Back/Singalonga-Scabies
STIFF RECORDS London, UK 25 Feb 1977

Dave Vanian Vocals
Captain Sensible Bass
Brian James Guitar
Rat Scabies Drums

Recorded at Pathway Studios
Produced by Nick Lowe

Third single from the group.

EATER

Outside View b/w You

THE LABEL London, UK 25 Mar 1977

Andy Blade Guitar
Brian Chevette Guitar
Ian Woodcock Bass
Roger 'Dee Generate' Bullen Drums

Recorded at Decibel Studios, London **Produced by** Dave Goodman

Early UK punk band formed in North London in 1976, first gig in Manchester in Nov 1976 supported by The Buzzcocks. Dave Goodman produced the early Sex Pistols demo sessions. The Label was Goodman's label with partner Cruzo Fuller, which also released Cash Pussies, The Bombers and Dave Goodman and Friends (which included Paul Cook and Steve Jones from The Pistols).

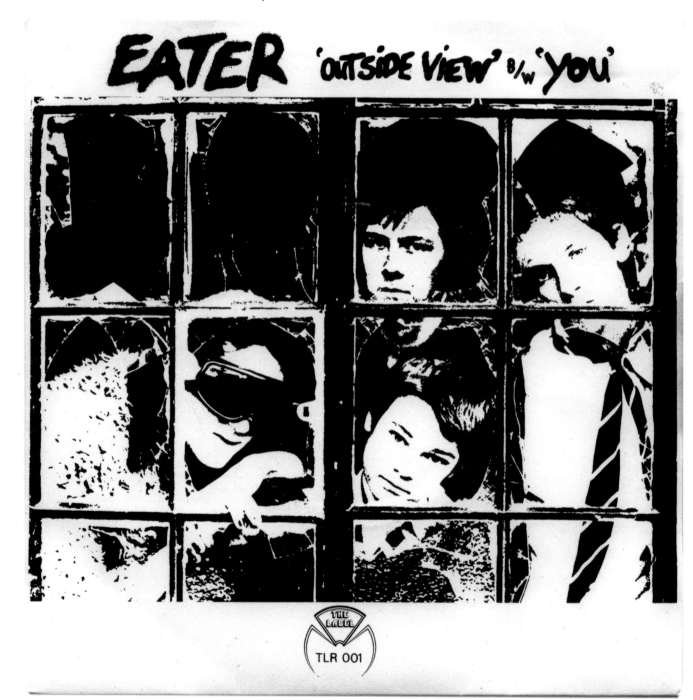

ULTRAVOX

Rockwrok b/w Hiroshima Mon Amour
ISLAND RECORDS *London UK* 14 Oct 1977

John Foxx Vocals
Chris Cross Bass, Vocals
Warren Cann Drums, Vocals
Stevie Shears Guitar
Billy Currie Violin, Keyboards

Produced by Steve Lillywhite and Ultravox

Formed in 1974, originally known as Tiger Lily. Signed to Island in 1976. In 1979 John Foxx left the group to start a solo career. Billie Currie joined Gary Numan. Ultravox then reformed with singer Midge Ure (who had played in Glen Matlock's Rich Kids). Currie and Ure had worked together in Steve Strange's group Visage. Their next album was the very successful Vienna, produced by Connie Plank.

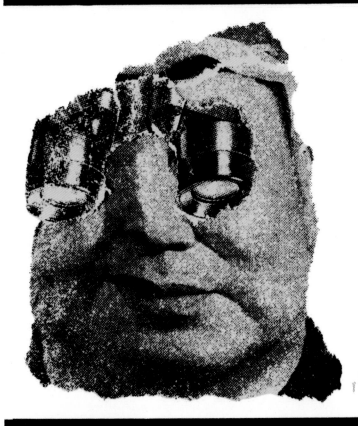
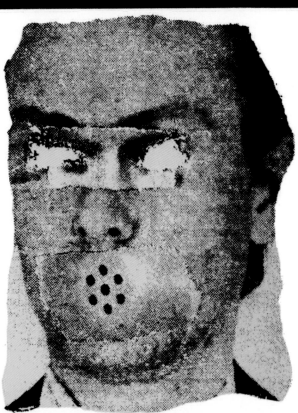

THE LURKERS

Shadow b/w Love Story (Free Admission Single)

BEGGARS BANQUET London UK 2 Sep 1977

Howard Wall Vocals
Arturo Bassick Bass
Esso Drums
Pete Stride Guitar

Recorded at Magrite Studios

Debut single from The Lurkers, who formed in Uxbridge, West London in 1976. This release was also the first release on the Beggars Banquet label, launched out of the West London record shop of the same name. To promote this single The Lurkers began a month long residency at The Red Cow in Hammersmith – hence the 'free admission single'. The Lurkers had five top forty hits between 1977 and 1979. The band split in 1980 (reuniting at various intervals).

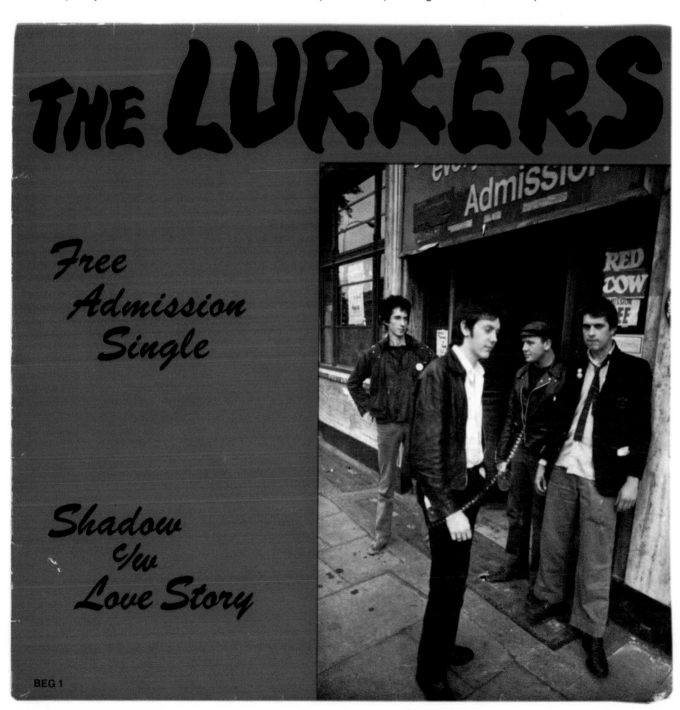

An interview with Martin Mills of Beggars Banquet.

The Beggars Banquet shop started in 1974 I think. When did you start selling the first punk singles in the shop and what were they?

'76, I think, when the Bizarre van service [run by Larry DeBay] started calling - American 45s from Richard Hell, etc, then the early Stiff and Chiswick ones, Nick Lowe and the Damned

What did you think of them? What were your favourite records from this time?

Incredibly exciting compared to everything else around - loved Nick Lowe, the Damned, the Buzzcocks, the Pistols of course.

Soon after punk started the Beggars Banquet label starts. The first release is the Lurkers and the first album a compilation of punk tracks from various bands. Did you want the label to be a punk label or was there a bigger picture already formed in your mind?

There was no plan! We just put out what was there that we liked.

Who designed the Lurkers sleeves? Quite a few are 'gimmick' orientated like The Lurkers' 'free with admission' single (was this a real claim?), and their Fulham Fallout free flexi. Was this humour and marketing all part of punk's identity or were these ideas already around?

An old friend did the first, Savage Pencil I think did the second. Yes the free admission single was real. The gold flexi and things were just fun marketing ideas.

Did you know any of the other labels at the time - Stiff, Chiswick, Factory, Rough Trade? Did you feel connected to them?

Yes, absolutely.

Would you describe Tubeway Army as a punk band at the start or different?

They were never punk, never wanted to be or pretended to be.

The Beggars Banquet label soon evolves out of punk into a much wider scope of music. Do you feel that nonetheless Beggars Banquet came out of punk?

Yes, though to be fair we only had one real punk band, we grew out of that scene and diversified from it.

Whilst expanding a roster to include a wide range of styles, and constantly updating itself as a label, do you think that Beggars Banquet nevertheless retains some of the ideals of punk?

Yes, absolutely - we may not have been as extreme as some, but the DIY spirit was always there and has remained.

BEGGARS BANQUET

VENUS AND THE RAZORBLADES

Punk-A-Rama b/w Alright You Guys

BOMP! RECORDS Los Angeles, California, USA 1977

Steven T Guitar, Vocals
Roni Lee Guitar
Danielle Faye Bass
Nicky Beat Drums
Dyan Diamond Guitar, Vocals
Vicki Razor Blade Vocals

Produced by Kim Fowley

UK edition picture-sleeve on Spark originally issued in USA on Bomp! Records. Enfant terrible Fowley's mostly-female sort of replacement to The Runaways. Slightly un-ironic homage to New York Dolls, Runaways, Sex Pistols (and The Hot Rods!). Formed by Fowley in Los Angeles in 1976, disbanded a year later.

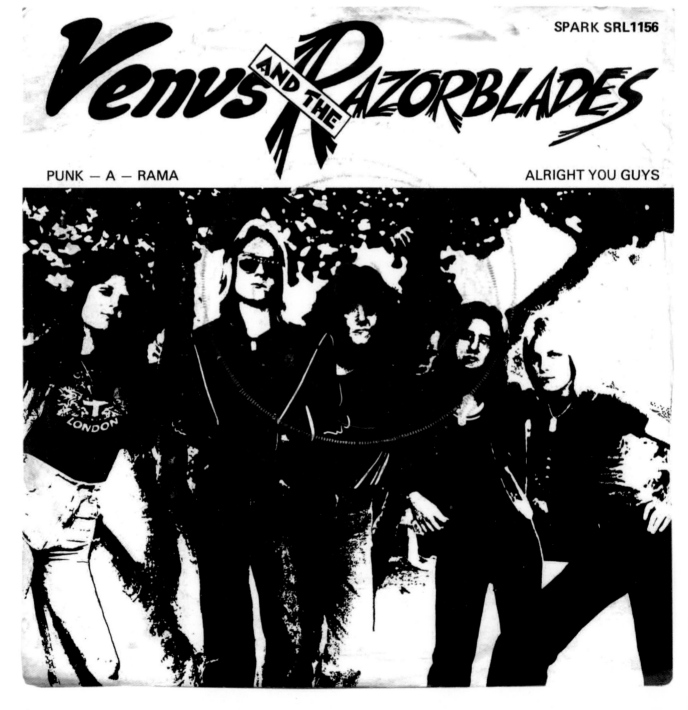

SPARK SRL1156

PUNK — A — RAMA   ALRIGHT YOU GUYS

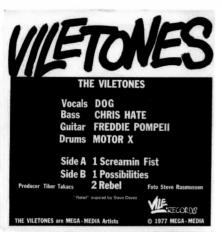

VILETONES
Screamin Fist b/w Possibilities/Rebel
Vile Records Toronto, Canada 1977

Steven Leckie ((Nazi) Dog) Vocals
Freddie Pompeii Guitar, Vocals
Michael Paputts Bass, Vocals
Mike Anderson (Motor X) Drums, Vocals.

Produced by Tibor Takacs
Photo by Steve Rasmussen

First-wave Canadian punk band who formed in Toronto in 1977.
This was their debut single on their own label.

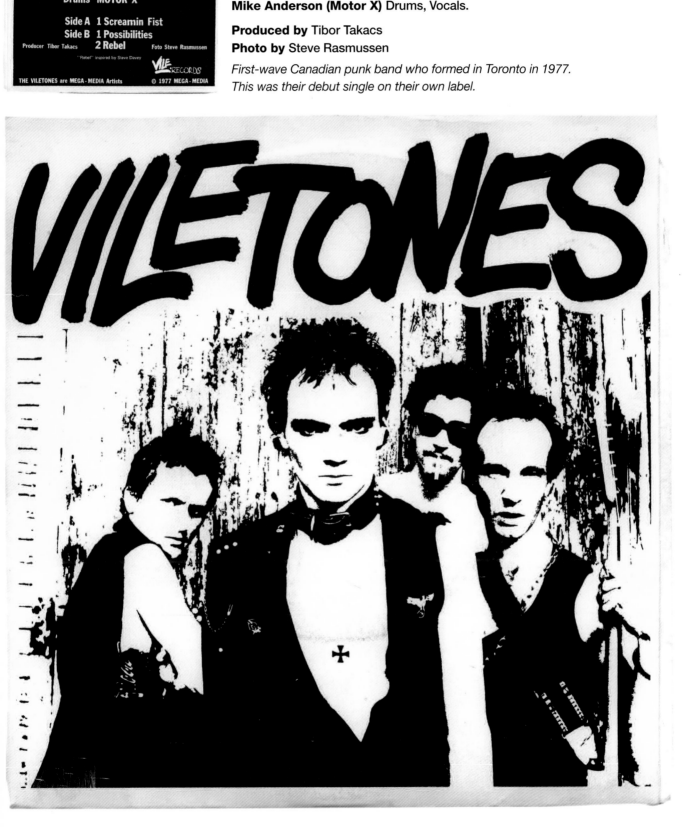

WIRE

Mannequin b/w Feeling Called Love/12XU

Harvest Records UK 11 Nov 1977

Colin Newman Vocals, Guitar
Graham Lewis Bass, Vocals
Bruce Gilbert Guitar
Robert Gotobed Drums

Produced by Mike Thorne

Formed in London in October 1976. Debut single. Proto-art-post-punk.

IAN DURY

Sex & Drugs & Rock & Roll b/w Razzle In My Pocket

STIFF RECORDS London UK 26 Aug 1977

Ian Dury Vocals
Norman Watt-Roy Bass
Charley Charles Drums
Chaz Jankel Guitar, Keyboards
Davey Payne Saxophone

Ian Dury was in pub rock group Kilburn and The High Roads from 1971-75 when they split-up. He then formed The Blockheads and signed to Stiff Records for this debut single. The ever-creative Stiff Records marketing team came up with the idea of deleting the record just two months after it came out – instant collectors item!

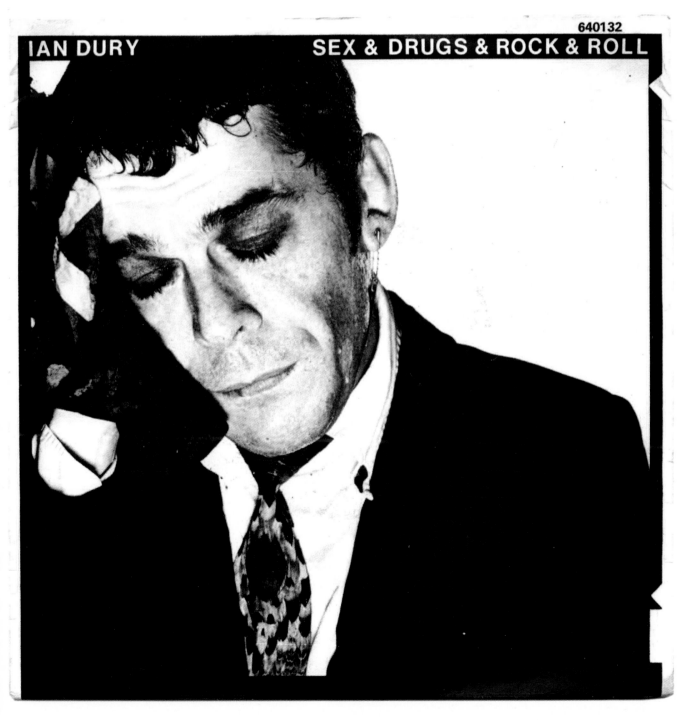

THE WEIRDOS

Destroy All Music/A Life Of Crime/Why Do You Exist?
BOMP! RECORDS Los Angeles, California USA 1977

John Denney Vocals
Dix Denney Guitar
Nickey 'Beat' Alexander Drums
Cliff Roman Bass

Producer by Craig Leon and Greg Shaw

The Weirdos formed in Los Angeles in 1976 and broke up in 1981 after one album, reforming occasionally. This is their first single.

'O' LEVEL
East Sheen b/w Pseudo Punk
Psycho Records London, UK November 1977

Ed Ball Vocals
John Bennett Drums
Gerard Bennett Bass

Artwork by Nic Aleg/Rodent

Formed in West London, 1976, linked to the equally ethically-DIY TV Personalities (who namecheck the group on their song Part-Time Punks) by various personnel. Ball later formed The Times and worked at Creation Records. One of three different sleeves.

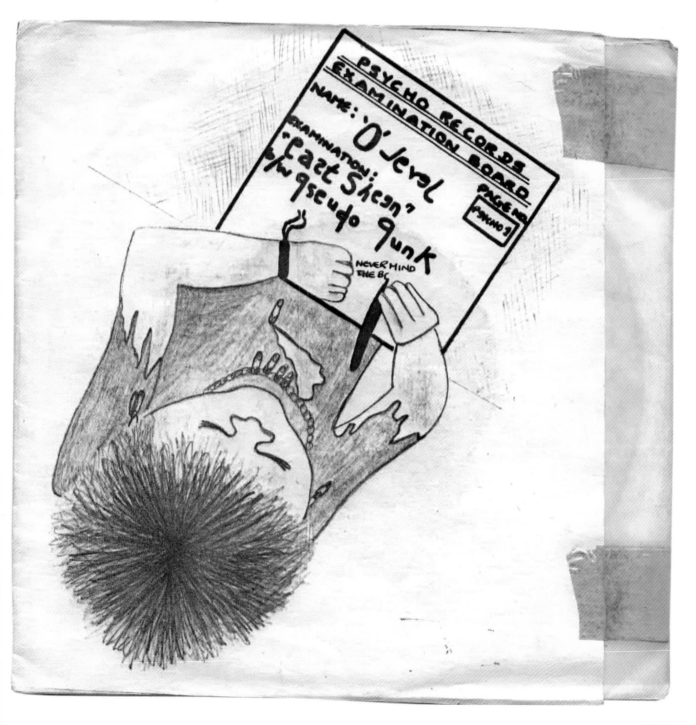

THE WAITRESSES

In 'Short Stack'
Slide b/w Clones

CLONE RECORDS Akron, Ohio USA 1977

Chris Butler Vocals and all instruments
Produced by Chris Butler

The Waitresses formed in Akron, Ohio created by Chris Butler as a side project whilst he was in the band Tin Huey. This is their first single on the local Clone label. Singer Patty Donahue would join shortly afterwards followed by full band when they signed to hipster New York label Ze Records.

GASOLINE
Killer Man b/w Radio Flic
EGG RECORDS FRANCE 1977

Alain Kan Vocals
J.P. Cayatte Bass
Olivier Burger Guitar

One of two singles (on the other they are called Gazoline) by early French punk band released on Egg Records, a sub-label of Barclay that also released experimental German artists such as Conrad Schnitzler, Asmus Tietchens and Popul Vuh.

THE UNWANTED
Withdrawal b/w 1984/Bleak Outlook
RAW RECORDS Cambridge, UK 1977

Ollie Wisdom Vocals
Vince Ely Drums
John Ashton Guitar
Paul Gardner Guitar
Paul Postman Bass

Graphics by David Jeffrey

Formed in March 1977 in London originally as Smak. Released two singles on Raw Records before they split-up in 1979 after singer Ollie Wisdom fooled the NME that he went to prison for six months for stealing a union jack flag in Bromley. The truth was more prosaic: 'We had a shit manager…' 'totally untogether'. Two of the band joined Psychedelic Furs, and Wisdom later started the Batcave club.

THE DESPERATE BICYCLES
Smokescreen b/w Handlebars

REFILL RECORDS London UK April 1977

Danny Wigley Vocals
Roger Stephens Bass
Dave Papworth Drums
Nicky Stephens Organ
Design Ingram Pinn

Debut single from the London-based group. Mono recording and both tracks are on both sides.
The British DIY music industry starts here.

THE VIBRATORS

London Girls (Live) b/w Stiff Little Fingers (Dead)

EPIC RECORDS UK 26 Aug 1977

Ian 'Knox' Carnochan Vocals
John Ellis Guitar
Pat Collier Bass
John 'Eddie' Edwards Drums

Produced by Lem Lubin and Simon Humphrey

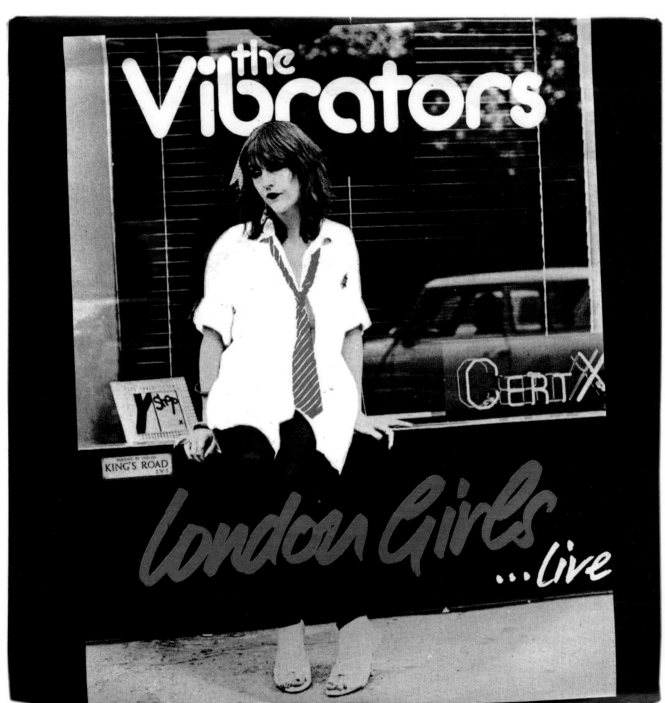

BLONDIE
Rip Her To Shreds/In The Flesh/X Offender
CHRYSALIS RECORDS UK Nov 1977

Deborah Harry Vocals
Gary Valentine Bass
Clem Burke Drums
Chris Stein Guitar
James Destri Keyboards

Produced by Richard Gottehrer

Formed in New York in 1974 by Chris Stein and Debbie Harry both of who had been in the earlier group The Stilettos. This was their first single after leaving Private Stock for Chrysalis and was not released in the US.

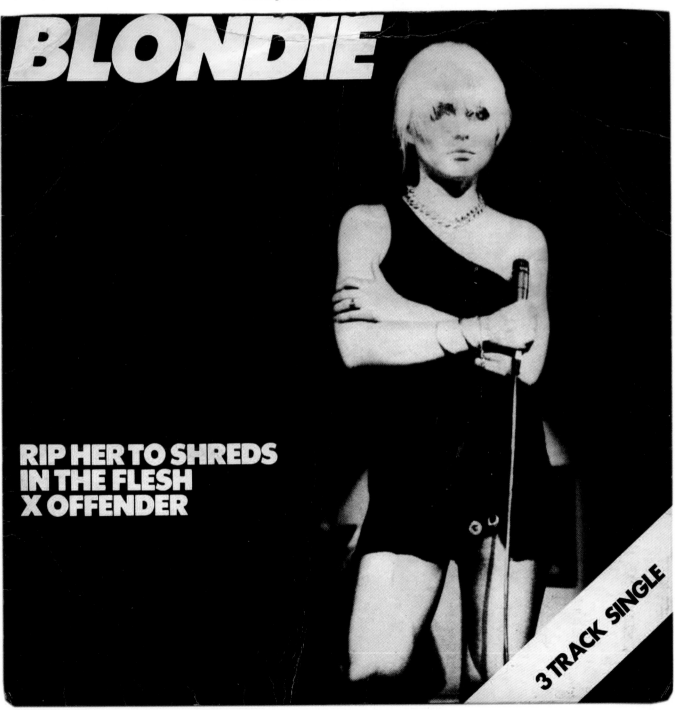

BLONDIE

RIP HER TO SHREDS
IN THE FLESH
X OFFENDER

3 TRACK SINGLE

THE DILS

I Hate The Rich/ You're Not Blank
What Records? Los Angeles, California USA 1977

Chip Kinman Guitar, Vocals
Tony Kinman Bass, Vocals
Endre Algover Drums

Formed by the Kinman brothers in 1976. Spent most of their time between San Franciso and Los Angeles scenes. One of the first California bands to tour. Influential band who nevertheless released just three seven-inch singles. This is second-press of their debut seven. Split-up in 1980. What Records? was also home to The Germs.

I HATE THE RICH
YOU'RE NOT BLANK

chip kinman-guitar,vocals
tony nineteen :bass&vocals
endre algover-drums

WHAT RECORDS?

PUB. BY NEW NOISE MUSIC

made in U.S.A.

THE BOYS

I Don't Care b/w Soda Pressing

NEMS RECORDS London, UK 12 April 1977

Matt Dangerfield Guitar, Vocals
Casino Steel Organ, Piano, Vocals
Hones John Plain Guitar, Vocals
Duncan 'Kid' Reid Bass, Vocals
Jack Black Drums

First single by The Boys on NEMS. Matt Dangerfield and Casino Steel left the London-based pre-punk London SS (which at some point included future members of The Clash, The Damned, Chelsea and Generation X) in September 1975 to form the Boys and signed to NEMS in January 1977, making them at the time the only British punk group to have a major deal (after EMI sacked The Sex Pistols). Switched to Safari in 1979, split in 1981 and then reformed with their name reversed as The Yobs!

THE RAMONES

Swallow My Pride b/w Pinhead/Let's Dance

SIRE RECORDS New York, USA 3 Feb 1977

Dee Dee Ramone Bass Vocals
Johnny Ramone Guitar
Joey Ramone Lead Vocals
Tommy Ramone (Erdelyi) Drums

Produced by T. Erdelyi and Tony Bongiovi

This is the UK picture sleeve which was issued in Britain five months after the US release.

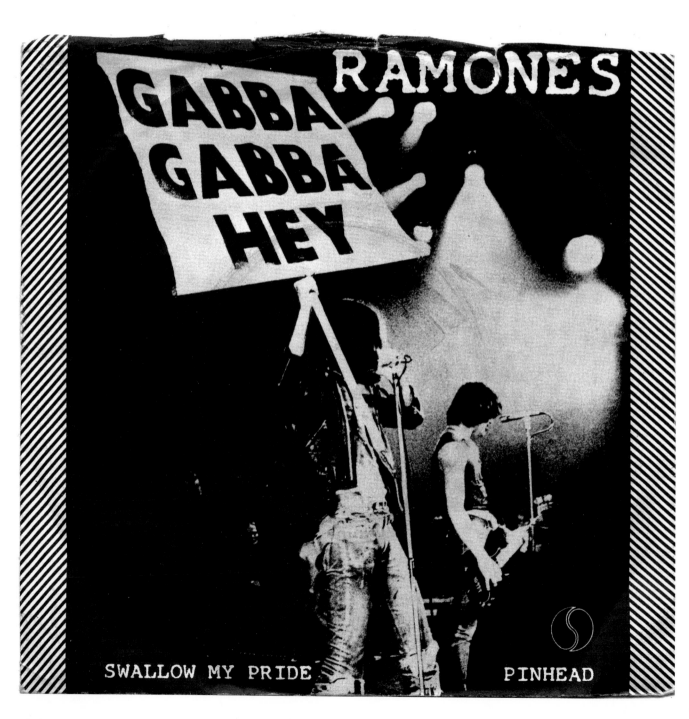

THE STRANGLERS

Grip b/w London Lady

UA Records UK 28 Jan 1977

Jean Jacques Burnell Bass, Vocals
Jet Black Drums
Hugh Cornwell Guitar, Vocals
Dave Greenfield Keyboards

Recorded at T.W. Studios, Fulham.
Produced by Martin Rushent
Photography by Chris Gabrin

Debut single from the band originally known as The Guildford Stranglers in 1974 (although none of the band came from Guildford!)

JOHN COOPER CLARKE

Innocents E.P.

RABID RECORDS Manchester UK Oct 1977

Eric Guitar
Middie Bass
Joe Viality Drums
John Scott Guitar
Zero Percussion

Produced by Martin Zero (Hannett)
Artwork and sleeve design by Kirk Van Gogh Studios

Debut release from Manchester poet JCC.
The band is The Nosebleeds without Ed Banger. One of two sleeve designs.

JOHN COOPER CLARK   INNOCENTS E.P.   CAT No. TOSH 103

THE TWINKEYZ
Aliens In Our Midst b/w One Thousand Reasons
GROK RECORDS Sacramento, California USA 1977

Donnie Jupiter (Don Marquez) Vocals, Guitar
Tom Darling Guitar, Vocals
Keith McKee Drums, Vocals
Walter Smith Guitar

*Twisted psychedelic pop garage formed in the wake of the birth of punk in
Sacramento in 1976. Sort of Jonathan Richman meets the Residents. This is
the second edition of their first single. Split-up in 1980. Donald Marquez now
produces sci-fi and fantasy comics.*

BIG IN JAPAN/ CHUDDY NUDDIES
Brutality, Religion And A Dance Beat
ERICS RECORDS Liverpool, UK Sep 1977

Bill Drummond Guitar, Vocals
Kevin Ward Bass, Vocals
Phil Allen Drums
Jayne Casey Vocals
Ian Broudie Guitar
Clive Langer Guitar

Formed in Liverpool in May 1977. Clive Langer was from the group Deaf School. Drummond later founded Zoo Records and formed KLF, Ian Brodie formed The Lightning Seeds. Future members included Holly Johnson who later fronted Frankie Goes To Hollywood and Budgie who later joined Siouxsie and The Banshees. Group split up on 26 Aug 1978 after last gig at the venue Eric's (whose subsidiary record label also released this single). The Chuddy Nuddies was the pseudonym of another Liverpool band, The Yachts.

Brutality
Religion
and a dance beat *

*e.g. Big in Japan
& The Chuddy Nuddies

THE STUKAS

Sport/I'll Send You A Postcard/Dead Lazy
SONET RECORDS London UK 1977

Paul Brown Vocals
Kevin Allen Bass
John Mackie Drums
Mick Smithers Lead Guitar
Raggy Lewis Guitar, Backing Vocals

Produced by Pat Collier

New wave band formed in Muswell Hill, London. This was their second single after their debut on Chiswick earlier in 1977. Sonet Records was a UK branch of Scandinavian label. Released one further single before splitting-up with band-members joining The Radio Stars, The Autographs and Blast Furnace And The Heatwaves.

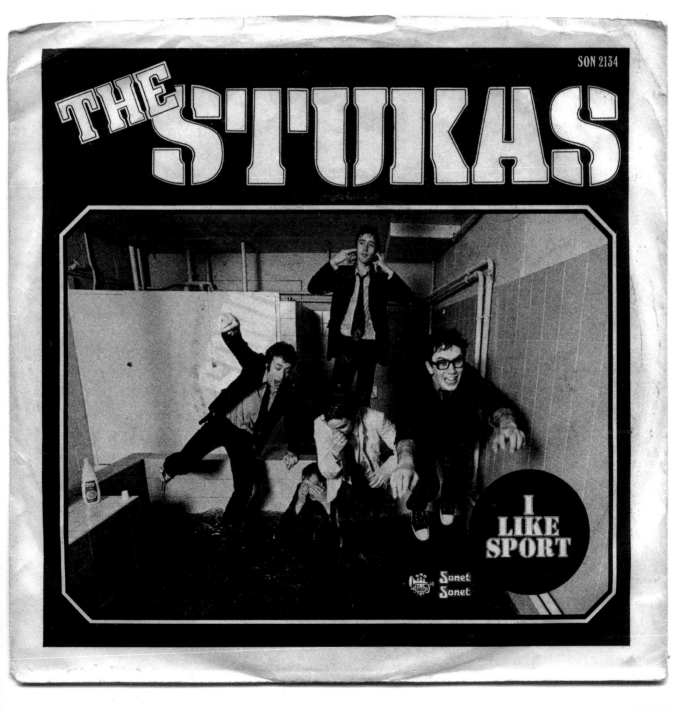

MIDNITE CRUISER

Rich Bitch b/w Striker

IT RECORD COMPANY Northern Ireland 1977

Paul West Vocals
Crow Guitar
Peege Guitar
Rodney Guitar
Jimmy Bass
Ger Drums

Band formed in 1977 in Portadown, came out of an earlier group called Speed. The It Record Company was run by Cliff Moore, who also ran a local record shop. Midnite Cruiser released just this one single.

THE FLYS
Bunch of Five EP
ZAMA RECORDS UK 2 Dec 1977

Dave Freeman Vocals, Guitar
Joe Hughes Bass
Neil O'Connor Vocals, Guitar
Pete King Drums

Recorded October 1977 at Pathways Studio, London
Produced by Chris King and The Flys

Formed in Coventry in 1976, came out of the earlier group Midnight Circus. By the time this self-released debut EP had come out the band had already signed to EMI. Lack of major label success led to the band splitting up in 1980 after just one album.

THE ADVERTS
Gary Gilmore's Eyes b/w Bored Teenagers
ANCHOR UK 12 Aug 1977

T.V. Smith Vocals, Guitar
Gaye Advert Bass
Howard Pickup Guitar
Laurie Driver Drums

Recorded at Pebble Beach Studios, Worthing, England
Produced by Larry Wallis and The Adverts

Sleeve Design Nicholas De Ville

Designer Nicholas de Ville had earlier collaborated with Bryan Ferry on Roxy Music's iconic record sleeves in the 1970s.

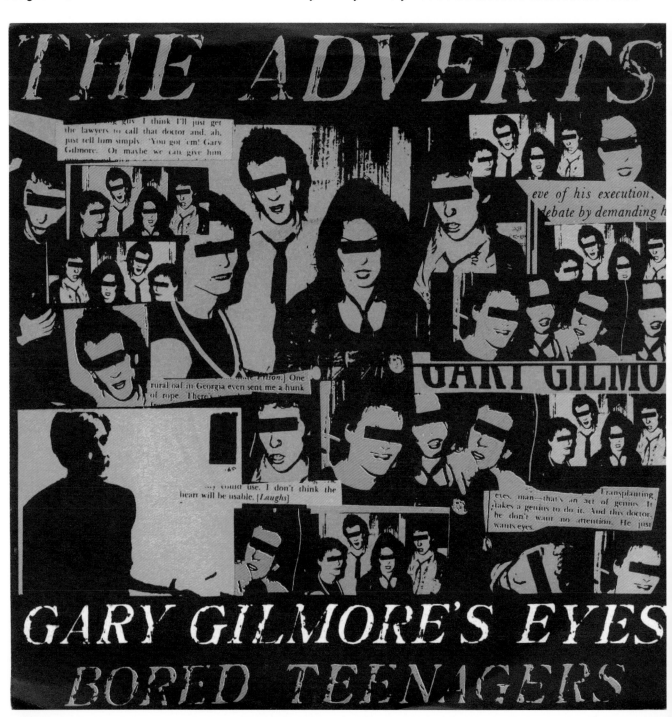

ALBERTO Y LOST TRIOS PARANOIAS

Snuff Rock EP **STIFF RECORDS** UK 9 Sep 1977

Bob Harding Vocals, Guitar
Bruce Mitchell Drums
C.P.Lee Vocals
Jimmy Hibbert Bass, Vocals
Simon White Guitar
Tony Bowers Bass

Produced by Nick Lowe

*Founded in Manchester in 1972. Comedy punk group – Snuff Rock is based on
the idea of a band who kill themselves for entertainment. Split-up in 1982.
Drummer Mitchell was also in Durutti Column.*

THE POP

Down on The Boulevard/I Need You/Easy Action
BACK DOOR MAN RECORDS
Los Angeles, California USA 1977

Roger Prescott Guitar, Vocals
David Swanson Bass, Vocals
David Robinson Drums
Produced by Allan Rinde

Los Angeles power pop with DIY credentials in existence from 1977-81.

THE DRONES
Bone Idol b/w Just Want To Be Myself
VALER RECORDS UK Sep 1977

M.J. Drone (Mike Howells) Vocals, Guitar
Gus 'Gangrene' Callendar Guitar,
Steve 'Whisper' Cundall Bass,
Peter 'Perfect' Howells Drums
Produced by Simon Humphrey

Band from Manchester, formed October 1976, (originally pub rock group Rockslide). First single produced by Paul Morley. Relocated to London at start of punk. Split-up in 1979.

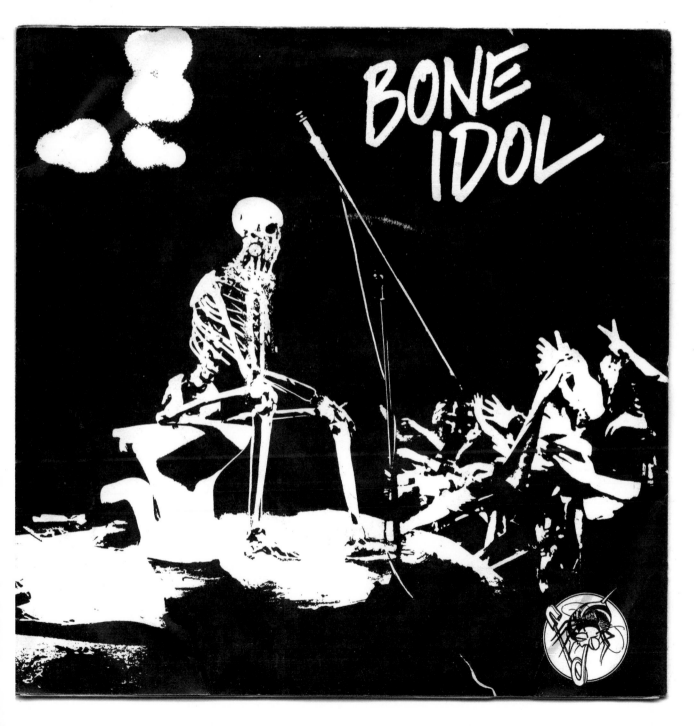

SQUEEZE
Packet of Three EP
DEPTFORD FUN CITY Deptford, London UK
July 1977

Glenn Tilbrook Lead Guitar, Vocals
Harri Kakoulli Bass
Gilson Lavis Drums
Chris Difford Guitar, Vocals
Jools Holland Keyboards

Recorded at Pathway Studios 1977 **Produced by** John Cale
Design and photography by Jill Furmanovsky

*Group founded in South London in 1974 and signed to Miles
Copeland's Deptford Fun City. This is their debut single.*

PACKET OF THREE

LEFT TO RIGHT: JOHNNY STRIKE, VOCALS and GUITAR; BRITTLEY BLACK, DRUMS; FRANKIE FIX, VOCALS and GUITAR; and RON THE RIPPER, BASS.

CRIME
Frustration b/w Murder By Guitar
Crime Music Records
Oakland, California, USA July 1977

Ron The Ripper Bass
Brittley Black Drums
Frankie Fix Guitar and Vocals
Johnny Strike Guitar and Vocals

Recorded at Mills College Recording Studio, Oakland, CA
Producer Novak
Photography by James Stark

Second single from this early San Francisco-based punk group.

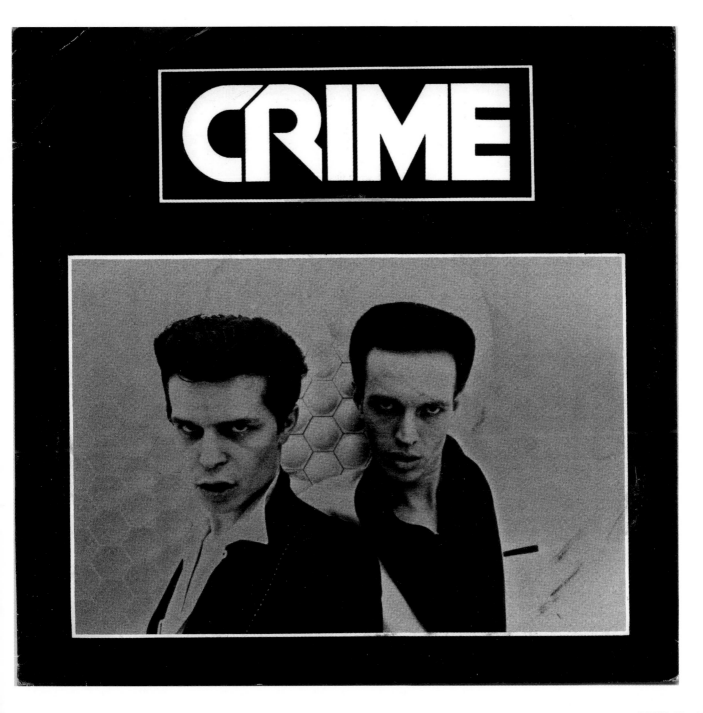

THE POLICE

Nothing Achieving b/w Fall Out

ILLEGAL RECORDS London, UK 1 May 1977

Henry Padovani Guitar
Stewart Copeland Drums, Guitar
Sting Bass, Vocals

Recorded at Pathway Studios, London **Produced by** Stewart Copeland & Bazza. **Photography by** Lawrence Impev

First single by The Police with Henry Padovani. First release on Miles (brother of Stewart) Copeland's Illegal Records. By the following year the band had signed to A & M and Padovani had been replaced by Andy Summers. This is the second-pressing 1979 sleeve.

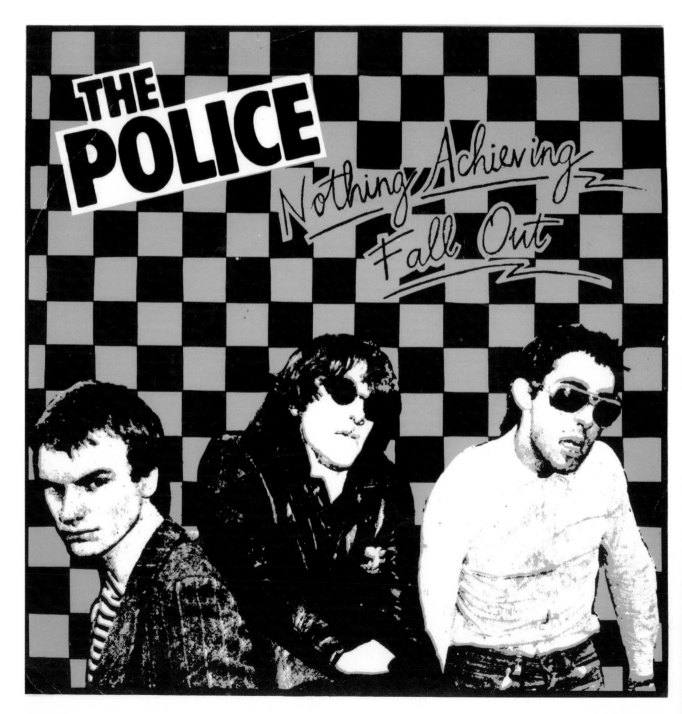

THE ZEROS

Don't Push Me Around b/w Wimp
BOMP! RECORDS
Los Angeles, California USA 1977

Javier Escovedo Guitar, Lead Vocals
Hector Penalosa Bass
Karton Chenelle Drums
Robert Alan Lopez Guitar, Backing Vocals

Recorded at Bonita Recording Studio **Produced by** The Zeros

*Early punk band from Chula Vista, California, formed in 1976, often played
with Los Angeles and San Francisco punk bands. Split in 1980,*

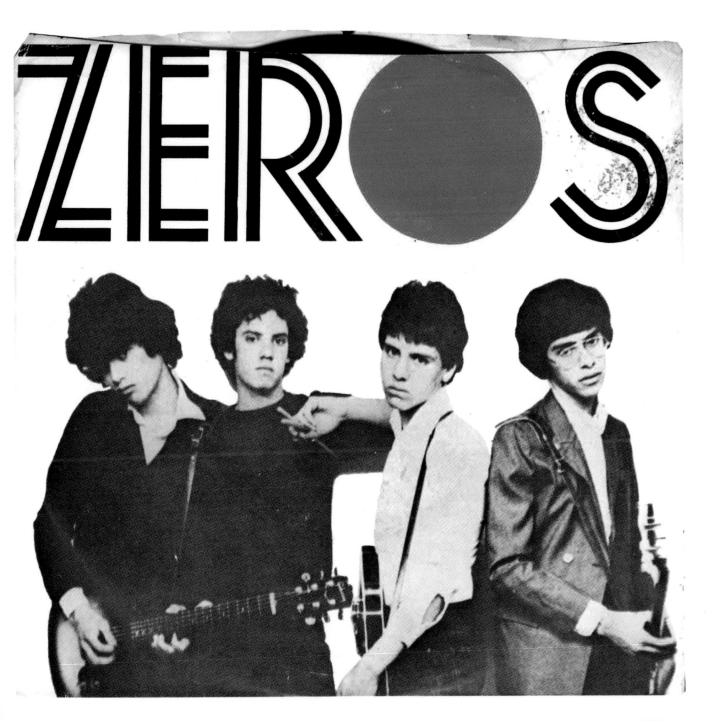

THE FEATURES
Drab City b/w Job Satisfaction
PROGRESS RECORDS Orpington, Kent UK 1977

Ian Fletcher Vocals, Guitar
Jerry Thornton Jones Vocals, Guitar
Tim Fletcher Vocals, Bass
Ron Kinner Drums

Band formed in 1976 in Opington (technically Petts Wood), Kent.
Sole self-released single recorded in September 1977.

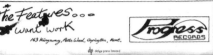

HARRY TOLEDO
AND THE ROCKETS

Busted Chevrolet EP

SPY RECORDS LTD. New York, USA 1977

Produced by John Cale

Design by Doo Da Post Inc

New York no wave punk released on John Cale's Spy Records, which he ran with Jane Friedman and Michael Zilkha. Toledo also had a track on the Max's Kansas City album. Cale's Spy Records went through Miles Copeland's IRS. Zilkha would later found Ze Records with Michel Esteban.

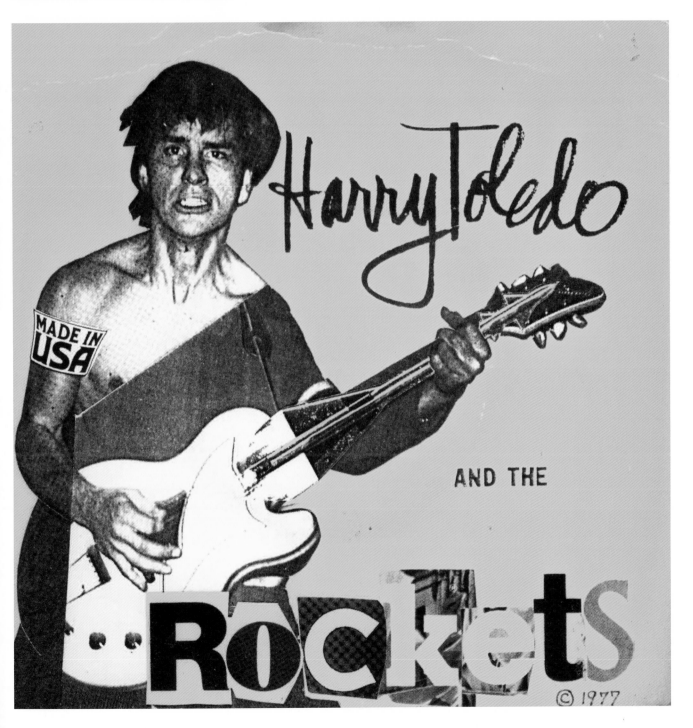

PLASTIC BERTRAND
Ça Plane Pour Moi b/w Pogo Pogo
RKM BELGIUM 1977

Produced by Lou Deprijck
*(who was also the singer on this as Plastic Bertrand never
actually performed on record)*

DEVO Mongoloid b/w Jocko Homo
BOOJI BOY RECORDS Akron, Ohio, USA Feb 1977

Mark Mothersbaugh Vocals, Keyboards, Guitar
Gerald V. Casale Vocals, Bass, Keyboards
Bob Mothersbaugh (Bob I) Lead Guitar, Vocals
Bob Casale (Bob II) Rhythm Guitar, Keyboards, Vocals
Alan Myers Drums

Layout by Jeff Seibert **Photography by** Greg Kaiser **Design by** Devo

*Devo members are from Kent and Akron, Ohio and the group formed in
1972. Apparently Richard Branson asked if they would consider John Lydon
joining the band shortly after the Sex Pistols split-up (they didn't). Stiff
Records three-tiered wraparound cover (pictured here) over Devo's own
Booji Boy Records seven-inch launched the Ohio-based group in the UK.*

JOHN CALE

Animal Justice/Memphis/Hedda Gabbler

ILLEGAL RECORDS London, UK August 1977

Jimmy Bain Bass
Kevin Currie Drums
Ritchie Fliegler Guitar
John Cale Vocals, Guitar, Piano, Viola
Bruce Brody Synthesizer

Produced by John Cale **Sleeve by** Jill Furmanovsky

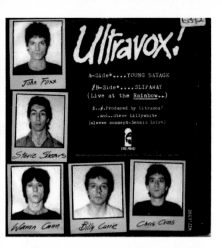

ULTRAVOX!
Young Savage b/w Slip Away
ISLAND RECORDS UK 28 May 1977

John Foxx Lead Vocals
Warren Cann Drums, Vocals
Chris Cross Bass, Vocals
Billy Currie Violin, Keyboards
Stevie Shears Guitar

Produced by Steve Lillywhite and Ultravox!

Second single.

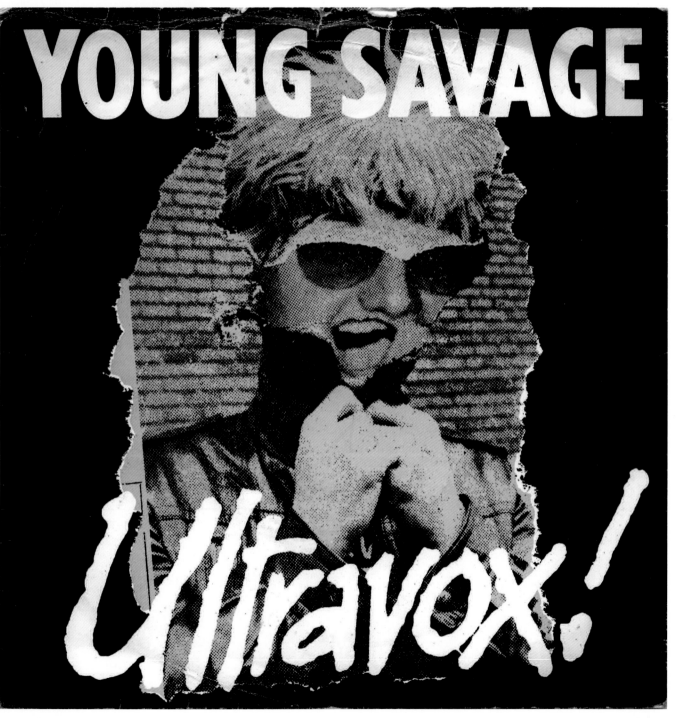

THE USERS

Sick Of You b/w (I'm) In Love With Today
RAW RECORDS Cambridge, UK 1977

James Haight Vocals
Bobby Kwok Bass
Andrew Bor Drums
Chris Free Guitar

Recorded at Spaceward Studios **Produced by** Mike Kemp
Photography by Cesare Bragetti **Graphics by** David Jeffrey

Formed in Cambridge, UK in 1976, released just two singles. The Users were the first band to make a record on local Raw Records.

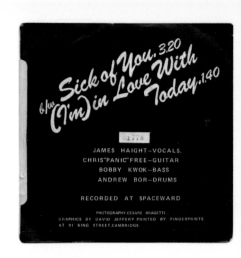

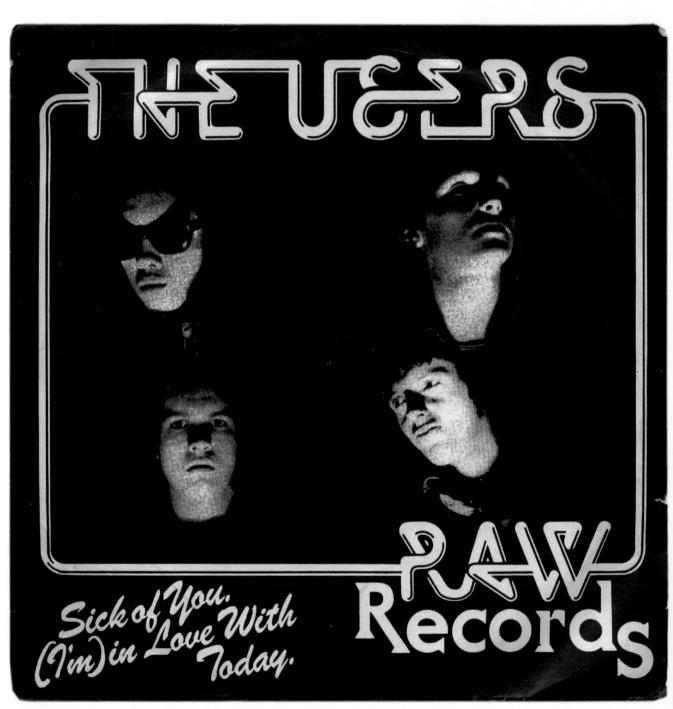

WRECKLESS ERIC
Whole Wide World b/w Semaphore Signals
STIFF RECORDS UK 12 Aug 1977

Wreckless Eric Vocals, Guitar
Nick Lowe Bass, Guitar
Steve Goulding/Ian Dury Drums
Denise Roudette Bass

Produced by Ian Dury/Nick Lowe

Debut single from Eric Goulden, AKA Wreckless Eric.

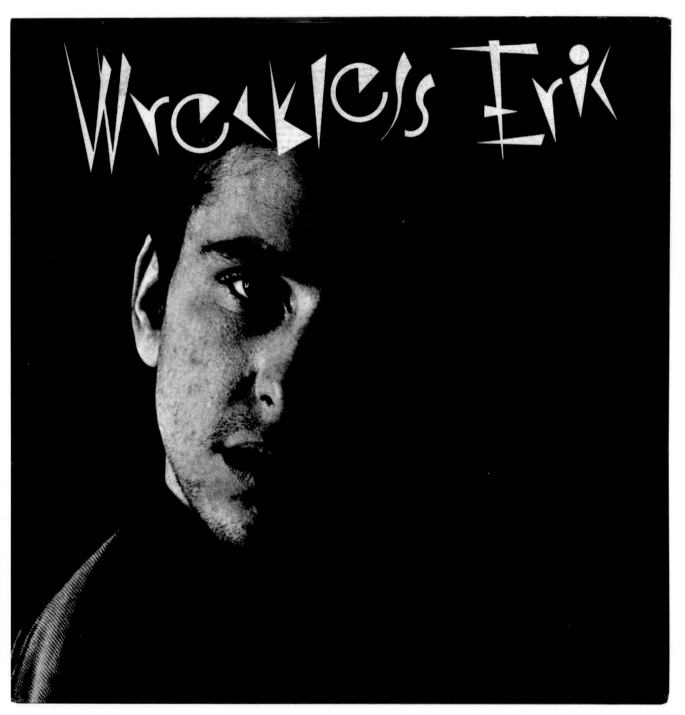

RANDOMS

ABCD b/w Let's Get Rid Of New York

DANGERHOUSE RECORDS

Los Angeles, California USA 1977

Pat Garrett Guitar, Vocals
K.K. Barrett Drums
John Doe Bass

All-star LA punk line-up. K.K. Barret of the Screamers on drums, John Doe from X on bass and Pat Garrett - who co-founded Black Randy And The Metrosquad and also one of the founders of Dangerhouse - on guitar and vocals.

LET'S GET RID OF NEW YORK CITY

An interview with David Brown of Dangerhouse Records.

David Brown had been a member of The Screamers, a Seattle-born group that became a part of the first wave Los Angeles punk scene. Also in this group were Tomata du Plenty, KK Barrett and Tommy Gear. In 1977 Brown formed Dangerhouse Records along with Pat 'Rand' Garrett (who produced the Screamers early demos) and Black Randy.

The label captured many of the first west coast punk bands on vinyl as well as presenting the releases in highly stylish picture sleeves, which came in a unique wraparound front-and-half-back style that has been copied ever since.

Dangerhouse released Los Angeles punk music by The Alley Cats, The Avengers, Bags, The Deadbeats, The Dils, Eyes, Randoms, Rhino 39, The Weirdos, Howard Werth and X over its short three-year existence.

Both Brown and Garrett played in Black Randy and The Metrosquad, which also released their music on Dangerhouse and we begin the interview with a discussion over Black Randy (John Morris), a notorious figure in the nascent Los Angeles punk scene.

Dangerhouse Records was run by yourself, Pat Garrett and Black Randy. Was Black Randy really a partner? Did that work well - was it a little tricky being partner with 'a constant liar'!?
Remember we were all quite young at the time ... Black Randy was definitely a partner. Some background: Randy had known the Screamers in Seattle and had filmed them doing awful things - things that would have you put in federal pen today for just watching them.

The night the Screamers threw me out of the band (this really didn't faze me at all as they were awful, manipulative people and I really wanted to make records), Randy did an impromptu rap on their front lawn, screaming through a mike in rhyme at their shabby behaviour in fucking me over.

Tomato came out in his bathrobe after about ten minutes and asked him to stop. Tommy Tibbetts (the foul little man who called himself Gear) actually had Pat Garrett remove my piano

tracks from the Screamers demo the next day. If you've ever listened to them and wondered why they sounded so thin, that's why.

Point being, Randy had a much greater level of loyalty, as well as the gift of gab. Since I could tell when he was lying, and he did it primarily for recreation, why would it bother me? ... He was an integral part of the whole thing, and he really pissed Pat and everybody else off which in turn pleased me greatly.

OK, he would steal money from the band members after a show for speed or heroin, but we all had other jobs - was the $50 or whatever that important? If it was, I just repaid it myself and went on my way.

But yes, tricky is the word - but he (and Joe Nanini) were the best ammunition in the world when the bands started to go sour on us. Once you had a couple of phone calls from them, it was sorted.

Were Dangerhouse the first to do a wraparound two-thirds sleeve in plastic? Yes, that was completely my idea. In those days the preparation of printed materials was done 'analog', meaning that colour repros had to be stripped with four negatives - a very expensive process if you were doing short runs. 'Real' record companies could absorb that if a record failed, but in our case the cost was prohibitive - a run of say, 1000 copies of a picture sleeve could actually cost more than the record itself.

Nonetheless, we were trying to have visual appeal on the cheap, hence the duotones printed on what was essentially trimmed $8^1/_2$ x 11 paper folded over. In all honesty, I could have done it with 14" paper (like the Weirdos cover) but I felt that if the label provided a sort of visual counterpart, why not flash a little of that as well?

Dangerhouse epitomises the DIY spirit of punk? Could you discuss this?
I agree. Take for example the picture sleeves just discussed; it must have been a good idea because everyone in town started copying it. We were somewhat lucky in finding the right engineer and studio as well, and were happy to share any

technical or professional information with other bands because (my opinion here) it wasn't like we were particularly clever, just took pride in what we did and made sure we did the best we could.

Notice how the life went out of bands like X the second they got somebody as predictably awful as Ray Manzarek producing them; we were breaking new ground all the time and frankly didn't care if we got rich or not (although Randy certainly wanted to).

I can only speak from experience, but I was fascinated with records and their production ever since I was a child, so it was merely the logical conclusion of a boyhood dream.

Consider this: when the Screamers did their first show at the Whisky a Go Go, we taped and stapled xerox posters all over west Hollywood - no one had done that up until then. If you went to Seattle in the grunge years, there were so many layers of flyers stapled to the phone poles of Capitol Hill that bums would sometimes set them on fire for a lark. So it was really just about making the best of what you have - and being the first to do it.

Could you talk a bit about the artwork of Dangerhouse? The designs seem so smart and instantly attractive – and different from other punk sleeves. Dangerhouse records seem to have a very clear and strong identity – separate from New York or British punk – that is very striking. Pat and KK both had very strong graphic art backgrounds, and Pat and I worked at various jobs that gave us access to typesetting which was very expensive in those days. Richard Gibson, the guy who still owns the original 'danger house' to this day, worked in a framing store and was a great idea man ... the point was to use very basic concepts of contrast and design to grab people's attention, nothing more than that.

Granted, some of it was quite crude - but clicked somehow. I believe the identity is more perception of those facts than anything else - some of the art was designed and produced by the bands themselves and I believe they appreciated the freedom to do so.

The only covers I did myself was for The Alleycats, Arcade and The Bags - but I was frequently left the task of pasting them up and stripping them for the printers, so sometimes things got a little jostly.

In any case we felt that the whole cut-out pasted-up ransom note approach taken by the Pistols was very rich but not something to endlessly imitate. We preferred something more striking and commercial where possible. It also helped that I had been a professional screen printer, huffing lacquer thinner all day long for years.

You mention the oil embargo as making it hard to make records in 1979. Could you explain this? A price-fixing embargo was orchestrated against the US in that year which made all products made from crude oil - including vinyl – go up in price; the price of these things doubled overnight, and suddenly there were people nationwide waiting in line for hours just to buy scarce gasoline.

Again the record companies likely had big stockpiles, and could always raise their prices anyway, but we did not (obviously) and could not - we got $.80 per single and $3.00 per album (even the silk-screened one) and that was that. Distributors and stores paid in cash in those days, however, so it wasn't the struggle like it is for today's independents.

Did LA punk exist in parallel to New York or London? Was it influenced more by England or New York or neither? What did you think of the New York scene? Your opinion is probably as valid as mine on that one. Tomato and Gear (The Screamers) and Randy were all very, very stuck on New York and England in the sense that they felt equals to that. It never really occurred to me that way, I was just grateful that I had moved the year previous to a place (LA) that was a blank slate for punk to take off in a different direction with its own flavour.

I detested the Dolls, Television and Blondie in particular, and had known Dee Dee Ramone when I was in college just as some freak you'd run into on the street constantly. The Ramones were so stylized that their record sales flamed out almost immediately but their image and persona lived on quite strong - even for people who had never seen them play. Again, everyone wanted to be David Bowie or Lou Reed which I found a sad situation in the extreme ... when the Metrosquad finally got to play the repulsive Mudd Club in 1980, we used it as an excuse to harass the owner and his crowd as much as possible, which was much more fun than actually succeeding with the NY 'scene' - which would never have happened anyway.

We stole things out of his apartment and club (broke into the liquor stash among other things), told him we wouldn't play if he didn't double the money since we already had tickets home. That's what *I* think of the New York scene, darlings of the smart set and junkies ... I just thought that No New York summed it up, dragging a poor old pseudo-intellectual out to produce cheap nihilism ... so Yes LA was meant to counter that with a 'fuck you, we're enjoying this, sorry about your lives' ...

I read quite a lot about The Damned coming to LA early on. A lot of LA bands seem to have a bit of the theatricality of this band. Is there any truth or sense in that? Perhaps. I remember well when the Damned stayed at the Screamers house; I had just returned from the East with a new used car to shlep the equipment in, and a treasure trove of 1950s sunglasses I'd found in a thrift store. If you've ever seen the picture of Captain Sensible playing naked at the Whiskey, he's wearing these sort of toilet-seat shaped sunglasses - they stole them all - and I was well pleased, always more cheap sunglasses where they came from. I just got this thrill when I first saw that record cover with Scabies licking whipped cream off his bandmate's head - this was exactly how I felt about the record industry and the sort of thing young people should be doing, instead of trying to be washed out urban cowboys etc.

Now having said that, the bands really all had their own approach, and I think we have to be fair to Randy and I that the Metrosquad had its own approach which required (a) never practicing, (b) making it up as you go along, (c) trying to create a 90-degree tangent from expectations, and (d) not giving a flip if it didn't work, we'd try again another day.

A large part of it was goading and reaming out the other musicians; having seen Joe Nanini dressed up as Exene with a corndog was worth any disappointments I've ever had in my life. The Weirdos, quite frankly, weren't weird enough, and the Bags only shtick was arguing during a set and walking off stage, and god knows Henry Rollins and his ilk were boring and predictable ... so I'm not sure about the theatricality, most of them were dull as toast!

You say in liner notes that the LA punk scene lacked commercialism – yet I think the songs from LA at this time are some of the catchiest in punk? Also the sleeves of Dangerhouse and the band identities seem very strong. Could you comment on this? Right, but being commercial is a fleeting thing; the Cheap Trick (*gaaak*) of yesterday are totally different from the Nickelback (*double gaaaak*) of today, for example. Commercial really means, 'will the record company give you money for it'?

If not, then you were a failure in the commercial sense - but once I freed myself from those faux shackles, anything was possible. It may be you are confusing recording quality with commercialism - Pat Garrett is an unbelievable genius, I can't believe he gave it up to marry someone who thought she should be a model in OK.

I was destined to continue the 40-hour a week grind, but if he had grit his teeth and followed through, he'd have been as famous as Rick Rubin or Quincy Jones today. I completely mean that, am still in awe of his knowledge, which was mostly innate.

His (and to a limited extent my own) ability to actually produce in the true sense of the word made good songs like The Weirdos - Solitary Confinement instant classics. It really is a shame we'll never know how it would have turned out. If anything we made it look too easy, which is why our imitators were so awful for the most part.

Dangerhouse seems to be completely at the centre of the early LA punk scene. Its demise also seems to come at the end of this scene – where it moves to the hardcore scene outside of the centre of LA. Is this correct? An accurate generalisation. Jon Savage disagrees with me on this, but I felt that bands like the Middle Class were very flat and predictable, they didn't try hard enough to do anything but slam at their instruments and bleat unintelligibly and humourlessly into their microphones.

The Germs sucked - everybody knew this - but their shows were fun to watch because they had personalities and were quite spontaneous. The early scenes, particularly in California and London were much more about people not following specific three-chord agendas (why I never cared for the Ramones or New York Dolls that much) but attempting any style or configuration that would get attention. There'll never, for instance, be another X Ray Spex or Rezillos or early Damned.

We had to throw off expectations to get anywhere - picking up an instrument you didn't know and playing it was a strong statement. I specialised in instruments that had been destroyed and I had rebuilt - you can't get that kind of sound out of a piano that hasn't been thrown downstairs (literally).

Did The Dickies major label signing confuse the Los Angeles punk scene a bit? Understand, I loved the Dickies as much as anyone, considered them good friends in the day, we even drove to San Francisco to see the Shit Pistols last show together. The greatest sadness I have from those days was the suicide of Chuck Wagon, who was quite introverted but would speak freely to me since we were keyboard players; he was another unsung genius, really made his Wurlitzer part of the act.

For all that, I always felt the reason the Dickies did so well out of the gate was that their songs were perfect, quick little packages with punchlines and catchphrases built right in. Who doesn't immediately get 'I'm O.K.' or their version of 'Banana Splits' (as kids we used to sniff glue while watching that show, so it was a great tease to hear it again)?

And of course they were great musicians, Joe Nanini always said Carlos C. was by far the best drummer on the scene, and they had snap. I won't say it confused things, but it initiated this insensate illogical greed on the part of others.

Even Randy thought he would be a star - can you imagine anything more ridiculous? But people bought into this silly idea and immediately I was the bad guy, holding them back from their true calling ... I would point to what happened after that.

No one from my label got any kind of contract outside of X, and they immediately started to suck when they did; Darby snuffed himself in hopes that he'd be a star beyond the grave - the week before John Lennon was shot; and the rest either foundered or continued doing the same shit for decades ... not how I wanted to spend my life.

The only exception to this was Wall of Voodoo, their Mexican Radio video being the only one to my knowledge to get a, 'hey that's cool' from Beavis and Butthead ... but they imploded in alcoholic ego which is better than continuing to do the same act for 35-fuckin years, isn't it?

SWELL MAPS

Read About Seymour/Ripped & Torn/Black Velvet
RATHER RECORDS UK 1977

Nikki Sudden Vocals, Guitar, Tambourine
Phones Sportsman Guitar, Vocals
Jowe Head Bass
Epic Soundtracks Drums

Recorded at Spaceward Sound, Cambridge August 1977
Produced by Swell Maps **Artwork by** Epic the Artist
Photography by Nikki Sudden
Formed in Birmingham in 1972 by brothers Epic Soundtracks and Nikki Sudden. After releasing two influential albums and four singles the group disbanded in 1980.

IGGY AND THE STOOGES
I'm Sick Of You/Tight Pants/Scene Of The Crime
BOMP! RECORDS Los Angeles, California USA 1977

Iggy Pop Vocals
James Williamson Guitar
Ron Asheton Bass
Scott Asheton Drums
Produced by James Williamson

First release (five years on) on Bomp! of three outtakes from the Stooges' classic Raw Power album made in 1972. The Stooges had split up in 1974 (reforming in 2003).

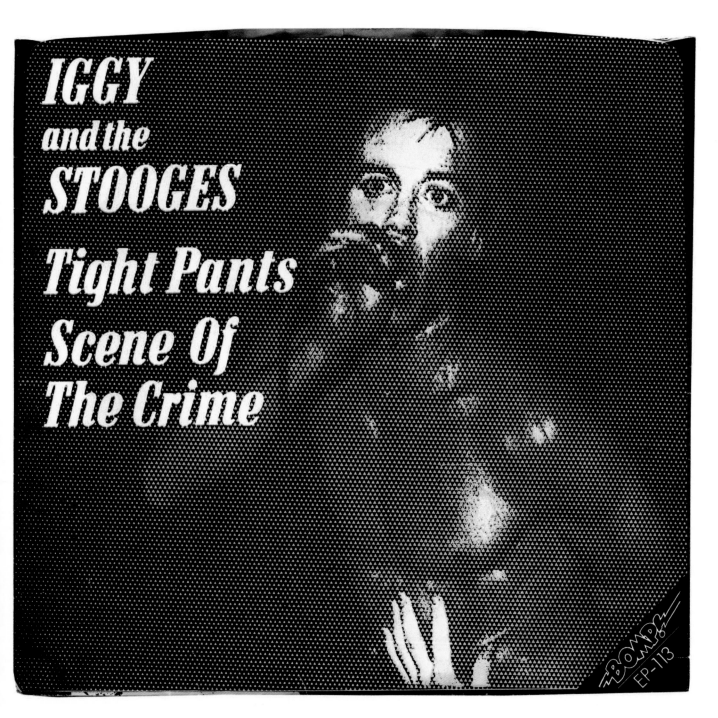

HEARTBREAKERS

One Track Mind b/w Can't Keep My Eyes On You/Do You Love Me?
TRACK RECORD London, UK 28 Oct 1977

Billy Rath Bass
Jerry Nolan Drums
Johnny Thunders Lead Guitar, Vocals
Walter Lure Lead Guitar, Vocals

Produced by Daniel Secunda, Speedy Keen **Photography by** Bob Ross

The Heartbreakers or Johnny Thunders and The Heartbreakers formed in New York in May 1975 after Thunders and Nolan quit the New York Dolls, originally with Richard Hell who himself had just quit Television. Hell was replaced the following year by Billy Rath. The band came to the UK just as punk arrived and were offered to play on The Pistols' Anarchy tour. They also signed to Track in the UK who released this their debut single as well as three further singles and an album L.A.M.F.

CHELSEA
Right To Work b/w The Loner
STEP-FORWARD RECORDS London, UK June 1977

Gene October Vocals
James Stevenson Guitar
Henry Daze Bass
Carey Fortune Drums

Produced by MC, MP **Photography by** Peter Kodick, Harry Murlowski
Design by Jill Furmanovsky

Debut release from Chelsea, made after the initial group members (alongside October) of Billy Idol, Tony James and John Towe had left to form Generation X.

THE GERMS
Forming b/w Untitled (Live)
WHAT RECORDS? Los Angeles USA July 1977

Bobby Pyn (Darby Crash) Vocals
Lorna Doom Bass
Donna Rhia Drums
Pat Smear Guitar

Debut single from LA punk group that existed from 1977-80. What Records also released The Dils, Kaos, The Controllers and others. The Germs released just one album on Slash Records in 1979. The following year the band split-up after the suicide of Darby Crash.

JOHNNY MOPED
No One b/w Incendiary Device
CHISWICK RECORDS London, UK Aug 1977

Slimy Toad Guitar
Johnny Moped Vocals
Fred Berk Bass, Piano
Dave Berk Drums

Sleeve Design by Barney Bubbles

Formed in Croydon in 1974 as Johnny Moped and the 5 Arrogant Superstars. Later became Assault and Buggery, then The Commercial Band before settling on Johnny Moped in Jan 1975. Released two albums and four singles. Band members included Captain Sensible (The Damned) and Chrissie Hynde (Pretenders).

THE PANIK

It Won't Sell EP
Modern Politics/Urban Damnation/Murder

RAINY CITY RECORDS Manchester, UK **Nov 1977**

Ian Nance Lead Vocals, Lead Guitar
Steve Brotherdale Drums
Hilton Bass
Random Rhythm Guitar

Produced by The Panik and Rob Gretton
Photography by Kevin Cummins **Sleeve Design by** Steve McGarry

And it didn't. Rainy City Records logo: 'We're so bored of London'

THE ELECTRIC CHAIRS

Stuck On You/Paranoia Paradise/The Last Time
ILLEGAL RECORDS London, UK Aug 1977

Wayne County Vocals
Greg Van Cook Guitar
Val Haller Bass
J. J. Johnson Drums

Recorded in London, 1977. **Produced by** Miles Copeland, Peter Crowley
Design by Jill Furmanovsky **Photography by** Vic Von Schwanberg-Kruehine, Harry Murlowski.

In 1974 County formed Wayne County and the Backstreet Boys, and in 1976 recorded three tracks for the Max's Kansas City album. County, who had earlier been an actress at Warhol's Factory, was also a DJ at Max's. In 1977 he relocated to London and formed The Electric Chairs, releasing music on both Illegal and Safari Records.

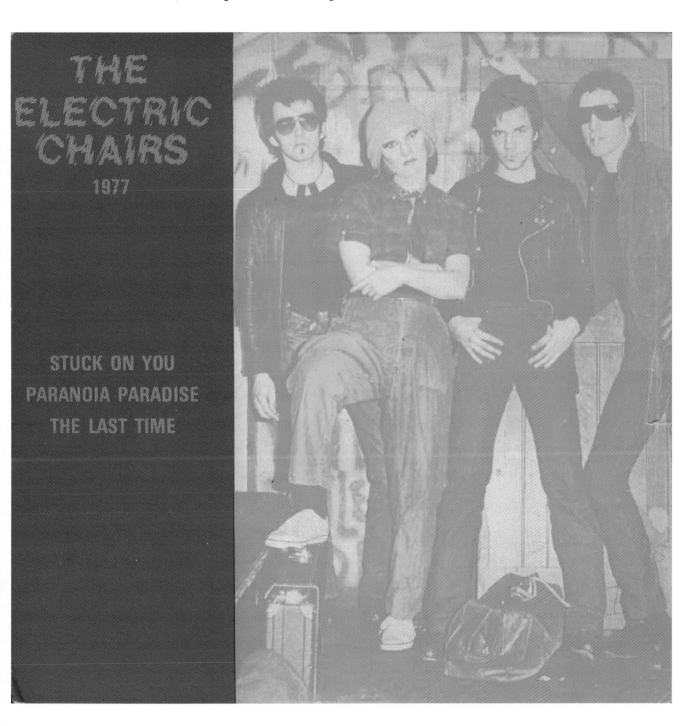

THE RADIATORS FROM SPACE

Television Screen b/w Love Detective

CHISWICK RECORDS *London, UK* 22 Apr 1977

Stephen Rapid Lead Vocals

Pete Holidai Guitar, Vocals

Philip Chevron Guitar, Vocals

Mark Megaray Bass

James Crash Drums

Produced by Roger Armstrong

Early Irish punk band formed in Dublin in 1976. This is their debut single.

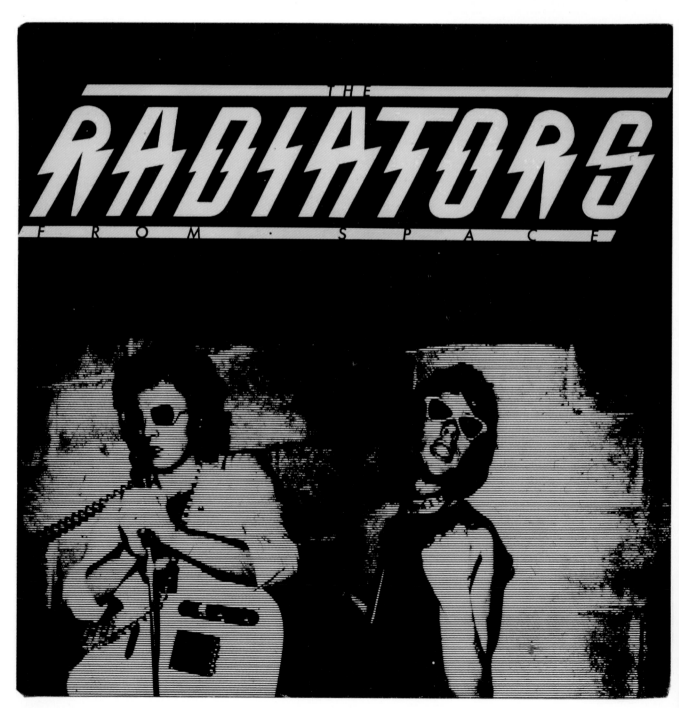

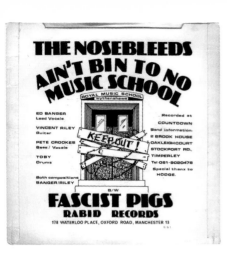

THE NOSEBLEEDS

Ain't Bin To No Music School b/w Fascist Pigs
RABID RECORDS Manchester, UK Aug 1977

Ed Banger Vocals
Pete Crookes Vocals, Bass
Toby Drums
Vincent Riley Guitar

Produced by Vini Faal

Formed in Wythenshawe, Manchester, England in 1976, originally known as Wild Ram, then Ed Banger And The Nosebleeds. After this single Vincent Reilly (Vinnie Reilly) formed Durutti Column, Morrissey (later to form The Smiths) replaced Ed Banger who joined Slaughter and The Dogs.

DMZ

Lift Up Your Hood/Busy Man b/w You're Gonna Miss Me/When I Get Off

BOMP! RECORDS Los Angeles, California USA 1977

Mono Mann Lead Vocals, Keyboards, Percussion
Peter Greenberg Lead Guitar
J.J. Rassler Guitar, Vocals
Rick Corraccio Bass
Paul Murphy Drums

Recorded at Dimension Sound, Boston **Produced by** Craig Leon
Photography by Lynn Ciulla **Design by** David Allen

Early garage punk formed in Boston, Massachusetts in 1976. First recording sessions produced by Craig Leon (who also produced the first Ramones album) resulted in this four track ep on Bomp! Records. DMZ then signed to Sire, and their sole album was released in 1978. After the failure of the album the band split-up shortly after.

THE JAM

In The City b/w Takin' My Love
POLYDOR UK April 1977

Paul Weller Lead Guitar, Vocals
Rick Buckler Drums
Bruce Foxton Bass, Backing Vocals

Produced by Chris Parry and Vic Smith
Photography by Walt Davidson
Design by Bill Smith

Formed in Woking in 1976. Split-up in 1982 after seven albums when Paul Weller went solo.

THE VALVES

Robot Love b/w For Adolfs Only

ZOOM RECORDS Edinburgh, Scotland UK

30 Aug 1977

Dee Robot Lead Vocals
Ronnie MacKinnon Lead Guitar
Gordon Scott Bass
G.Dair Drums

Recorded 11th August 1977 at REL Studios, Edinburgh

Band formed in Edinburgh, Scotland, in existence 1977-79. Debut release on Bruce Findlay's local Zoom Records, which also released Simple Minds. After four Simple Minds singles Zoom was licensed through Arista. The Valves made two further singles.

MARIE ET LES GARÇONS
Rien a Dire b/w A Bout de Souffle/Mardi Soir
REBEL RECORDS FRANCE 1977

Jean-Pierre Bass, Guitar
Marie Girard Drums
Patrick Vidal Bass, Vocals
Eric Fitoussi Guitar, Vocals

Produced by Marie et Les Garçons and Michel Esteban

Formed in Lyon, France in 1976. This track was produced by Michel Esteban and released on his new Rebel Records. The group then went to New York, where they were produced by John Cale and made a record on Esteban and Michael Zilkha's new Ze Records. Shortly after Marie Girard left the group, which then carried on as Les Garçons before splitting-up in 1980.

THE CORTINAS
Fascist Dictator b/w Television Families
STEP-FORWARD RECORDS London UK 1977

Jeremy Valentine Vocals
Mike Fewins Lead Guitar
Nick Sheppard Guitar
Dexter Dalwood Bass
Daniel Swan Drums

Debut single from Bristol-based band The Cortinas and the first release on Step-Forward Records, run by Mark Perry (from Sniffin' Glue and ATV) and Miles Copeland. After one more single signed to CBS for an album, True Romances, before splitting-up in September 1978.

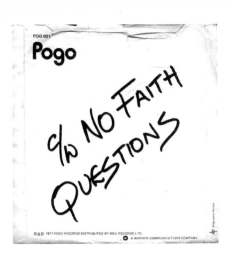

SUBURBAN STUDS
No Faith b/w Questions
POGO RECORDS LTD. *UK* 4 Nov 1977

Eddy Zipps Vocals, Guitar
Keith Owen Guitar
Paul Morton Bass
Steve Poole Drums

Formed in Birmingham in 1976. Independent Pogo Records Ltd. went through WEA Records. This is the second pressing of the single, with added picture sleeve. Suburban Studs released two singles and one album before splitting-up, occasionally reforming.

ELVIS COSTELLO

Watching The Detectives b/w
Blame It On Caine/Mystery Dance

STIFF RECORDS London, UK 14 Oct 1977

Elvis Costello Vocals, Guitar
Steve Goulding Drums
Andrew Bodnar Bass
Steve Nieve (Steve Nason) Keyboards

Produced by Nick Lowe
Sleeve Design by Barney Bubbles

Second single by Elvis Costello. The Attractions were Costello's new band who feature on the B-side only. The earlier recorded A-side features Goulding and Bodnar from Graham Parker's band The Rumour.

THE MIRRORS
Shirley b/w She Smiled Wild
HEARTHAN RECORDS Cleveland, Ohio USA 1977

Jim Crook Lead Guitar, Vocals
Jim Jones Bass, Vocals
Michael Weldon Drums
Paul Marotta Piano, Organ
Jaime Klimek Guitar

Recorded at Owl Studios/live in the Basement in June and August 1975.
Photography by Joyce Faust and Jill Marotta. **Sleeve design by** Michael Weldon.

Proto-punk from the fertile ground of Cleveland, Ohio. The Mirrors were active between 1973 and 1975.

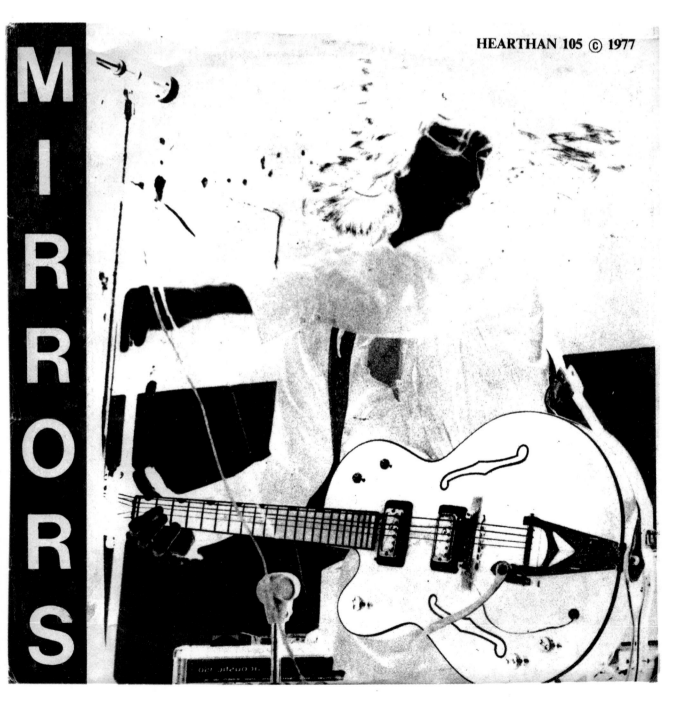

JOHN OTWAY
AND WILD WILLY BARRETT

Really Free b/w Beware of The Flowers (Cos I'm
Sure They're Gonna Get You Yeah!)
POLYDOR UK 11 Nov 1977

John Otway Guitar, Vocals
Wild Willy Barrett Guitar

*Twisted folk-guitar duo who got caught up with and fitted nicely into punk,
signed a five album £250,000 deal with Polydor and it was commercially
downhill ever since. Still touring and Otway delivers occasional lectures
entitled 'Making success out of failure'.*

DESPERATE BICYCLES

The Medium Was Tedium b/w Don't
Back The Front
REFILL RECORDS London, UK

July 1977

Danny Wigley Vocals
Roger Stephens Bass
Dave Papworth Drums
Nicky Stephens Organ

Sleeve designed by Ingram Pinn

From the back sleeve: "The Desperate Bicycles were formed in March 1977 specifically for the purpose of recording and releasing a single on their own label. They booked a studio in Dalston for three hours and with a lot of courage and a little rehearsal they recorded 'Smokescreen' and 'Handlebars' It subsequently leapt at the throat. Three months later and The Desperate Bicycles were back in a studio to record their second single and this is the result. "No more time for spectating" they sing and who knows? they may be right. They'd really like to know why you haven't made your single yet. "It was easy, it was cheap, go and do it" (the complete cost of "Smokescreen" was £153) The medium may very well have been tedium but it's changing fast. So if you can understand, go and join a band. Now it's your turn…"

ALTERNATIVE TV

Life After Life b/w Life After Dub

DEPTFORD FUN CITY London, UK 1977

Dennis Burns Bass
Chris Bennett Drums
Kim Turner Guitar
Mark Perry Vocals
Jools Holland Piano

Produced by Joe Sinclair

Formed in March 1977 by Mark Perry and Alex Fergusson. Perry had started Sniffin' Glue magazine in July 1976 and formed the band when he stopped the magazine after becoming disillusioned with the punk scene.

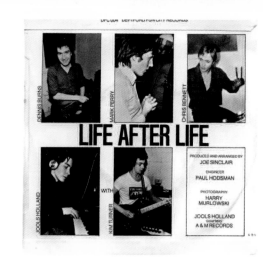

HAMMERSMITH GORILLAS
You Really Got Me b/w Leavin' Ome
RAW RECORDS UK 1977

Allen Butler Bass
Gary Anderson Drums
Jesse Hector Vocals, Guitar

The Hammersmith Gorillas (later shortened to The Gorillas), formed in Hammersmith, London in 1974. Their high-energy sound was a precursor to punk and by 1977 the group had achieved enough of a cult following in this new era for Raw Records to reissue their 1974 version of the The Kinks classic.

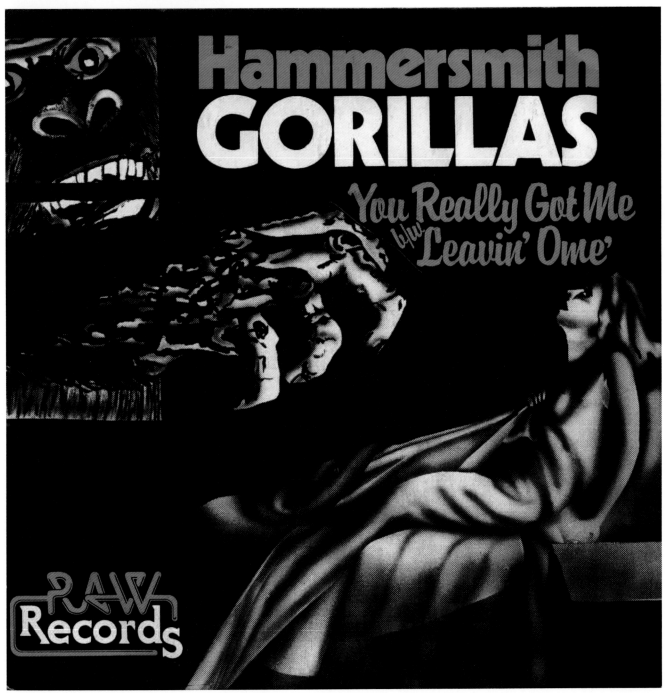

THE CORTINAS
Defiant Pose b/w Independence
STEP-FORWARD RECORDS London, UK 1977

Jeremy Valentine Vocals
Dexter Bass
Daniel Swan Drums
Nick Sheppard Guitar
Mike Fewings Lead Guitar

Photography by Peter Christopherson
Design by Hipgnosis

1978 PUNK 45s

Side One.
WARSAW
NO LOVE LOST

Side Two
LEADERS OF MEN
FAILURES

Pic. bottom left, left to right:
Bernard Albrecht, Guitar. Ian Curtis, Vocals.
Stephen Morris, Drums. Peter Hook, Bass.

All tracks written by JOY DIVISION

Recorded at Pennine Sound Studio, Dec. 77
Photography Gareth Davy.
Cover designed by Bernard Albrecht.
This is not a concept E.P. it is an enigma.
All complaints — Terry Mason

Up until the recording date of this E.P.
we were known as WARSAW.

JOY DIVISION

An Ideal For Living EP **ENIGMA** Manchester, UK June 1978

Ian Curtis Vocals
Bernard Albrecht (Sumner) Guitar
Stephen Morris Drums
Peter Hook Bass

Recorded at Pennine Sound Studio, Dec. 77
Cover Design Bernard Albrecht **Photography** Gareth Davy
First release by the band on their own label. The band was known as Warsaw at the time of the recordings but changed their name to Joy Division by the time the record was made. 'This is not a concept E.P. it is an enigma. All complaints - Terry Mason' [Mason was an early member of the group who instead became manager before the appointment of Rob Gretton]

THE NORMAL

T.V.O.D b/w Warm Leatherette

MUTE RECORDS London UK May 1978

Performed by Daniel Miller

Photo courtesy of The Motor Industry Research Association!

The first release on Mute Records

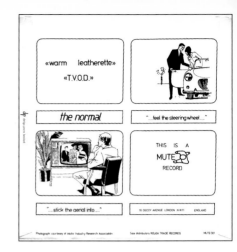

GANG OF FOUR
Damaged Goods b/w Love Like Anthrax/Armalite Rifle
FAST PRODUCT UK Oct 1978

Jon King Vocals
Andy Gill Guitar
Dave Allen Bass
Hugo Burnham Drums

Recorded at Cargo Studios, Rochdale, June 1978

Debut single from the Gang of Four, who formed in Leeds in 1977. Released on Bob Last's Fast Product label in Edinburgh, Scotland. Band split-up in 1983, occasionally reforming.

THE DEADBEATS

Kill The Hippies/Brainless/Final Ride/Deadbeat
DANGERHOUSE Los Angeles, California USA

July 1978

Scott Guerin Lead Vocals, Percussion
Geza X Guitar
Pasquale Amadeo Bass
Shaun Guerin Drums
Pat Delaney Sax

Produced by Geza X. Gedeon
Cover Art David Williams

Early LA art punk band on the legendary Dangerhouse Records label. In 1978 they released their first and only EP titled Kill The Hippies.

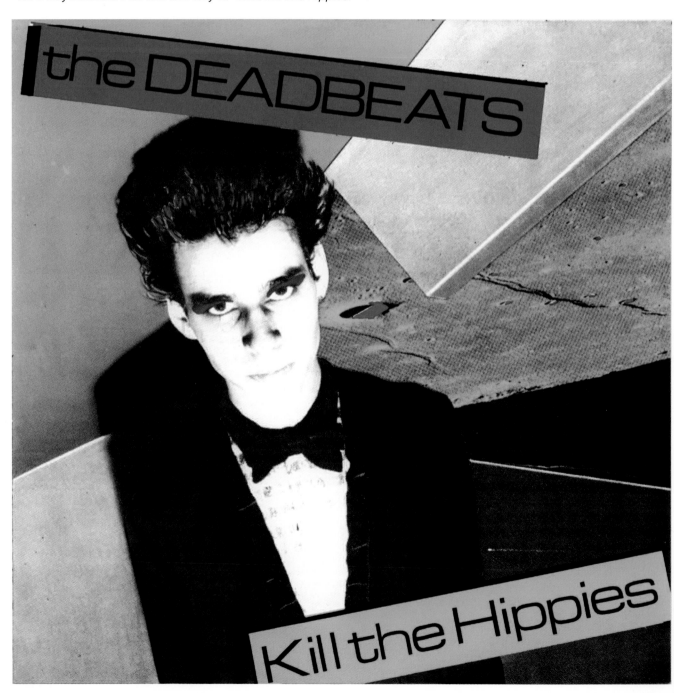

SUBWAY SECT
Nobody's Scared b/w Don't Split It
BRAIK RECORDS London, UK 24 Mar 1978

Vic Goddard Vocals
Rob Simmons Guitar
Paul Myers Bass
Bob Warde Drums

Produced by George Alexander

Formed in London, Sep 1976. This was their first single.

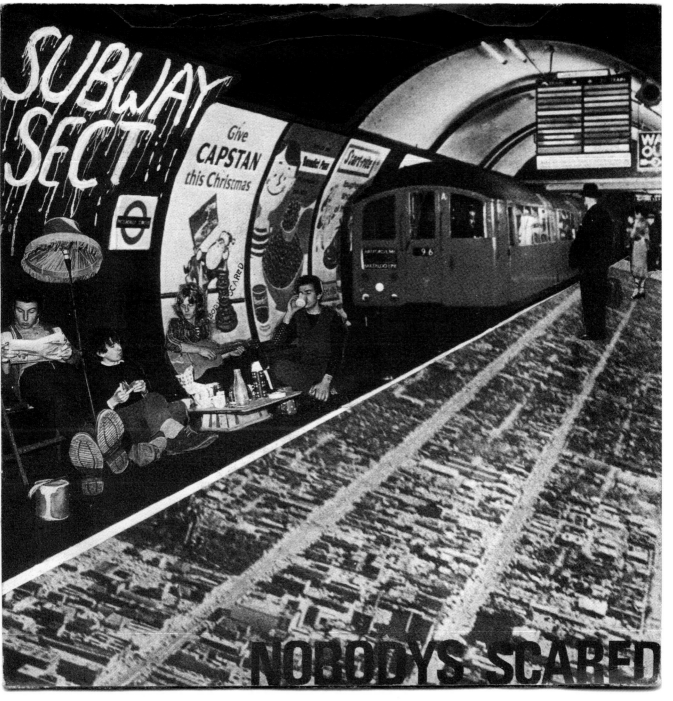

TALKING HEADS

Take Me To The River b/w
Thank You For Sending Me An Angel
SIRE RECORDS New York, USA 1978

Tina Weymouth Bass
Jerry Harrison Guitar, Keyboards, Vocals
David Byrne Guitar, Vocals
Chris Frantz Drums

Produced by Brian Eno and Talking Heads **Cover Art** David Byrne

Homage to soul singer Al Green

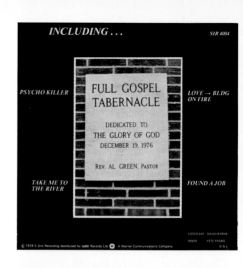

999

Emergency b/w My Street Stinks

UNITED ARTISTS UK January 1978

Nick Cash Vocals, Guitar
Guy Days Lead Guitar
Jon Watson Bass
Pablo LaBrittain Drums

Produced by Andy Arthurs
Sleeve Design by Snow - George

Formed in London, Dec 1976. Nick Cash had been in Kilburn and The High Roads.

THE ART ATTACKS

I Am A Dalek b/w Neutron Bomb
ALBATROSS UK March 1978

Edwin Pouncey Vocals

Steve Spear Guitar, Backing vocals

M.S. Bass

J.D.Haney Drums

Edwin Pouncey is also known under the alias of Savage Pencil, music writer and graphic artist.

EDWIN POUNCEY AKA Savage Pencil, is an illustrator, comic artist and music journalist. He also co-founded the short-lived punk band The Art Attacks in London in 1978.

How did you get into punk? I arrived in London at the point when the UK punk rock scene was just emerging. At that time it was still pretty underground, which is one of the reasons I was attracted to it. The main accessible source for this information was the Rock On record stall in Soho market. Rock On specialised in all things rock 'n' roll related, so punk rock was something they embraced and wanted to promote. I bought my copy of New Rose by The Damned from them on the day of release, and was advised to check out the 100 Club on Oxford Street if I wanted to catch any of this music being played live.

The term punk rock had not really established itself by then. Punk was a term that referred to the hordes of late 60s/early 70s US garage bands who were only just being recognised and appreciated by the mid 70s. Lenny Kaye's Nuggets compilation for Elektra Records was the touchstone for those wishing to explore primal punk, but bands like the Stooges, MC5, Flamin' Groovies and the New York Dolls were already being acknowledged as the originators of the genre. As I was to discover, however, UK punk was a completely different animal, with an agenda that railed against authority and made a demand for real social, political and cultural change, all of which would steadily unfold as the popularity of the bands concerned accelerated.

The Sex Pistols' televised 'interview' with Bill Grundy proved to be the spark that ignited the tabloid press to howl outrage and, in doing so, made punk rock identifiable to those who might have previously thought it was just another teenage fad. For my part, I felt that the Grundy incident sounded the death knell for punk's innocence, which was the main reason I had been attracted to it in the first place. Seeing the Pistols at the 100 Club pre-Grundy was a completely different experience to seeing them after they had signed to EMI – the band's almost intimate performances (played to an audience of 50 or 60 regular or curious punters) had sounded hungry, powerful and spiked with a mock menace. 'There's a few hippies here tonight,' Johnny Rotten would snarl as he cast a baleful eye around the room, before signalling with a nod to the rest of the band to explode like a musical nail bomb. These early shows (culminating with the now legendary Screen on the Green gig) were my personal highlights of the UK punk rock live experience. The energy they projected made you want to form your own band – regardless of whether you could play or not.

Can you talk a bit about The Art Attacks?
The Art Attacks were formed by myself and guitarist Steve Spear while

we were at the Royal College of Art. The band lasted just under a year and in that time we released two singles and appeared on two compilation LPs (Streets and Live at the Vortex). The band also toured with The Lurkers, playing at a variety of northern pubs, clubs and derelict institutions before escaping back to London. It was grim back up north, and shortly after I decided that I wanted to concentrate on getting my art degree and left the band.

How did the design for The Fall's 'Lie Dream of a Casino Soul' come about? Mark E Smith had already namechecked me on a song for The Fall's Dragnet LP, mainly because I had featured him in a Rock 'n' Roll Zoo comic strip I had done for [music weekly] Sounds that showed him being beaten up by punks for being too different. It happened, apparently. Mark was saying in the song that I shouldn't worry and he could fight his own battles. I had great empathy with what The Fall were doing and admired their very original creative stance in a scene that was rife with pale imitations of the Sex Pistols and The Clash. Some distant camaraderie was definitely there.

When The Fall signed to Kamera, Mark got in touch with me and asked if I would do the cover for 'Lie Dream of a Casino Soul'. He sent me some grainy black-and-white pictures and a brief suggestion of what he had in mind. I did my usual monster portraits of Mark and Karl Burns hanging outside a sort of Wigan Casino locale. I wanted it to look dark, sinister and full of Lovecraftian threat. As though Salford had being transformed into his mythical town of Arkham. I knew that Mark had read HP Lovecraft, so I thought this approach might amuse him. I hope it did.

What other punk releases did you do?
Quite a few. The early ones I did were the cover for the Streets compilation, the lettering for The Saints' 'I'm Stranded' single, 'Freak Show' by The Lurkers, 'Jimmy Jukebox' by Kim Fowley and something for a band called The Upp. All of this was triggered off by my weekly Rock 'n' Roll Zoo comic strip in Sounds, a funny animals strip that commented on the various aspects of the music scene. I was working at Sounds as a layout artist/writer/cartoonist for almost five years before I left to go freelance. I went on to do cover art for many other bands including Sonic Youth, Big Black and Sunn O))).

THE RUDE KIDS

Raggare Is A Bunch of Motherfuckers b/w Charlie

Polydor SWEDEN 1978

Lasse (Throw It) Drums

Bona Vocals

Lasse Guitar, Backing Vocals

Spaceman Bass

Recorded at BMB Studio, Stockholm, May 1978

Produced by The Rude Kids and Morgan

Photo Bengt Eklof

Band formed in Stockholm, Sweden in 1977 and existed until 1984. First Swedish punk band released on a major label.

X

Adult Books b/w We're Desperate

DANGERHOUSE Los Angeles, USA April 1978

John Doe Vocals, Bass
Exene Cervenka Vocals
Billy Zoom Bass
Don Bonebrake Drums

Produced by Jimmy Nanos and Pat Rand **Photos and Concept** Jules Bates

Debut single from X, formed in Los Angeles, 1977. First of two releases on Dangerhouse before signing to a different Los Angeles independent label, Slash Records, for 'Los Angeles', their debut album. Later signed to major label Elektra. Band split-up in 1993, occasionally reforming.

SIOUXSIE AND THE BANSHEES

Hong Kong Garden

POLYDOR UK 18 August 1978

Siouxsie Sioux Vocals

Kenny Morris Drums

John McKay Guitar

Steve Severin Bass

Produced by Nils Stevenson and Steve Lillywhite.

Formed in London, 1976. Debut single

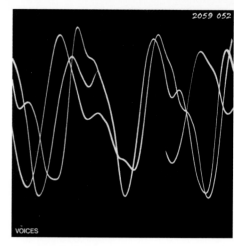

DEVO
Satisfaction b/w Sloppy
BOOJI BOY RECORDS Akron, Ohio USA 1978

Bob Casale Guitar, Keyboards, Vocals
Gerald V. Casale Bass, Keyboards, Lead Vocals
Bob Mothersbaugh Lead Guitar, Backing Vocals
Mark Mothersbaugh Keyboards, Guitar, Lead Vocals
Alan Myers Drums

Photos Moishe Brakha **Production and Graphic Concept** Devo

'The name Devo comes from their concept of 'de-evolution', the idea that instead of continuing to evolve, mankind has actually begun to regress, as evidenced by the dysfunction and herd mentality of American society.' This Booji Boy release was distributed by Bomp! Records in Los Angeles.

another fine product of
THE DE-EVOLUTION BAND

THE HUMAN LEAGUE

Being Boiled b/w Circus of Death
FAST PRODUCT UK June 1978

Martyn Ware Keyboards
Ian Craig Marsh Keyboards
Phil Oakey Vocals

First single by The Human League, formed in Sheffield in 1977. Recorded on a domestic tape recorder in an abandoned factory at a cost of £2.50 – presumably the cost of the cassette. Third release on the fledgling Fast Product label.

MENACE

GLC b/w I'm Civilised

SMALL WONDER London UK 10 Mar 1978

Morgan Webster Vocals
Steve Tannett Guitar
Charlie Casey Bass
Noel Martin Drums

Group formed in Islington, London in 1976.
Split-up in 1979 after five singles.

TIN HUEY

Breakfast With The Hueys EP
Robert Takes The Road To Lieber Nawash b/w Squirm You Worm
CLONE RECORDS Akron, Ohio USA 1978

Mark Price Bass, Vocals
Nappy Lemans Drums, Percussion
Ralph Carney Saxophone
Michael Aylward Vocals, Guitar
Harvey Gold Vocals, Guitar, Keyboards

Recorded at Bushflow Studio, Akron, Ohio.

Formed in Akron, Ohio around 1972, out of an earlier band called Rags. This is their second single on Clone Records. Shortly after this Chris Butler joined the group and they recorded their sole album for Warner Brothers, Contents Dislodged During Shipment but left the major label shortly afterwards. Butler then formed The Waitresses. Akron's Clone Records was run by Nick Nicholis, who had originally been vocalist for another Akron band, The Bizarros.

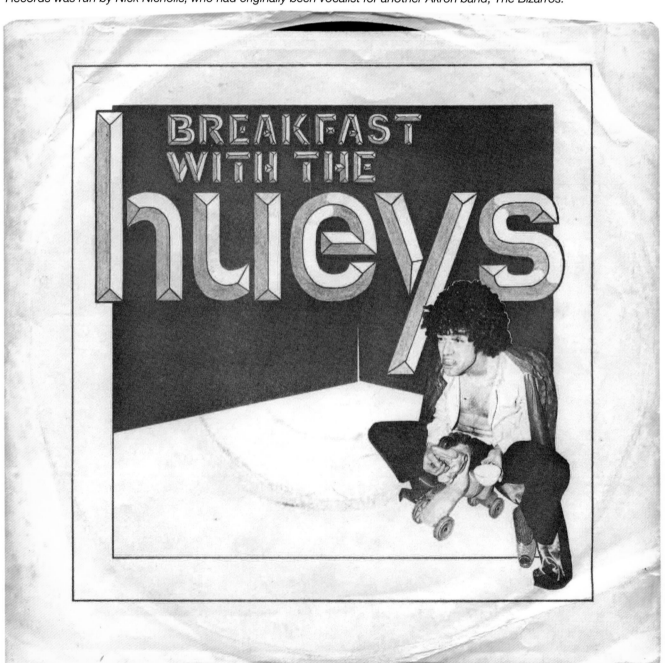

THE BAGS

Survive b/w Babylonian Gorgon
DANGERHOUSE RECORDS Los Angeles, California USA Dec 1978

Terry Dad Bag Drums
Alice Bag Vocals
Rob Ritter Guitar
Pat Bag Bass
Craig Lee Guitar Vocals

Produced by Geza X. Geden **Cover Pic by** Melanie Nissen

Sole single from Los Angeles punk band.

CABARET VOLTAIRE

Extended Play EP
Talkover/Here She Comes Now/
Do The Mussolini-Headkick/The Set Up
ROUGH TRADE London UK November 1978

Richard H. Kirk Guitar, Voice
Chris Watson Electronics, Tape, Voice
Stephen Mallinder Bass, Voice

Produced and recorded at Western Works by Cabaret Voltaire
Photography by Rod **Sleeve Design** C.V.

The experimental electronic sound group formed in Sheffield in 1973. This is their first single release on Rough Trade.

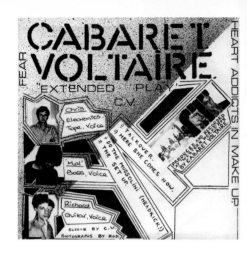

What is the relationship between punk and Cabaret Voltaire?
Cabaret Voltaire were recording from around '73/'74 and started becoming aware of the first British punk stirrings from around 1975. It was as if the punks had been on a parallel trajectory to us and the notions of anarchy and confrontation were very familiar. The first ever Cabaret Voltaire performance in 1975 ended in a mini riot. Also, the fashion of punk (ripped clothes/charity shop retro/paint splashed shirts) was something that CV were already exploring via an interest in Dada and Surrealism. CV had quite a reputation around Sheffield as being kind of strangely dressed weirdos and people almost knew us for that before they'd even heard a note of our 'music'.

I remember visiting Malcolm McLaren's shop in its various incarnations (Let it Rock/Too Fast to Live Too Young to Die/Sex) many times in the early to mid 70s. There were a few others in Sheffield who were hip to all that, you'd see people in PVC and winklepicker shoes and stuff like that before the whole thing became commodified by the media.

I think the big difference between the punks and CV was that even though we liked the energy and aggression of the music, to us it was a bit retro. We wanted to have that same vibe but make the music more electronic, more forward looking.

What is the connection between Cabaret Voltaire and Factory Records at the start. How did it come about? Factory became interested in CV after we'd been sending tapes to Richard Boon at New Hormones. Mal [Stephen Mallinder] and myself had started going to Manchester for the nightlife and shops in the mid 70s and really enjoyed it. Clubs like The Ranch and Pips were better than what was happening in Sheffield at the time.

Once Tony Wilson got to hear our tapes he invited us to play at the early Factory shows at the PSV club in Moss Side. After that we became regular visitors, getting to know Rob Gretton, Alan Erasmus and Joy Division, who often played on the same bill as CV. Tony was left some money and decided to invest it in a record label so he asked CV for a couple of tracks for the Factory Sample EP.

This was after the first EP for Rough Trade and at one point we may have decided to work with Factory, but Rough Trade came up with some cash so that we could upgrade our studio, Western Works to four-track.

How did it come about that you signed with Rough Trade? Why did you sign to Rough Trade? Most bands did one off-singles but you recorded with them extensively. Was it a good experience? CV didn't actually sign with Rough Trade. Every record we did was a separate agreement and did not tie us exclusively under contract with them, hence we could record for Factory as well. It worked well for us. They left us alone and when we had a new release we'd deliver the master tapes and artwork then go back to Sheffield. I really liked Geoff Travis as a person and admired his taste in music at this time, especially his enthusiasm for dub, but we dealt a lot of the time with the late Peter Walmsley and later Mayo Thompson, Scott Pearing and Claude Bessey. It was pretty cool, but later on became frustrating and hence the move to Some Bizarre/Virgin in 1983.

Did you consider making the records yourself at the beginning? Yes in fact before the Extended Play EP we were considering borrowing money to self-release. Also, Throbbing Gristle were going to release us through Industrial but in the end didn't have the finance to do it, so pointed us in the direction of Rough Trade. Jon Savage had a hand in persuading Geoff that he should put our records out.

Were you a fan of the first wave of punk? If so who did you like? The first wave of punk to me was in the 60s - the Seeds, Iggy and The Stooges, ? And the Mysterions, Count Five, 13th Floor Elevators, Velvet Underground, even early Rolling Stones ,The Who and The Kinks - but yes I enjoyed the Sex Pistols, The Clash (first LP),The Damned, Subway Sect, The Prefects, Siouxsie and the Banshees, Wire and The Fall.

Did you like any music from USA? In terms of punk, yes – see above. But also The New York Dolls, The Ramones, Television, Richard Hell, Talking Heads, Patti Smith, The Residents, Devo, Chrome and especially Suicide.

Or Jamaica maybe? Jamaican dub was always on the stereo. King Tubby, Augustus Pablo, Lee Scratch Perry, Dr Alimantado, Tappa Zukie, Scientist, Keith Hudson.

Did you see a connection with, say, The Pistols and Cabaret Voltaire? Maybe in attitude, if not music? If so, how did punk shape Cabaret Voltaire? I do remember buying an electric guitar from someone at art school in 1975 for £3.50. Mal got a bass guitar and Chris bought a cheap electric organ, all of which we used to go through various processors/treatments. It was for sure an encouragement to pick up a guitar and get more primal. I remember seeing the Sex Pistols at the Black Swan pub in Sheffield around '76, then on the anarchy tour in Leeds (it was banned from Sheffield) and later on Christmas day

CABARET VOLTAIRE

SILENT COMMAND
SILENT COMMAND

SILENT COMMAND

remember buying an electric guitar from someone at art school in 1975 for £3.50. Mal got a bass guitar and Chris bought a cheap electric organ, all of which we used to go through various processors/treatments. It was for sure an encouragement to pick up a guitar and get more primal. I remember seeing the Sex Pistols at the Black Swan pub in Sheffield around '76, then on the anarchy tour in Leeds (it was banned from Sheffield) and later on Christmas day in Huddersfield, when Sid was in the group. The Sheffield and Leeds gigs were revelatory but Huddersfield was a bit chaotic. Definitely the attitude thing. It was great to know there were some kindred spirits at large!

What, if anything, are the musical roots/lineage of Cabaret Voltaire's music. ie What came before for you?
The list is very long, but here's a few. BBC Radiophonic Workshop, the German scene of late 60s early 70s - Neu, Can, Kraftwerk, Popul Vuh, Harmonia, Faust, Tangerine Dream. Joe Meek, Phil Spector productions, The Velvet Underground, the Nuggets album, Jamaican dub. Black dance music – James Brown, Fatback Band, Hamilton Bohannon, Brass Construction, Miles Davis, John Coltrane, Sly Stone, Funkadelic, Parliament, George Clinton, soul , funk, northern soul, Fela Kuti, Stockhausen, John Cage, Steve Reich, Roxy Music, David Bowie, Iggy Pop, Brian Eno, Walter/Wendy Carlos.

Is industrial music a product of decaying industrial cities? Or is that too corny?
The term industrial music was coined by Throbbing Gristle – 'industrial music for industrial people' – but I think because of Sheffield's industrial past we somehow got labelled with that tag.

Certainly Sheffield in those days was decaying, bleak and monochrome and still had a lot of heavy industry so perhaps subconsciously it was reflected. I know Kraftwerk described their music at one time as industrial folk music, which I quite like as a descriptive term.

Were you a fan of Throbbing Gristle. Or vice versa? How did you come to record on Industrial Records? V
ery much so. And I think they liked us as well. Still in touch with the surviving members after all these years. We got in touch with them after getting the Second Annual Report LP and started a dialogue, sending down tapes and Xerox art, etc. Finally met up with them at a show of theirs at the Industrial Training College Wakefield, July 1978 and even got a ride back to Sheffield in their van. Went on to play a few

shows together and when they started releasing cassette only LPs on Industrial they asked CV and myself for releases, one being CV's Outer Limits album (material from '74 -'76) and the other being Disposable Half Truths, my first ever solo release. They were always very forthcoming with advice and help regarding the perils of the music bizz, having started releasing music and running their own label. I think we all really admired their self-suffiency as well as their art.

Who designed Cabaret Voltaire's sleeves?
The early sleeves were done by myself - Extended Play/Nag Nag Nag/Mix up/Voice of America. I was doing a lot of Xerox /Mail Art in the mid 70s, plus reading a lot of William Burroughs, so it seemed just natural … I was also at art school from 74-75, dabbling in installation projects and working with standard and super 8 film and slides for the CV live shows. The photographic images for some of the sleeves (Red Mecca/The Covenant the Sword and the Arm of the Lord/Plasticity/The Conversation/Methodology) were also my handy-work.

From 2x45(1982) onwards we worked with Neville Brody. This continued until Code (1987). Phil Barnes also created images for The Crackdown and Micro-phonies albums as well as for a number of my solo works (Time High Fiction/Ugly Spirit/Black Jesus Voice/Virtual State and Sandoz - Digital Lifeforms) and some later CV albums. The Designers Republic did quite a few of the later period sleeves.
For me it was always seemed to work better when the people who designed were supplied with images to work with.

Was it clear what the covers should represent?
Being a big fan of Dada and Surrealism it was always important to have an element of strangeness or 'fuckedupness'/bending of reality/alienation, which was really a reflection of the content of the records.

Which cover is your favourite?
I was always fond of the Voice of America collage.

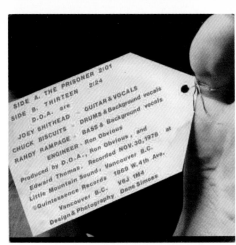

D.O.A.
The Prisoner b/w Thirteen
QUINTESSENCE RECORDS Vancouver, CANADA 1978

Joey Shithead Guitar & Vocals
Randy Rampage Bass
Chuck Biscuits Drums

Recorded Nov. 30, 1978 at Little Mountain Sound, Vancouver
Produced by D.O.A., Ron Obvious & Edward Thomas
Design & Photography Dane Simoes

Hardcore group founded in Vancouver 1978 by Joey 'Shithead' Keithley who had been in the earlier local punk group The Skulls. D.O.A. have released around 20 albums and are still active. Keithley, the only original member, also runs Sudden Death Records.

THE PAGANS
Street Where Nobody Lives b/w What's This Shit Called Love?
DROME RECORDS Cleveland USA 1978

Mike Hudson Lead Vocals
Tim Allee Bass
Brian Morgan Drums
Tommy Metoff Guitar

Recorded at Suma, Ohio in March 1978
Produced by Johnny Dromette **Cover design by** Dromette

Formed in Cleveland, Ohio in 1977, released four singles before splitting-up in 1979, occasionally reforming. Drome Records was run by John Thompson (Johnny Dromette) and came out of his Cleveland record store of the same name. Thompson also designed the artwork for Drome releases and many Pere Ubu and Hearthan products.

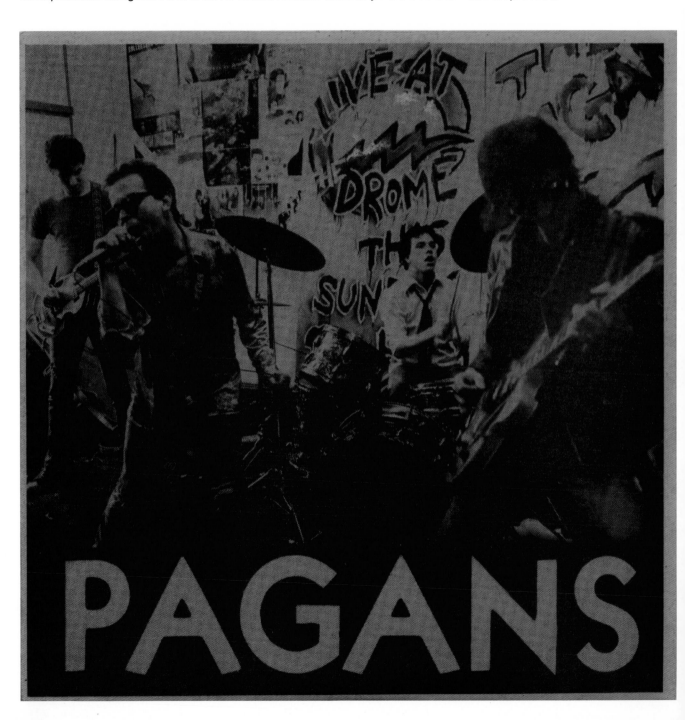

FILTH

Don't Hide Your Hate b/w Sex, Nothing For Me
PLUREX MODERN LABEL HOLLAND 1978

Only single from Dutch punk band formed in Amsterdam in Jan 1978.
Plurex Modern was an indie label started by Wally Van Middendorp, singer
of another Dutch punk band, The Tits

THE OFFS Johnny Too Bad b/w 624803
ROTTEN RECORDS San Francisco, USA 1978

Don Vinil Vocals
Billy Hawk Guitars
Robert Morgan Bass
Chris Olson Drums

Cover and credits Jack Off (Jack Johnson)

Proto-punk/ska band from San Francisco. The cover features an image from Jean Genet's Un Chant d'Amour (a man sucking a gun barrel) backed with a negative photograph of Dan White, who had recently assasinated San Francisco Mayor Moscone and Harvey Milk, being taken into custody. Their album First Record, released in 1984, featured artwork by Jean Michel Basquiat.

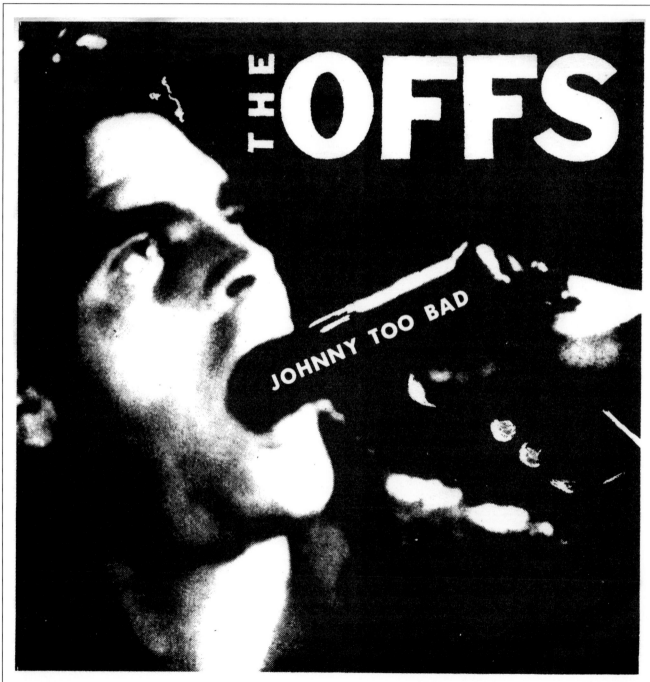

BRIARD: Fuck the Army / Product of the
TV -generation

POKO REKORDS PIS 009

Briard:
Pete Malmi   -laulu
Andy McCoy   -kitara
Sam Sodamy   -basso
Serious Lee Insane -rummut

äänitetty microvoxissa 20.6.1978
äänitys pekka nurmikallio
tuottaja briard

kiitokset pekan äidille kahvista ja leivoksista
kansi j.situkonen 1978

BRIARD

Fuck The Army b/w Product of The TV-Generation
POKO RECORDS FINLAND 10 August 1978

Pete Malmi Vocals
Timo Huovinen Bass
Sidi Vainio Drums
Andy McCoy Guitar

Produced by Briard

The first Finnish punk band, released their first single in November 1977.
Split-up in 1979 after four singles occasionally reforming.

THE CURSE

Shoeshine Boy b/w The Killer Bees

HI-FI RECORDS CANADA 1978

Mickey Skin Lead Vocal
Trixie Danger Guitar
Dr. Bourque Bass
Patzy Poizon Drums

Recorded at Marigold Studios, Toronto, Canada
Produced by Gabor Hegedus
Photo by Carol Starr

Only single from all female punk band from Toronto, Canada formed in May 1977.

THE VICTIMS

Television Addict b/w Flipped Out Over You
No label Perth, AUSTRALIA 18 March 1978

Dave Flick Vocals, Guitar
James Baker Drums
Rudolph V Bass

*Australian punk band from Perth, Western Australia, in existence
1977-79, put out two self-released singles.*

ROBERT RENTAL

Paralysis b/w A.A.C.

REGULAR RECORDS Battersea, London UK 1978

Robert Rental Voice and all instruments
Produced by Robert Rental and Thomas Leer

Original DIY pressing of 500, re-released the following year on Company Records.

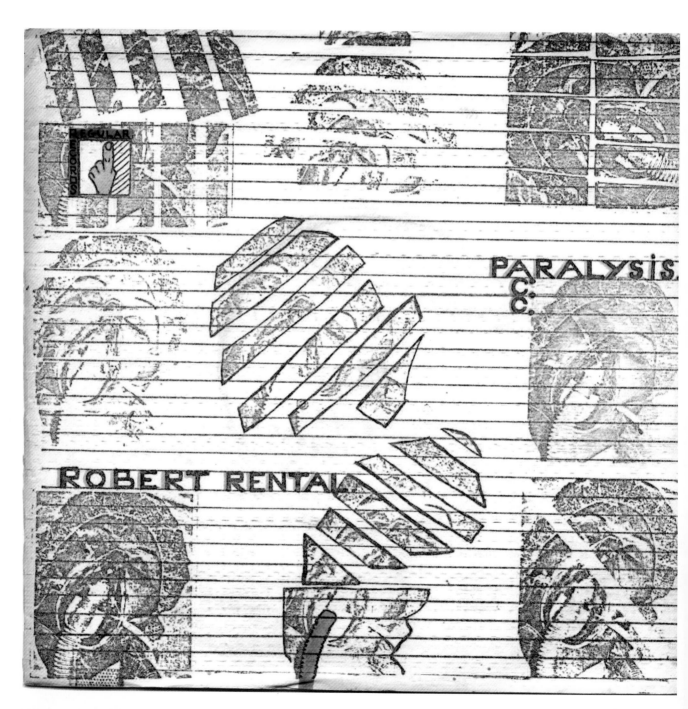

THE TIGHTS,
Grease EP Bad Hearts b/w It & Cracked
CHERRY RED RECORDS London, UK 2 June 1978

Barry Island Bass
Rick Mayhew Drums
Robert Banks Guitar
Malcolm Orgee Vocals

Recorded at Millstream Studios, Cheltenham **Produced by** John Acock

Band from Great Malvern, Worcester who released just two singles before splitting-up, presumably to form the stockings. This was the first release on Cherry Red Records, founded by Iain McNay. Cherry Red quickly brought together an eclectic catalogue releasing music by Destroy All Monsters from Detroit (featuring ex-members of The Stooges and MC5) and The Runaways, Kim Fowley's protégées in Los Angeles, alongside the label's roster of successful British artists.

THE FALL

Bingo-Master's Break-Out! EP
Psycho Mafia/Bingo-Master/Repetition
STEP-FORWARD RECORDS London UK 11 Aug 1978

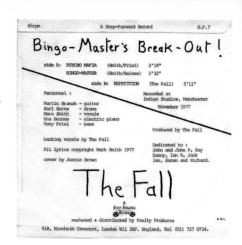

Mark E. Smith Vocals
Martin Bramah Guitar, Backing Vocals
Karl Burns Drums, Backing Vocals
Una Baines Electric Piano, Backing Vocals
Tony Friel Bass, Backing Vocals

Recorded at Indigo Sounds, Manchester
Produced by The Fall **Cover by** Jonnie Brown

Debut single from The Fall, formed in Manchester late 1976.

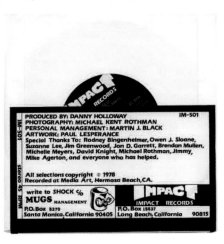

SHOCK
This Generation's On Vacation/Spoiled/Overseas
IMPACT RECORDS Los Angeles, California USA 1978

Paul Lesperance Lead Vocals
Steve Reiner Bass Guitar
Gaylord Drums
Kip Brown Guitar

Recorded at Media Art, Hermosa Beach, CA
Photography by Michael Kenny Rothman **Artwork by** Paul Lesperance

Formed in 1976, Shock were one of the first punk groups to come out of Los Angeles scene. Adrenaline-charged power pop. Released just two singles.

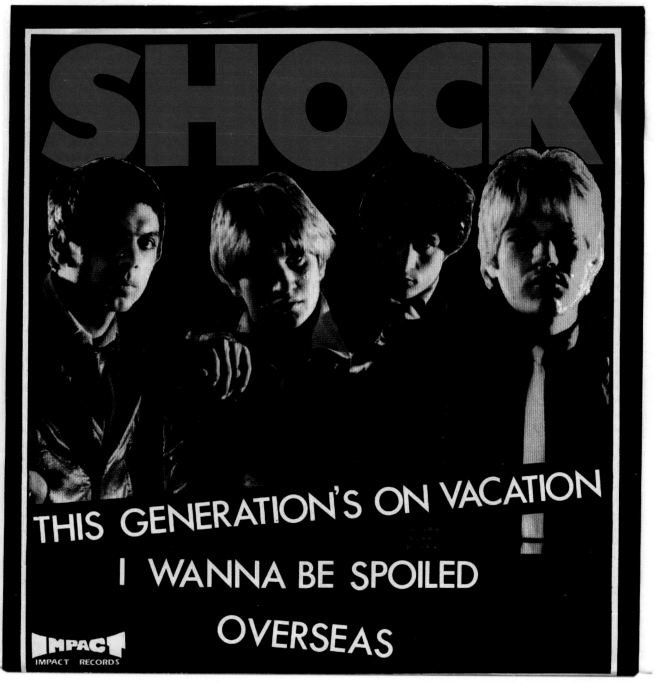

84 FLESH
Salted City b/w D-Section
SKYDOG RECORDS Paris, FRANCE 1978

Flesh Vocals
Louis W Bass
Belock and Goddard Guitars
Goddard Drums

Produced by Marc Zermati **Artwork by** Bazooka, Loulou Picasso, Olivia Clavel

Only release from French punk band originally known as 1984. Artwork is by Bazooka, a collective of mainly French artists active from 1974-1978 that included Christian Chapiron (Kiki Picasso), Jean-Louis Dupré (Loulou Picasso), Olivia Clavel (Electric Clitoris), Lulu Larsen , Bernard Vidal (Bananar), Jean Rouzaud and sporadically Philippe Bailly (Ti5 Hard).

KLEENEX Beri Beri/Ain't You b/w Hedi's Head/Nice
Sunrise SWITZERLAND 1978

Klaudia Schiff Bass
Lisot Ha Drums
Marlene Marder Guitar
Regula Sing Vocals

Photographs by **P. Mattioli** Design by **Peter Fischli**

All-female band formed in Geneva 1978. Kleenex later changed their name to LiliPUT to avoid legal problems with the tissue manufacturer. Fold-out poster sleeve. Subsequently released on Rough Trade with two of the tracks (Ain't You and Hedi's Head). Sunrise was the label of Swiss composer Etienne Conod. Sleeve designer Peter Fischli formed Fischli/Weiss a collaborative art duo with Daniel Weiss.

THE CURE

Killing an Arab b/w 10.15 Saturday Night

SMALL WONDER RECORDS London, UK Dec 1978

Robert Smith Vocals, Guitar
Porl Thompson Guitar
Michael Dempsey Bass
Lol Tolhurst Drums

Produced by Chris Parry **Design by** Bill Smith, Chris Parry

Debut single by The Cure, formed in Crawley, West Sussex in 1976. This record was also reissued the following year on Chris Parry's Fiction Records, which became the home of The Cure releases for the next 20 years. The song is based on Albert Camus' book The Stranger and was not, as a sticker on the later edition was keen to point out, racist.

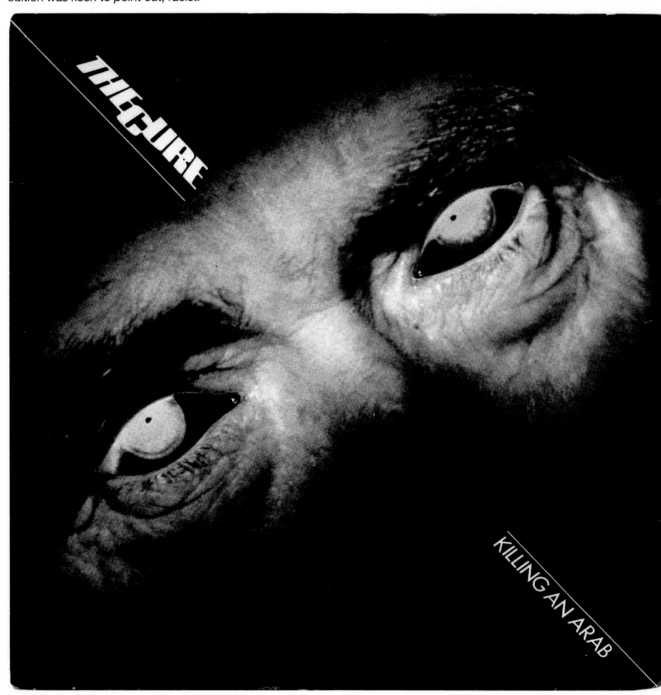

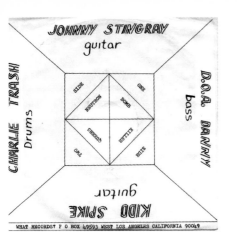

WHAT RECORDS? P O BOX 49593 WEST LOS ANGELES CALIFORNIA 90049

THE CONTROLLERS
Neutron Bomb b/w Killer Queers
WHAT RECORDS? *Los Angeles, California USA* 1978

D.O.A. Danny Bass, Vocals
Kid Spike Guitar, Vocals
Johnny Stingray Guitar, Vocals
Charlie Trash Drums, Vocals

Formed in Los Angeles in July 1977. Released two singles, split-up in 1979, reforming occasionally.

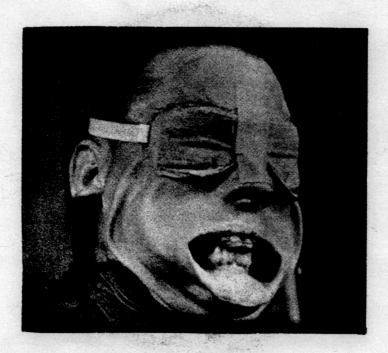

TELEVISION PERSONALITIES

Where's Bill Grundy Now? EP
Part-Time Punks/Where's Bill Grundy Now?/Happy Families/Posing At The Roundhouse
KINGS ROAD RECORDS UK November 1978

Dan Treacy Vocals
Ed Ball Drums, Guitar, Backing Vocals
John Bennett Drums
Gerard Bennett Bass

Includes 'Part-Time Punks'. Could anything be more biting than a young punk's sarcasm? Ouch. TV Personalities second single released on their own Kings Road Records. The single was later re-released in conjunction with Rough Trade. The band went on to make eight albums. "They play their records very loud, they pogo in the bedroom, but only when their mum's gone out. They pay five pence on the buses and they never use toothpaste, though they got £2.50 to go and see the Clash." (la la la la la …)

THE GERMS
Lexicon Devil b/w Circle One & No God
SLASH RECORDS
Los Angeles, California USA May 1978

Darby Crash Vocals
Lorna Doom Bass
Pat Smear Guitar
Nicky Beat Drums

Produced by Geza X

Second single from The Germs. Sleeve comes in four different colours. The Germs disbanded when Darby Crash committed suicide on December 7, 1980.

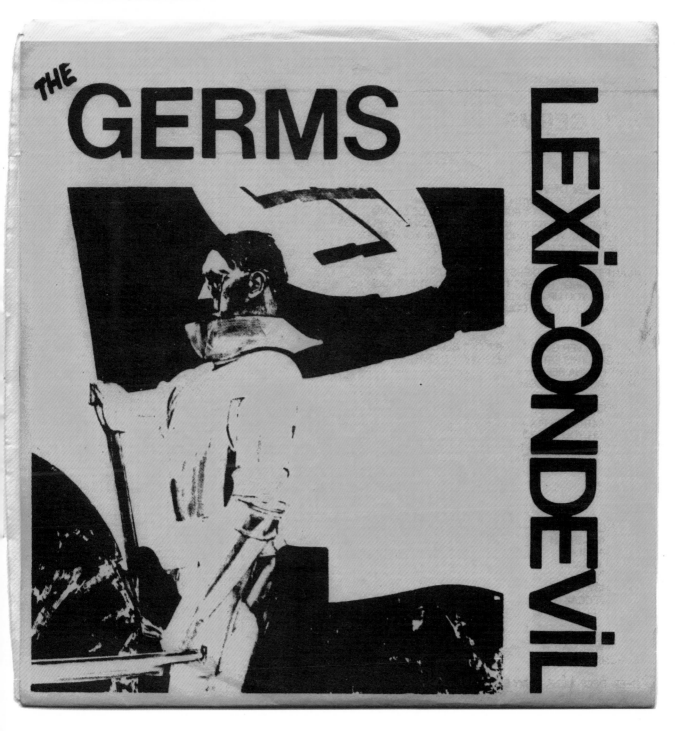

THE SKIDS

Charles EP
Charles/Reasons/Test-Tube Babies
NO BAD RECORDS Edinburgh, Scotland Feb 1978

Richard Jobson Vocals
Alexander Bass
Thomas Kellichan Drums
Stuart Adamson Lead Guitar

Recorded at REL Studios, Edinburgh **Produced by** The Skids

Band formed in Dunfermline, Fife, Scotland in 1977. Debut single released on local record shop owner Sandy Muir's No Bad Records. Shortly afterwards signed to Virgin Records.

45 r.p.m.
STEREO

SRTS/78/CUS 231
(LOO 2)

REVENGE

'A' SIDE "WE'RE NOT GONNA TAKE IT"

'B' SIDE "PORNOGRAPHY"

BOTH TITLES WRITTEN AND PRODUCED BY REVENGE.
REVENGE ARE:-
LOL HAMMOND - GUITAR & LEAD VOCALS.
IAN STRANGE - BASS & BACKING VOCALS.
DAVE EDGAR - DRUMS & BACKING VOCALS.
RECORDED AT GATE WAY STUDIOS IN BALHAM SOUTH LONDON.

MANY THANKS TO OUR ROADIE JOHN AND ALL OUR MATES.
THIS RECORD SHOULD BE PLAYED AS LOUD AS POSSIBLE.
FORGET ABOUT THE NEIGHBOURS AFTER ALL LET'S FACE IT
THEY'RE ONLY GOOD FOR LENDING SUGAR, ALCOHOL AND
UNDERWEAR, ETC.
SLEEVE NOTES BY THE VERY UNDERATED TONY JOHNSON.

MANUFACTURED BY
SRT PRODUCTIONS Ltd.
LONDON

REVENGE

We're Not Gonna Take It b/w Pornography
LOONY RECORDS London UK 1978

Lol Hammond Lead Vocals, Guitar
Ian Strange Bass, Backing Vocals
Dave Edgar Drums, Backing Vocals

Recorded at Gate Way Studios In Balham, south London
Produced by Revenge

Formed in Cheshunt, Hertfordshire, released two singles on the Looney Records label in 1978.

REVENGE

"WE'RE NOT GONNA TAKE IT"

THE MEKONS

Where Were You/ I'll Have To Dance Then (On My Own)

FAST PRODUCT UK 1978

Andy Corrigan Vocals

Mark White Vocals

Ken Guitars

Tong Guitars

Ros Allen Bass

Jon Langford Drums, Vocals

Recorded 20th and 22nd October 1978 at Spaceward Studios, Cambridge

Formed in Leeds in 1977 at same college as Gang of Four and Delta 5 who all came into existence during same period. The Mekons are now based in Chicago, USA. This is another release from the astute A&R stable of Bob Fast and Fast Product. A truly great record.

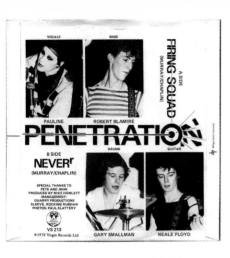

PENETRATION
Firing Squad b/w Never
VIRGIN RECORDS UK 1978

Pauline Murray Vocals
Robert Blamire Bass
Gary Smallman Drums
Neale Floyd Guitar

Produced by Mike Howlett
Photos Paul Slattery

Band formed in Ferryhill, County Durham in 1976. This is their third single.

SCRITTI POLITTI

Skank Bloc Bologna b/w Is and
Ought The Western World/28/8/78

ST. PANCRAS RECORDS

London UK **Nov 1978**

Green Gartside Guitar, Vocals
Niall Jinks Bass
Tom Morley Drums

*Scritti Politti formed in Leeds in 1977, after seeing the
Sex Pistols play at Leeds Poly in Dec 1976, on the first
date of their Anarchy tour. Like the Desperate Bicycles,
the group helped launch the DIY ethic, with the fold out
cover listing the costs of the manufacture of this record.*

THE ZEROS
Wild Weekend b/w Never
BOMP! RECORDS Los Angeles, California USA 1978

Javier Escovedo Guitar, Lead Vocals
Robert Alan Lopez Guitar, Backing Vocals
Hector Penalosa Bass
Karton Chenelle Drums

Recorded at Kitchen Sync Studio.
Produced by Greg Shaw and The Zeros
Photography by Dead / Nissen **Design, Art Direction by** Allen

Second single, released on Bomp!

PRAG VEC

Existential/Bits/Wolf/Cigarettes

SPEC RECORDS London UK 16 Oct 1978

David Boyd Bass
Nick Cash Drums
Susan Gogan Vocals, Wasp, Guitar, Bass
John Studholme Guitar, Wasp, Bass, Drum Machine, Tapes, Vocals

Recorded at Rockstar Recording Studio, London. **Sleeve design by** Prag Vec and Pete **Photography by** Mike Laye

Gogan and Studholme were in earlier Trotskyite R&B band The Derelicts which folded in 1976. In Feb 1978 formed Prag Vec in London. After Virgin A&R told the band they had just signed Penetration, and said, 'Sorry – you're too like Pauline', they were also turned down by five management agencies so decided instead to self-release two singles on their own Spec Records. Made one further single on Celluloid before splitting up.

SHAM 69

Borstal Breakout b/w Hey Little Rich Boy
POLYDOR UK 6 Jan 1978

Jimmy Pursey Vocals
Dave Parsons Guitar
Dave Tregunna Bass
Ricky Goldstein Drums

Produced by Jimmy Pursey and Peter Wilson

Sham 69 formed in Hersham, Surrey in 1975. This is their first single after leaving Step Forward and signing with major label Polydor.

STIFF LITTLE FINGERS

Suspect Device b/w Wasted Life

RIGID DIGIT RECORDS

Belfast, NORTHERN IRELAND 1978

Jake Burns Lead Guitar, Vocals
Henry Cluney Rhythm Guitar
Ali McMordie Bass
Brian Faloon Drums

Influential first wave Irish punk band formed in Belfast in 1978, moved to London the following year. This record later came out via Rough Trade. After one album on Rough Trade they signed to Chrysalis. Split-up in 1983.

WIRE

I Am The Fly b/w Ex-Lion Tamer

HARVEST RECORDS UK Dec 1978

Colin Newman Guitar, Vocals
Graham Lewis Bass, Vocals
Robert Gotobed Drums
Bruce Gilbert Guitar
Produced by Mike Thorne

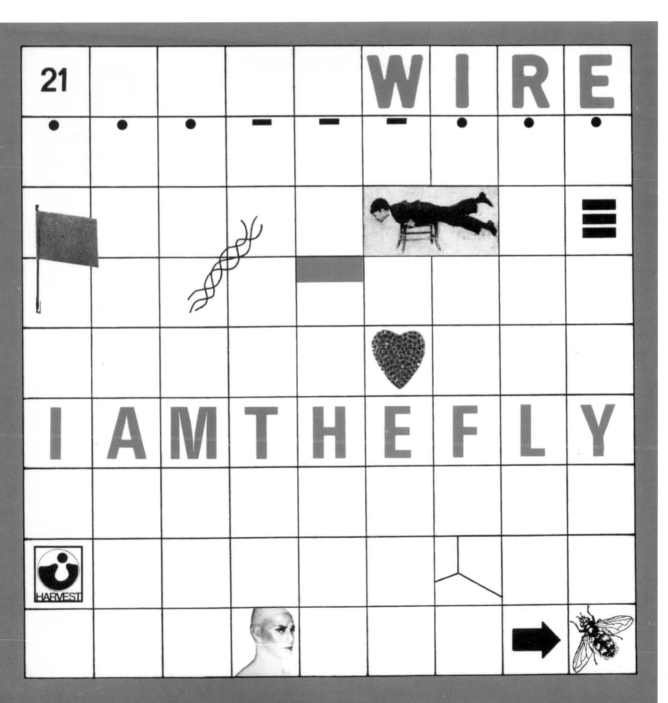

THE HOLLYWOOD SQUARES
The Hillside Strangler b/w Hollywood Square

SQUARE RECORDS Los Angeles, California USA 1978

Eddie Vincent Guitar, Vocals
Spider Cobb Bass
Tad Malone Drums

Produced by Ron Hitchcock Hand stamped paper sleeve.

Formed in Los Angeles in 1977. This song is about the Hilllside Strangler, the then unknown serial killer (which was actually two men, Kenneth Bianchi and Angelo Buono) terrorizing the city at the time.

A FACTORY SAMPLE
JOY DIVISION/DURUTTI COLUMN/ JOHN DOWIE/CABARET VOLTAIRE

FACTORY RECORDS Manchester, UK Dec 1978

Recorded at Cargo Studios, Rochdale, 11 October 1978
Produced by Martin Zero (Martin Hannett), Laurie Latham, CP Lee, Cabaret Voltaire **Sleeve Design by** Peter Saville

This is the first record released on Factory (FAC 1 was a concert at The Factory). The cover of the EP is made of rice paper, dyed silver and sealed inside a thin plastic bag. Contains 27 min and 40 seconds of music on two 7"s.

THE SLEEPERS

Seventh World/No Time /Flying/She's Fun/Linda

WiN RECORDS San Francisco, California USA 1978

Ricky Williams Vocals
Paul Draper Bass
Tim Mooney Drums
Michael Belfer Guitar

Recorded Jan - Mar 1978 at Tres Virgos studios, Mill Valley, CA
Produced by Paul Draper **Photography by** Richard Peterson
Designed by Paul Draper and Richard Peterson

From Palo Alto, California in 1978, became first-wave San Francisco punk band.
Vocalist Ricky Williams was originally the drummer in Crime. Split in 1979 and
again in 1980 after releasing a second single and album.

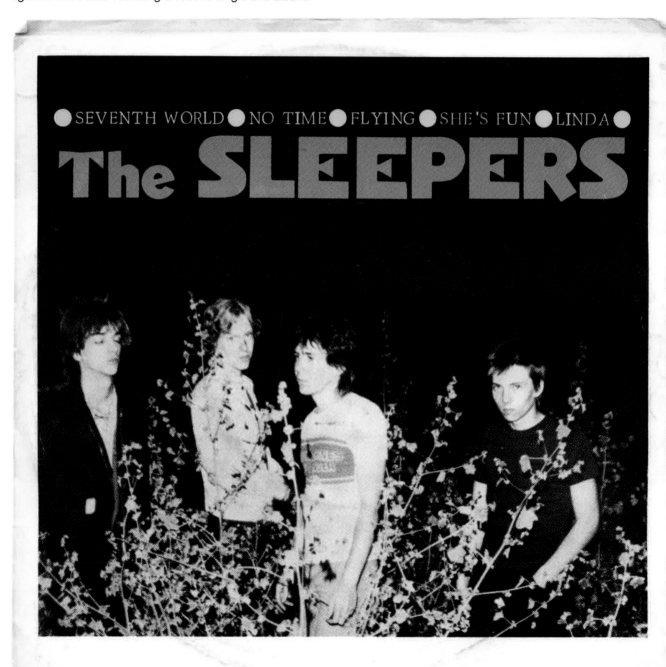

THE NORMALS
Almost Ready b/w Hardcore
LECTRIC EYE RECORDS
Jefferson, Louisiana, USA 1978

Steve Walters Bass
Chris Luckett Drums, Backing Vocals
David Brewton Guitar, Vocals
Charlie Hanson Guitar, Vocals

Recorded at Rosemont Studios, New Orleans.
Produced by Charlie Hanson **Photo by** Harry Crescioni

Formed in Jefferson, Louisiana in 1977. This is their only single and was recorded in an old gospel studio in New Orleans.

THEORETICAL GIRLS

U.S. Millie b/w You Got Me
THEORETICAL RECORDS New York USA 1978

Jeffrey Lohn Guitar, Vocals
Glen Branca Guitar
Margaret DeWys Keyboardist
Produced by Wharton Tiers

Only release from the group Theoretical Girls.

NEW YORK NO WAVE

An interview with Glenn Branca.

Following the success of the first wave of punk bands in New York – The Ramones, Television, Talking Heads and Blondie – and their subsequent evacuation of the city, no wave became the black hole to fill this void. No wave pushed further the confrontational aspect of punk music, as exemplified by the first-wave group Suicide.

No wave also linked New York's art and music worlds. The no wave bands included Theoretical Girls, The Contortions, Teenage Jesus and The Jerks, Mars and DNA.

Here, avant-garde composer Glenn Branca talks about this period.

Aside from releasing his own music as Theoretical Girls, The Static and under his own name, Glenn Branca also launched Normal Records, which released the music of a new generation of groups including Sonic Youth, Swans and Y Pants.

Would you describe the Theoretical Girls and The Static as no wave? Are you kidding me?

What did you take from punk in the music you were making during this period?
I loved punk. But while I was living in Boston and checking out the proto-punk bands of the early to mid-70s I was already visualising an experimental rock band.

You've commented that the difference between the East Village and the Soho no wave scenes was that the East Village bands were more into drugs. This makes them part of a musical lineage that goes back to The Velvet Underground. What was the musical lineage of the Soho music scene? How did this split between West and East Village no wave music scenes occur?
If I said drugs, I meant heroin. That has absolutely nothing to do with music. Our musical lineage was exactly the same. The differences weren't musical but locational - they lived east of Broadway and we live west of Broadway - and simply the fact that they knew and worked with each other, and we knew and worked with each other.

The real split came when Brian Eno decided to work with only the East Village bands on the No New York album. There was no real antipathy, at least from our side. We also played CBGB's and Max's. Actually, I think a lot of this may have been created by Diego Cortez, a conceptual artist in the Soho scene, who was a heavy backer of the Contortions.

If he was the guru of the East Village bands, Dan Graham, another and much more important conceptual artist, had that role on the Soho side as the backer of Theoretical Girls and later Sonic Youth.

Which of the earlier first generation New York punk did you like? I saw Patti Smith and the Ramones in Boston. In New York I saw Suicide and absolutely everybody else. Debbie Harry was the most beautiful woman I'd ever seen on stage anywhere, just ten feet away at CBGB's. It was amazing that she could put out so much energy while always staying physically calm. Cool and always sensual as hell.

Did you hang out at Max's or CBGB's?
CBGB's was closer, so I hung out there. Richard Hell was there at the bar almost every night. I think he lived, like, two doors down. I don't know why, I never met him, but when he walked by me in the lobby of the building where Roir records had its office he turned around, looked at me, and said, 'Asshole!' I was at Max's one night when Sid Vicious was there at the bar. I exchanged hellos with Warhol one afternoon before a soundcheck. We had never met, although I did see him around the galleries a lot.

How did no wave bring together the worlds of punk and art? Music is art. But these worlds can never meet. It's just that if you can't hang it on the wall as a one-off or limited edition, it can't be considered art. The conceptualists railed against this attitude, but failed - there's just too much money involved.

The Theoretical Girls and The Static made so few records - one apiece. Did you see a value in making records, as opposed to performing or writing?
Ha, what a fucking joke! We were all broke. We couldn't make records. We all would have done albums if we could have - but after the Sex Pistols, the labels wouldn't touch anything that smelled like punk. Sire was bought up by Warners and moved to London. All of the small New York labels went out of business. That's why I started Neutral Records with Josh Baer, who had some money - we released 16 records, including one of mine.

How did you hook up with 99 Records?
I was looking to release an album. I knew Ed. I walked into the store one day and asked him if he wanted to start a label and release one of my records. He said he didn't know anything about the recording, manufacturing and distributing of records. I told him that I did, from the three records released on Theoretical Records. He said, after thinking about it, ok.

THE WEIRDOS

We Got The Neutron Bomb/Solitary Confinement
DANGERHOUSE RECORDS
Los Angeles, California USA 1978

John Denney Vocals
Dave Trout Bass
Nickey Beat Drums
Cliff Roman Guitar
Dix Denney Lead Guitar

Recorded in Hollywood at Kitchen Sync. **Produced by** Pat Garrett and The Weirdos **Photography by** D.Burt **Artwork by** J. Denney

Influential band formed in Los Angeles in 1976. Broke up in 1981 and reformed sporadically ever since.

RUDI

Big Time b/w No One
GOOD VIBRATIONS Belfast, NORTHERN ISLAND April 1978

Ronnie Matthews Guitar, Vocals
Gordon Blair Bass, Backing Vocals
Graham Marshall Drums
Brian Young Guitar, Backing Vocals

Rudi formed in 1975 and were the first release on Good Vibrations, Northern Ireland. The label, founded by Terri Hooley, which grew out of the record shop of the same name, released music by local bands Rudi, The Nerves, The Gas, Protex and most successfully The Undertones. Rudi came to London in late 1978 and later signed to the Paul Weller-funded Jamming! label which became defunct when the Jam split-up. Rudi split-up shortly afterwards themselves.

THE HUMAN SWITCHBOARD

I Gotta Know b/w No!

CLONE RECORDS Akron, Ohio, USA 1978

Robert Pfeifer Vocals, Guitar
Myrna Marcarian Vocals, Organ
Ron Metz Drums
Mark McCracken Percussion

Recorded 22 March at Bushflow, Akron.
Front artwork by Myrna Marcarian Back artwork by Meir Goren

Garage punk band formed by Bob Pfeifer and Myrna Marcarian at Syracuse University in 1977. First single recorded in Cleveland, mixed by David Thomas of Pere Ubu. This is their second single released on Akron's Clone Records, home of The Bizarros, Tin Huey, Waitresses and other local bands. The Switchboard went on to release three albums and four singles before splitting-up in 1985.

LEYTON BUZZARDS
19 & Mad/Villain/ Youthenasia
SMALL WONDER London UK July 1978

Nick Nayme Vocals
Dave De Prave Bass
Gray Mare Drums
Chip Monk Guitar

Produced by Andre Jacquemin and The Buzzards

Formed in Leyton, East London in 1976. Released one single on Small Wonder then signed to Chyrsalis where they had a hit with Saturday Night (Beneath The Plastic Palm Trees). Split-up in 1980. Later went on to form not great new romantic/pop group Modern Romance.

THE CLASH
Clash City Rockers b/w Jail Guitar Doors
CBS RECORDS UK 17 Feb 1978

Joe Strummer Vocals, Guitar
Paul Simonon Bass
Mick Jones Guitar
Nicky 'Topper' Headon Drums

Produced by Micky Foote
Photo by Roco Macanley

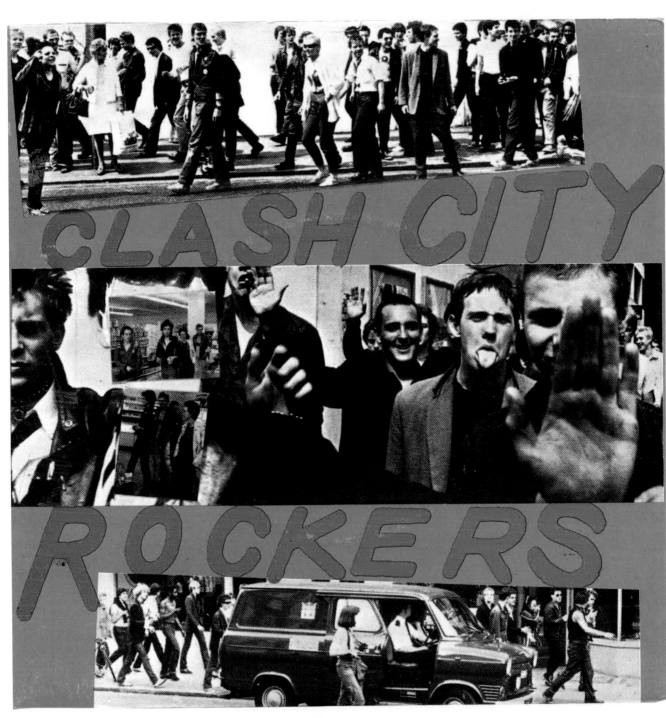

LLYGOD FFYRNIG

N. C. B. b/w Sais/Cariad Y Bus Stop
PWDWR RECORDS
Abertawe (Swansea), WALES 1978

Pete Williams Bass
Julian Lewis Drums
Gary Beard Guitar
Hywel Peckham Guitar
Dafydd Rhys Vocals

Only single from Welsh punk band (whose name translates as Ferocious Mice).

DESTROY ALL MONSTERS
Bored b/w You're Gonna Die
IDBI RECORDS Detroit, USA 1978

Niagara Vocals
Ron Asheton Guitar
Larry Miller Space Guitar
Rob King Drums
Ben Miller Saxophone

Photography D.B. Keeps and Sue Rynski **Sleeve Design** Niagara
Produced by Destroy All Monsters

Infamous group formed in Ann Arbor, Michigan in 1973. In 1977 Ron Asheton from The Stooges and Mike Davis from MC5 joined the group. Although released in 1978, the single Bored was their first official release, by which time the group had also started to fall apart. Eventually split in 1985, reforming occasionally.

SOFT SOUTH AFRICANS

THE HOMOSEXUALS

Hearts in Exile b/w Soft South Africans
LORELEI No. 1 RECORDS *London UK* 1978

Debut release from The Homosexuals, formed by Bruno Wizard and Anton Hayman in Battersea, South London in 1978. Came out of earlier group, The Rejects. Pioneering DIY group alongside Desperate Bicycles, TV Personalities etc.

PHYSICALS
All Sexed Up EP
PHYSICAL RECORDS London, UK 1978

Alan Lee Shaw Vocals, Guitar
Steve Schmidt Guitar
Crister Sol Bass, Vocals
Steve Bye Drums

Recorded at Minet Ave, London **Produced by** Ian Dickson and The Physicals
Photography by DeCourcy-Wheeler **Design by** Piss Artistes NYC

After The Rings (with Twink from The Pink Fairies) and The Maniacs this was Alan Lee Shaw's third punk group, the New York Dolls-esque Physicals which released two singles and lasted from 1977-80

THE MIDDLE CLASS
Out Of Vogue/You Belong/Situations/Insurgence
JOKE RECORDS
San Francisco, California USA 1978

Jeff A Vocals
Mike Patton Bass
Bruce Atta Drums
Mike A Guitar

The Middle Class was the first hardcore Orange County band to break into the early LA punk scene.

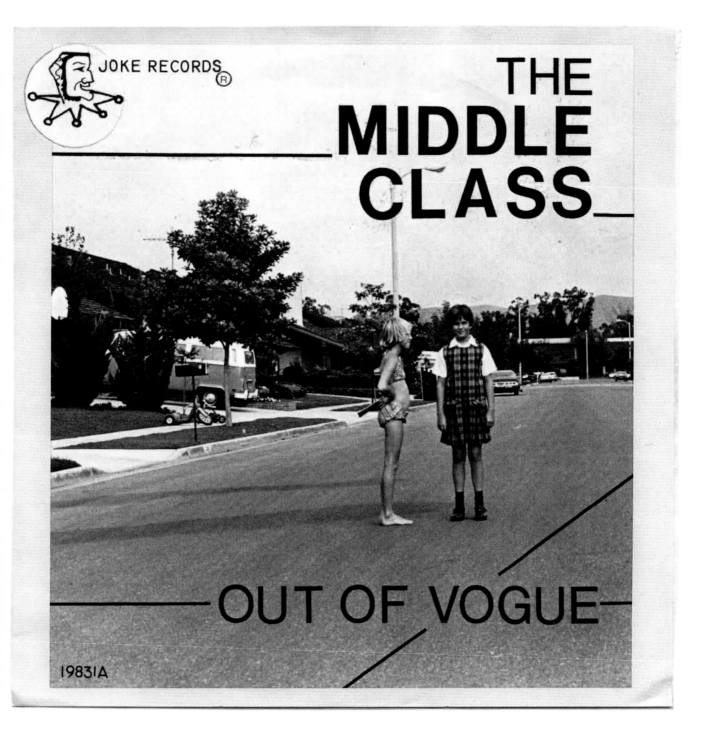

TUBEWAY ARMY
Bombers/Blue Eyes/O.D.Receiver
BEGGARS BANQUET London, UK July 1978

Gary Numan Vocals, Keyboards, Guitar
Barry Benn Drums
Sean Burke Guitar
Paul Gardiner Bass

Produced by Valerian **Photography by** Mike Stone

Formed in London in 1978. Numan had been in an earlier punk band Mean Streets. Tubeway Army were one of the first new wave bands to use synthesizers.

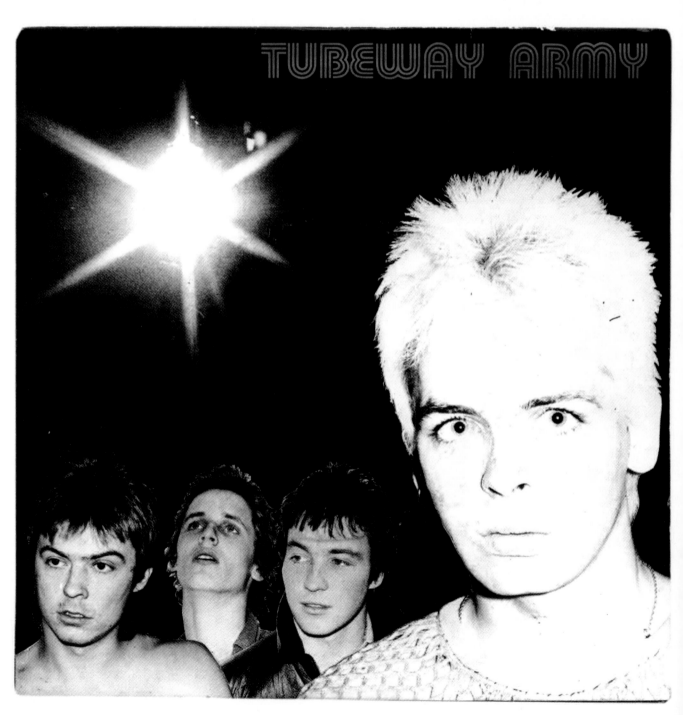

THE MAD

Eyeball b/w Hate Music
DISGUSTING RECORDS New York, USA 1978

Hisashi Ikeda Bass
Bowery Choir Chorus
Jun Nakanishi Drums
Danny Ipana Lead Guitar
Julien Hechtlinger Rhythm Guitar
Johnny 19 Sax
Screaming Mad George Vocals

Recorded at Songshop Studios **Produced by** D. Zelonky
Design by Screaming Mad George

The first of two singles from New York art/thrash/hardcore/horror punk band The Mad – the horror referring to their penchant for gore and prosthetics on stage. This was no mere whimsy – Osaka-born lead singer Screaming Mad George later went to Hollywood to work on special effects and as a make-up artist on Predator, Re-Animator, Nightmare on Elm Street 4 and others. In 1998 Playstation also released in Japan a horror fantasy game of George's creation.

THE DOLE

New Wave Love B/w Hungry Men No Longer Steal
Sheep But Are There Hanging Judges?
THE ULTIMATE RECORD LABEL Peterborough, UK
1978

Ian 'Emu' Neeve Vocals
Pete Howsam Keyboards
Simon Page Guitar
Matt Gillatt Bass
Paul Vjestica Drums

*Formed in Peterborough in 1977. Released just one-single,
split-up the following year.*

THE DOLE

invite you to lend an ear (or two if you prefer stereo) to their debut single

New Wave Love / Hungry Men

NEW WAVE LOVE

(Howsam - Page - Vjestica - Neeve - Gillatt)

THE DOLE

An Ultimate Music Production by Roger Slater and Adrian Knight.

DOUBLE   MCPS

A SIDE   **ULT. 402 - A**

Copyright Control
Ⓟ 1978

the ultimate
record label

the ultimate record label

All rights of the manufacturer & of the owner of the recorded
works reserved. Unauthorised Copying, Public Perform-
ance & Broadcasting of this Record Prohibited.
Recorded by Ultimate Music Ltd.,
Peterborough PE2 OES.
Made in Great Britain.

This is a high quality microgroove gramophone record and gives full stereophonic sound when played on stereo
equipment. Always handle it by the edges and avoid damage to the music surface. Equipment: The turntable
should be perfectly level and run at a constant speed of 45 r.p.m. The pick-up arm should be free to move
parallel to and perpendicular to the turntable surface. Check the stylus for wear regularly - a chipped or worn
stylus can permanently damage your records.

So keep your sweaty maulers off the disc; and, as for
using grotty gear - forget it.

THE ROTTERS
Sit On My Face Stevie Nix b/w Amputee
ROTTEN RECORDS Los Angeles USA 1978

Nigel Nitro Vocals
Phester Swollen Guitar
Rip Chord Bass
Johnny Condom Drums

Archly cynical debut single by the Rotters to which Fleetwood Mac strangely took offense after Rodney Bingenheimer played it on the radio, leading to the single being 'banned in LA'. The follow up was the much less prosaically titled Sink The Whales Buy Japanese Goods, which, in their own words, the band 'couldn't give away'. The group split in 1980, occasionally reforming with differing line-ups.

BIG IN JAPAN
From Y To Z And Never Again EP
ZOO RECORDS Liverpool, UK Nov 1978

Jayne Vocals
Kev Ward Vocals
Ian Broudie Guitar
Bill Drummond Guitar
Dave Balfe Bass
Holly Bass
Budgie Drums
Phil Allan Drums

First release on Bill Drummond's Zoo Records.

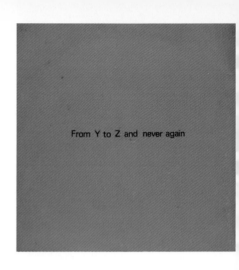

From Y to Z and never again

BLACK FLAG

Nervous Breakdown EP
Nervous Breakdown/Fix Me/I've Had It/Wasted
SST RECORDS Long Beach, California USA Oct 1978

Keith Morris Vocals
Gary McDaniel Bass
Robo Drums
Gregory Ginn Guitar

Recorded at Media Art Studio, Hermosa Beach, California, January 1978.

Debut single from first US hardcore band Black Flag founded in Hermosa Beach, California in 1976 by Gregg Ginn. Black Flag are influential not just in their sound but also their focus on an autonomous punk DIY approach to their music. Split-up in 1986, reforming occasionally.

PUBLIC IMAGE LTD
Public Image b/w The Cowboy Song
VIRGIN RECORDS UK 1978

John Lydon Vocals
Jah Wobble Bass
Keith Levene Guitar
Jim Walker Drums

Sleeve Design by Zebulon **Photography by** Dennis Morris

Fold-out newspaper sleeve. Debut single from John Lydon's post-punk, post-Pistols Public Image Ltd founded in London in 1978.

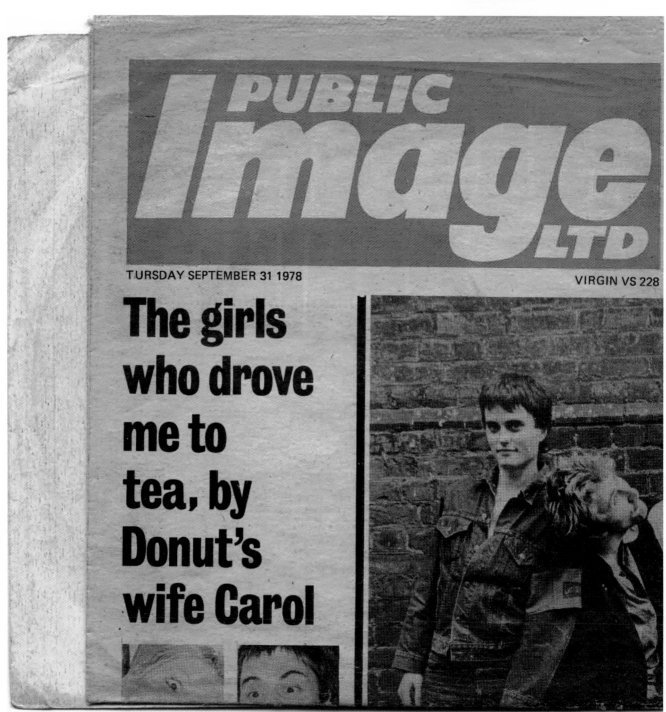

MARLEY, PISTOLS AND PiL

An interview with Dennis Morris.

Dennis Morris is a photographer, designer and artist who began his career as a teenager when Bob Marley invited him to come on tour with The Wailers. Morris had bunked off school to see the group soundcheck at the Speakeasy club on Margaret Street in Fitzrovia, central London.

His subsequent photographs of The Wailers appeared on the front covers of Melody Maker and Time Out and were noticed by, among others, Johnny Rotten, who asked Morris (who was the same age as the Pistols) to take the first official shots of the Sex Pistols when they signed to Virgin. Morris later accompanied Johnny Rotten to Jamaica, worked as A&R and art director at Island and led his band the Basement 5.

How did you come into contact with Bob Marley?
I came into contact with Bob Marley in 1974 when he came over to promote the Catch a Fire album. They were playing their first gig at the Speakeasy club in London.

From the Speakeasy club they went on a short tour of the UK. It was winter and they had never experienced a winter like this. One morning they woke up and wanted to play football, but it was snowing heavily. They were shocked by the intensity of the snow - Peter and Bunny said it was 'Babylon', and they should go home. After much arguing between Peter, Bunny and Bob, they decided to go back to Jamaica and so after a few dates the tour collapsed.

How did you come into contact with the Sex Pistols?
I made contact with the Sex Pistols through Virgin Records. I was well aware of the band and wanted to work with them. Although Johnny Rotten and Sid Vicious both went to Hackney technical college in Dalston, where I grew up, our paths at that point had never crossed. When they got signed to Virgin we met, and the rest is history.

What was it like working with the Pistols?
Working with the Pistols was absolute chaos. Everything was random, Malcolm made sure of it. At the height of the paranoia Malcolm, put together the SPOT [Sex Pistols on Tour] tour. It was a secret magical mystery tour, as the band was banned from playing in any venues. The idea was, we were on a coach, traveling around up the M1. The roadie would pull into a petrol station, phone Malcolm's office to see if the gig we were heading to was still happening, and he would say yes or no. The problem was, if the council had found out about the gig, they would pull the license of the venue. So if it was no, we would head to another venue, hoping the council hadn't found out. As you can imagine, it was quite frustrating, criss-crossing the country.

Can you tell us a bit about going to Jamaica with John Lydon and Richard Branson?
When Richard Branson and Simon Draper had decided to get involved with reggae music, they contacted me, and we had a meeting where it was decided I would go to Jamaica with Richard. As Richard would sign the bands, I would do the photos for album sleeves and press shots. I said to Richard and Simon that it would also be a good idea to take Johnny Rotten - aka John Lydon - as he had just left the Sex Pistols, and was bored. They decided this was a good idea. Don Letts also turned up out of the blue one day in Jamaica, but was not part of the project.

I know you did artwork and A&R, among other things. Did you work at Virgin?
I never worked at Virgin, I actually worked at Island Records as an art director with A&R capacity. I signed Linton Kwesi Johnson to the label and did all the artwork for Forces of Victory, Bass Culture and LKJ in Dub. I also signed the Slits to Island Records, and it was my idea for Dennis Bovell to produce them.

How did the idea for the Public Image Ltd newspaper come about? Did you do it in consultation with the band? Did Richard Branson like it? Was it expensive?
The idea for the PIL single was my concept. The band had very little to do with it. It was actually cheaper than a conventional sleeve as it was printed like a newspaper. It was very much liked by the record company and Richard Branson.

Could you talk a bit about the PIL logo - how did it come about? Did you do all the PIL artwork?
The PIL logo is based on an aspirin. John had the idea to call the band Public Image Ltd, and I broke it down to PIL. I was in a phase of abbreviation: Linton had become LKJ, so it was logical to break it down to PIL. Hence the logo. Very simple, very direct, subliminal. I did all the PIL artwork - the first single, the first album and the Metal Box and the logo.

How long were you at Island and what did you do next?
I spent two years at Island and after that I created Basement 5, as it is known now, and created the logo, the concept, the imagery and the sound.

DENNIS MORRIS

THE REZILLOS

Top Of The Pops b/w 20,000 Rezillos Under The Sea
SIRE RECORDS UK 14 July 1978

Fay Fife Vocals
Eugene Reynolds Vocals
Jo Callis Guitar
Simon Templar Bass
William Mysterious Bass
Angel Patterson Drums

*Formed in Edinburgh, Scotland in 1976. Split in 1978 and came back
as The Revillos a year later.*

STIFF LITTLE FINGERS
Alternative Ulster b/w '78 Revolutions A Minute
ROUGH TRADE London, UK Oct 1978

Jake Burns Vocals, Guitar
Henry Cluney Guitar
Ali McMordie Bass
Brian Faloon Drums

Produced by Ed Hollis **Photography by** Milton Haworth

ALTERNATIVE ULSTER
RT 004   45 r.p.m.

STIFF LITTLE FINGERS

"In '69 it was fine
You say
But by '79
It's gonna be mine
I say
For now is here
Our New Year"

"Get up and grab it
It's yours
Ignore the bores
And their laws
Be an anti-security
Force   Alter
Your native land"

'78 REVOLUTIONS A MINUTE.

Jake Burns - vocals,
lead guitar
Henry Cluney -
rhythm guitar
Ali McMordie - bass
Brian Faloon - drums

A ROUGH TRADE-RIGID DIGITS
COLLABORATION
FOR JOHN PEEL
WHO MADE IT POSSIBLE

Remixed at Olympic
Studios
Engineer
Doug Bennett
Cover photo
Milton Haworth

MAGAZINE
Shot By Both Sides b/w My Mind Ain't So Open
VIRGIN RECORDS UK 20 Jan 1978

Howard Devoto Vocals
Barry Adamson Bass
Martin Jackson Drums
John McGeoch Guitar, Saxophone

Produced by Magazine and Mick Glossop

Formed in Manchester in April 1977. A-side written by Howard Devoto and Pete Shelley. Debut release of Magazine, Devoto's new band after leaving The Buzzcocks in early 1977.

VS 200

MAGAZINE

SHOT BY BOTH SIDES
Words by Howard Devoto
Music by Howard Devoto & Peter Shelley

MY MIND AIN'T SO OPEN
Words by Howard Devoto
Music by Howard Devoto & John McGeoch

HOWARD DEVOTO – VOCALS
BARRY ADAMSON – BASS GUITAR
MARTIN JACKSON – DRUMS
JOHN MCGEOCH – GUITAR & SAX

ABSTRUSE IMAGES

℗ 1978 Virgin Records Ltd

ADAM AND THE ANTS

Young Parisians b/w Lady

DECCA UK 1978

Adam Ant Vocals, Guitar
Andy Warren Bass
Dave Barbarossa Drums
Matthew Ashman Guitar, Piano
Jo Julian Piano
Greg Mason Saxophone

Produced by Jo Julian and Adam Ant
Photography by Julie Stone
Illustration by Stuart Leslie Goddard

Stuart Goddard (Adam Ant) was the former front man of Bazooka Joe, who supported The Sex Pistols at their debut concert at St Martins art college on 6 Nov 1975. Following this he quit to form a new band originally known as The B-Sides, later Adam and The Ants. This was their debut single.

XTC

Are You Receiving Me b/w Instant Tunes
VIRGIN RECORDS UK 29 Sep 1978

Andy Partridge Vocals, Guitar
Colin Moulding Bass
Barry Andrews Keyboards
Terry Chambers Drums

Formed in Swindon, Wiltshire, UK in 1977.

BLACK RANDY AND HIS ELITE METRO SQUAD

Idi Amin EP

Idi Amin/I'm Black & Proud Part 3/I'm Black & Proud Part 14/I Wanna Be A Nark

DANGERHOUSE RECORDS

Los Angeles, California USA 1978

Black Randy Vocals
Bod Dread Guitar, Vocals
K.K. Barrett Guitar
Pat Garrett Bass
David Brown Keyboards

Band formed in Los Angeles in 1977 around Black Randy (John Morris) and including all-three founders of the Dangerhouse Records label (Randy, Garrett and Brown).

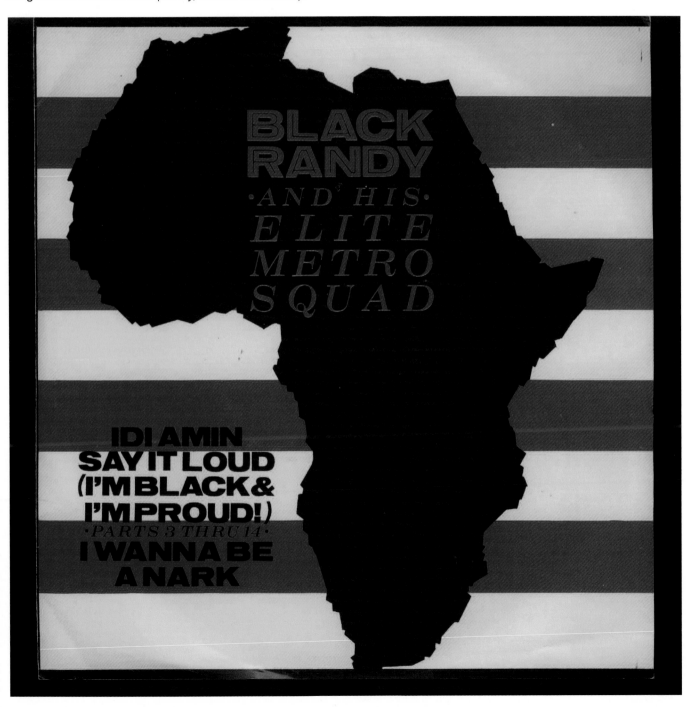

THE UNDERTONES

Teenage Kicks EP

GOOD VIBRATIONS Belfast, Northern Ireland Sep 1978

Feargal Sharkey Vocals
John O'Neill Guitar
Damian O'Neill Guitar
Michael Bradley Bass
Billy Doherty Drums

Recorded at Wizard Sound Studios **Photography by** Paddy Simms
Layout by Terri Hooley and Paddy Simms

Formed in Derry, Northern Ireland in 1976. Debut single released on Terri Hooley's Good Vibrations label out of Belfast. Subsequently signed to Sire Records. Wraparound sleeve in various colours.

THE UNDERTONES

TEENAGE KICKS

THE PATHETIX
Aleister Crowley/Don't Touch My Machine/Snuffed It
NO RECORDS Lancashire UK 1978

Knickers (Andrew Nicholson) Vocals
Jack Frost (Gary Brown) Bass
Star (Terry Sanders) Drums
Phil Image (Phil Husband) Guitar
Pete Hectic (Pete Rowlands) Lead Guitar
Pokey (Peter Leeper) Sax

Recorded at Amazon Sound Studio Oct 1978 **Produced by** The Pathetix

Post-punk band from Nelson, Lancashire, formed in 1976. Released one single on their own No Records, then one further single on TJM in Manchester. Split-up in 1981.

TRB

Up Against The Wall/I'm All Right Jack
EMI UK 5 May 1978

Tom Robinson Vocals
Danny Kustow Guitar
Brian 'Dolphin Taylor' Drums
Mark Ambler Bass

Produced by Chris Thomas **Photography by** Syd Shelton
Design by Hot Pink Heart/Red Wedge Graphics

Formed in London, 1976. Signed to EMI 1977. Split-up in 1979 when Kustow left the group and Tom Robinson went solo.

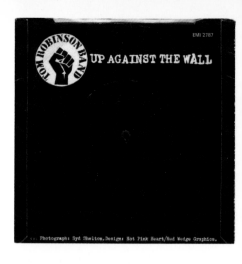

THE VICTIMS

No Thanks To The Human Turd EP
I Understand/Open Your Eyes/
High School Girls/T.V. Freak/Disco Junkies
No label Perth, AUSTRALIA 1978

Dave Flick (Faulkner) Vocals
Rudolph V Bass
James Baker Drums
Dave Flick Guitar
Rockin' Rod Saxophone

*From Perth, Western Australia, active 1977-79, came out of earlier group
The Geeks. This was their second and final self-released single. After split,
Faulkner and Baker formed The Hoodoo Gurus.*

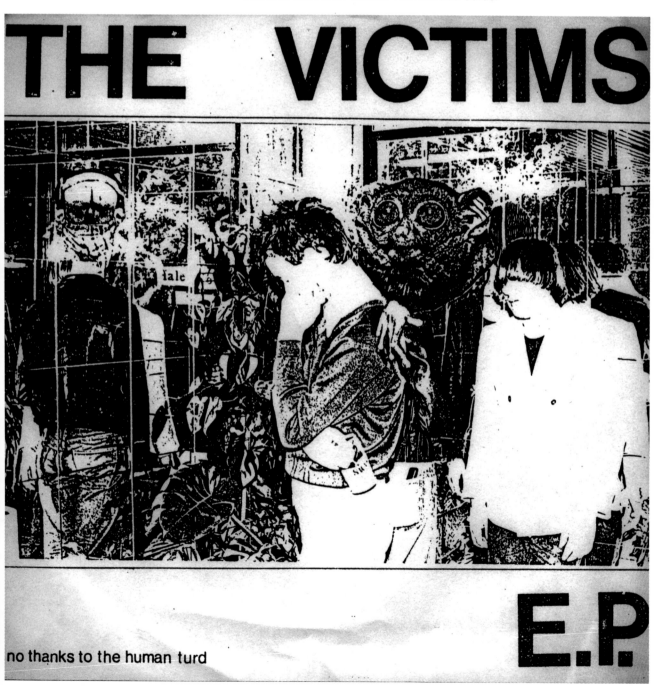

BLONDIE
Denis/Contact In Red Square/Kung Fu Girls
CHRYSALIS UK Feb 1978

Chris Stein Guitar
Debbie Harry Vocals
Clem Burke Drums
Jimmy Destri Keyboards
Gary Valentine Bass

Recorded at Plaza Sound Studios
Produced by Richard Gottehrer

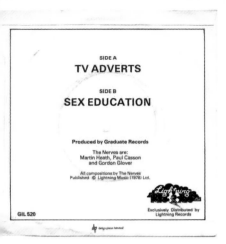

THE NERVES

TV Advert b/w Sex Education
LIGHTNING RECORDS London, UK 1978

Martyn Heath Vocals, Guitar
John Glover Drums
Paul Casson Bass

Produced by Graduate Records

Band from Staffordshire, formed in 1977, disbanded one year later after this single.

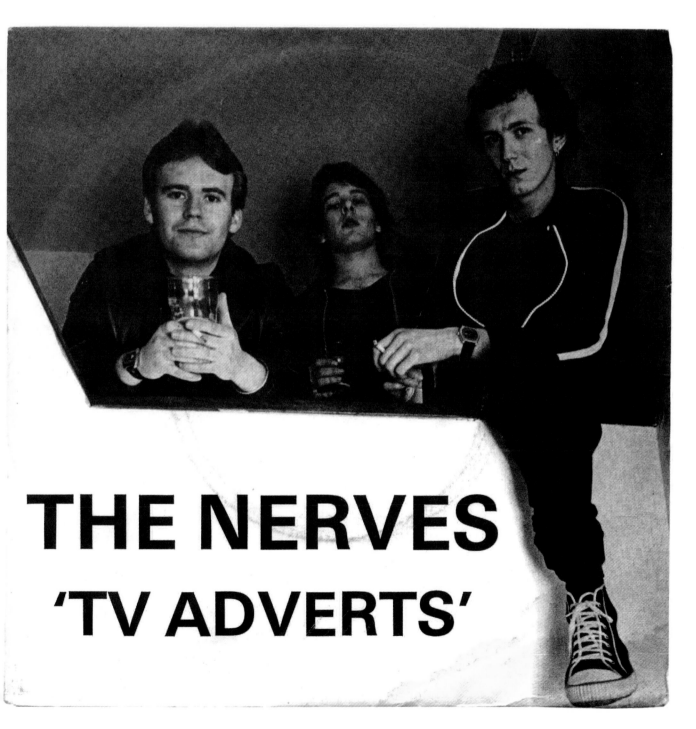

THE NERVES
'TV ADVERTS'

UK SUBS

CID/Live In A Car/B1C

CITY RECORDS *London, UK* 22 Sep 1978

PIN 22

Charlie Harper Vocals
Paul Slack Bass
Peter Davis Drums
Nicky Garratt Guitar

Recorded at Spaceward Studios 11 July 1978
Produced by U.K. Subs

Initially called The Subversives, formed in London in 1976.
Still going after 26 albums!

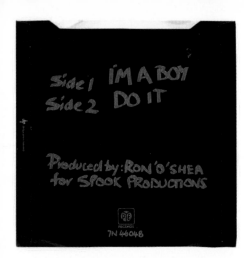

CYANIDE

I'm A Boy b/w Do it

PYE RECORDS *UK* 1978

Bob de Vries Vocals
Dave Stewart Guitar
Mick Stewart Drums
Jock Marston Bass

Recorded at Pye Studios December 1977
Produced by Ron O'Shea

Formed in York, North Yorkshire in 1977.
Released one album and three singles.

TEENAGE JESUS AND THE JERKS

Orphans b/w Less of Me

MIGRAINE RECORDS New York, USA 25 April 1978

Lydia Lunch Guitar, Vocals
Gordon Stevenson Bass
Bradly Field Drum

Produced by Bob Quine **Photography by** Bill Arning

Debut single from the no wave group formed in New York in 1976 which initially included James Chance. Released on sub-label of Charles Ball's Lust/Unlust New York label.

& THE JERKS

Guitar
& Vocals:
LYDIA LUNCH

Drum:
BRADLY FIELD

Bass:
GORDON
STEVENSON

PRODUCED BY BOB QUINE
LUST/UNLUST MUSIC P.O. BOX 3208 GRAND CENTRAL STATION NYC, NY 10017

PHOTOS BY BILL ARNING

TEENAGE JESUS

ORPHANS

b/w

LESS OF ME

THE NIPPLE ERECTORS
King of The Bop b/w Nervous Wreck
SOHO RECORDS London UK June 1978

Shane MacGowan Vocals
Shanne Bradley Bass
Roger Towndrow Guitar
Arcane Vendetta Drums

Recorded at Chalk Farm Studios **Produced by** Stan Brennan

Photography by Michael Clifford **Scribbles and Letraset by** Phil Smee

Formed in London in 1976 by Shanne Bradley, notable as Pogues frontman Shane MacGowan's first musical group. After this single the group renamed itself The Nips. Split-up in 1981. Shane Macgowan helped form The Pogues, Shanne Bradley co-founded The Men They Couldn't Hang.

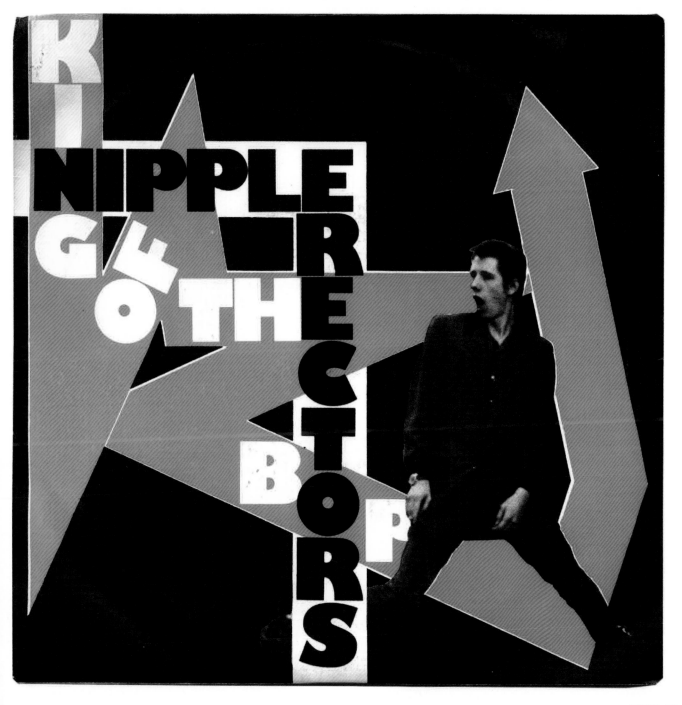

IAN DURY AND THE BLOCKHEADS

Hit Me With Your Rhythm Stick b/w There Ain't Half
Been Some Clever Bastards

STIFF RECORDS London UK 23 Nov 1978

Ian Blockhead (Dury) Vocals
Charlie Charles Drums
Chaz Blockhead (Jankel) Keyboards
Davey Payne Saxophone
John Turnbull Guitar
Michael Gallagher Keyboards
Norman Watt-Roy Bass

Sleeve Design by Barney Bubbles

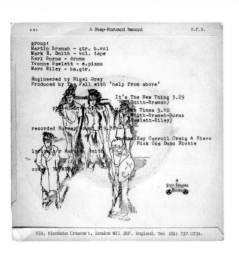

THE FALL

It's The New Thing b/w Various Times

STEP-FORWARD RECORDS UK 14th July 1978

Mark E. Smith Vocals, Tape
Martin Bramah Guitar, Backing Vocals
Karl Burns Drums
Yvonne Pawlett Electric Piano
Marc Riley Bass

Produced by The Fall with 'help from above'
Recorded at Surrey Sound
Cover by KC, MES and YP

TUXEDOMOON

Joe Boy T.E.G. b/w Pinheads On The Move
TIME RELEASE RECORDS

San Francisco, California 1978

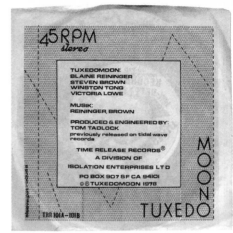

Blaine Reininger Keyboards, Violin, Electric Guitar
Steven Brown Keyboards, Clarinet, Saxophone
Victoria Lowe Vocals
Winston Tong Vocals

Recorded by 1978 in San Francisco, California.
Produced by Tom Tadlock **Artwork by** Pat Roques

Formed in San Francisco in 1977. This is their second single (first pressing was on Tidal Wave). Group signed to the Residents' Ralph Records in 1979. In the early 80s the group relocated to first Rotterdam and then Brussels. Split in early 1990s, reformed ten years later.

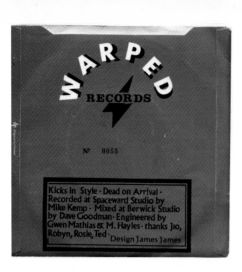

THE USERS

Kicks in Style b/w Dead On Arrival
WARPED RECORDS Cambridge, UK 1978

James Haight Vocals
Bobby Kwok Bass
Andrew Bor Drums
Chris Free Guitar

Recorded at Spaceward Studios

Second and final single from The Users formed in Cambridge, UK in 1976

IGGY POP & JAMES WILLIAMSON

Kill City b/w I Got Nothin'
RADAR RECORDS UK Feb 1978

Iggy Pop Vocals
Scott 'Troy' Thurston Bass, Keyboards
Brian Glascock Drums
'Strait' James Williamson Guitar
John 'The Rookie' Harden Saxophone

Produced by James Williamson **Design by** Barney Bubbles

Recorded in 1975. The album, Kill City, eventually came out in 1977 on Bomp! Records and this single was licensed to Radar in the UK.

FLESH EATERS
Disintegration Nation EP
UPSETTER RECORDS Los Angeles, USA 1978

Scott L Bass
Dennis W Drums
John C Guitar
Chris D Vocals

Producer by Flesheaters and Randy Stodola **Illustration** Bonnie Ballistic
Photography by CD, J. Jennik, John C **Back Cover collage** Richard
Paulsen **Letters/Label** G Hitler, J Bell **Cover** CD
*Debut single from The Flesh Eaters, founded in Los Angeles by lead vocalist
Chris Desjardins, known as Chris D, in 1977.*

THE MIRRORS

Cure For Cancer b/w Nice Vice

LIGHTNING RECORDS London, UK 13 Jan 1978

Gary Lloyd Vocals, Rhythm Guitar
Andy Smith Lead Guitar
Alan Jones Bass
Trevor Tarling Drums

Recorded at Berry Street Studios

Band from Newport, Wales released two singles on Lightning Records in 1977 and 1978.

CHINA STREET

You're A Ruin b/w (I Wanna Be) Your M.P.

CRIMINAL RECORDS UK Feb 1978

Dusty Hall Vocals, Saxophone, Harmonica
Martin Pilkington Guitar
Adam Williams Bass
Dave Willan Drums

Produced by Don Mooney

Band from Lancaster formed late 1970s. Released one further single.

PATRICK FITZGERALD

Safety Pin Stuck In My Heart EP
Banging & Shouting/Safety Pin Stuck In My Heart/
Work Rest Play Reggae/Set We Free/
Optimism/ Reject
Small Wonder Records UK 27 Jan 1978

Patrick Fitzgerald Guitar, Vocals
Produced by Pete **Art** Final Solution **Typing** Jackie

*Punk poet Fitzgerald was a regular customer at Pete Stennett's Small
Wonder record shop and this was his debut release.*

SMALL 4

PATRIK
FITZGERALD

THE B-52'S
Rock Lobster b/w 52 - Girls
DB RECORDS Atlanta, Georgia USA 1978

Fred Schneider Vocals, Cowbell
Kate Pierson Vovals, Farfisa Organ, Bass
Cindy Wilson Vocals, Tambourine
Ricky Wilson Guitar
Keith Strickland Drums Percussion

Produced by The B - 52's and Kevin Dunn **Photo** Ann States

The B-52's formed in Athens, Georgia in 1976. Danny Beard's independent DB Records came out of the Wax N Facts record store in nearby Atlanta and this single was the label and band's debut release. After this single the band signed to Warners.

THE POP GROUP
She Is Beyond Good And Evil/3.38
RADAR London UK Mar 1979

Mark Stewart Vocals
Gareth Sager Guitar
Simon Underwood Bass
John Waddington Guitar
Bruce Smith Drums

Producer by Dennis Bovell

Debut single from post-punk band from Bristol, England, formed in 1978 and disbanded 1981. Highly influential group whose members were later involved in Pigbag, Maximum Joy, The Slits and Rip Rig + Panic. Mark Stewart launched a successful solo career, which began on Adrian Sherwood's On-U Sound label.

A CERTAIN RATIO

All Night Party b/w The Thin Boys
FACTORY RECORDS Manchester UK May 1979

Jeremy Kerr Bass
Martin Moscrop Guitar, Trumpet
Peter Terrell Guitar
Simon Topping Vocals

Recorded at Cargo Studios, Rochdale.
Produced by Martin Zero (Hannett)
Design by Peter Saville

"Detail from FAC 5, 1979 Paper and vinyl construction in an edition of 5000"

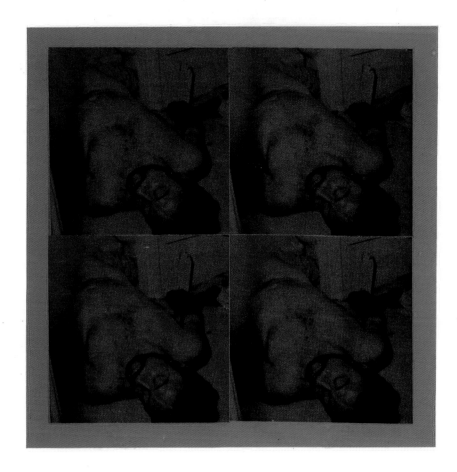

A Certain Ratio *All Night Party*

Detail from *Fac 5*, 1979
Paper and vinyl construction in an edition of 5000
Produced by Martin Zero at Cargo Studios, Rochdale

45 rpm, a Factory Product

G & L

Certain Ratio formed in 1977. Was the band a consequence of punk?
Because of punk you didn't have to be a musician to play in or start a band. Usually bands were formed from a group of friends with the same musical taste and sometimes it helped if one or two of you had an instrument but it wasn't essential.

Peter Terrell and Simon Topping were old school friends who used to go to Pips Disco, which had three rooms; a punk room, a northern soul room and a Bowie and Roxy room. They decided to form a band and it started off with just the two of them and because Pete couldn't play any chords he learnt how to tune his guitar to an E major chord so that all he had to do was bar his finger across the frets and move it up and down. Simon's mate made a noise generator which did what it says on the tin and Simon played it and attempted singing.

A Certain Ratio were born and at their first gig at Pips, Jez [Jeremy Kerr] was in the audience. Jez owned a bass guitar and because of this possession he was made a member of the band. The next gig they played was at Band on the Wall with the three of them and the glam punk band I was in, Alien Tint, played on the same bill. The three members of ACR thought that I looked out of place with Alien Tint because I was dressed the same way as them - in a D-mob suit with short back and sides and a quiff. Because of this and because I had a good guitar amp they asked me to join ACR.

We had all been into punk at the start, which is why it was so easy to form the band the way we did. After punk we were listening to Wire, Brian Eno, The Velvet Underground, David Bowie, Iggy Pop, northern soul, James Brown and many diverse types of music. This collection of influences matched with the fact that we couldn't really play our instruments was how our style and sound was forged.

Did you go the Sex Pistols' Free Trade Hall gigs in Manchester?
We didn't go to the Free Trade Hall gigs. I was 15 so just a little too young.

If punk was the impetus behind ACR how come you did not want to sound like the first wave of punk bands - why was your sound so much more experimental? Punk was very short lived for those who got into it when it first started. It was good for a year or two and then it just got too mainstream. We were part of the Manchester Musicians Collective where most bands were experimental and we all tried to outdo each other to be top of the 'weird' table. The more experimental you were the more people respected you.

We were born out of punk but definitely post-punk in musical style. If I remember correctly the only band that resembled anything like punk in the Musicians Collective was Mick Hucknall's band The Frantic Elevators. Punk was frowned on in the Musicians Collective because I suppose it was the start of post-punk.

All Night Party All Night Party was an example of writing and performing a song where you do not have the musical knowledge to do something intentionally. The sound, song and structure develops from what you know and where you push to the limit what you can actually play. Simon's lyrics are different because he writes what he knows or imagines. The song is very dark and reflects what Manchester was like at the time. Donald always said that the guitars took the place of the drums and we thrashed away because we didn't have a drummer providing the beat. I suppose it is a weird form of punk without the shouting.

Shack Up Shack Up was released about a year later than All Night Party but you can hear how the band have developed as musicians. For a start we have now got the best drummer in Manchester in the band - a black funk drummer [Donald Johnson]. We had chosen Shack Up to do as a cover because it was so simple to play and effective. The two-note trumpet riff is a good example of punk trumpet playing. Because we are not accomplished musicians and have come from the punk scene we are all playing slightly ahead of the beat which makes it different from our funk heroes who always played slightly behind the beat in a less urgent manner.

The front sleeve of All Night Party is of Lenny Bruce lying dead in his hotel bathroom after overdosing. Jez had a few Lenny Bruce albums that we used to listen to and we loved the way he tried to shock people. I suppose that picture was supposed to do the same thing and shock people. We also used phrases from Lenny on some of our early recordings. The other pictures are all of Anthony Perkins who looks a bit like four members of ACR.

How would you describe Factory. Did it come out of punk? I suppose the idea of Factory Records did come out of punk. Tony Wilson used to have loads of punk bands on his So It Goes programme and Granada Reports. Because he had access to these bands through being a TV presenter he started the Factory club and quite often he would have bands on at the club that he had had on his show. From the club came the label. A lot of the bands that Tony booked for the club did not have records out so he thought it would be a good idea to start a label. The club and the label grew out of the punk DIY ethic.

Did you like bands like The Ramones or Talking Heads? What were your favourite bands? I personally liked Iggy Pop more than say The Ramones. Talking Heads were also excellent but they weren't a punk band, they came later. I think the first time I saw talking Heads was when they supported Blondie on their tour. We supported Talking Heads on their first headlining tour of the UK. The Sex Pistols got more from David Bowie than they did from The Ramones.

At 16 my favourite bands were The Buzzcocks, The Clash, Penetration, X-Ray Spex and the band that really taught me that anyone could form a band were the Manchester band The Worst.

A Certain Ratio were not directly influenced by punk bands but indirectly because we were trying to be anti-punk in our music. Even the early drummer-less stuff was a reaction to punk. We were listening to Kraftwerk, The Velvet Underground, James Brown, Brian Eno and anything that wasn't punk.

THE STATIC

My Relationship b/w Don't Let Me Stop You
THEORETICAL RECORDS New York 1979

Glenn Branca Guitar, Vocals
Barbara Ess Bass, Backing Vocals
Christine Hahn Drums, Backing Vocals

Produced by Dan Graham and Mark Bingham

Only release from the experimental New York group.

The RAS-controlled auditory screening process called the cocktail-party effect is working properly at left, as the RAS allows the voice of the close conversational companion to go through (green dot), effectively obscuring all other voices (red dots). At right the RAS of the schizophrenic fails to do its screening job, transmitting all of the voices to the cortex in a jumble.

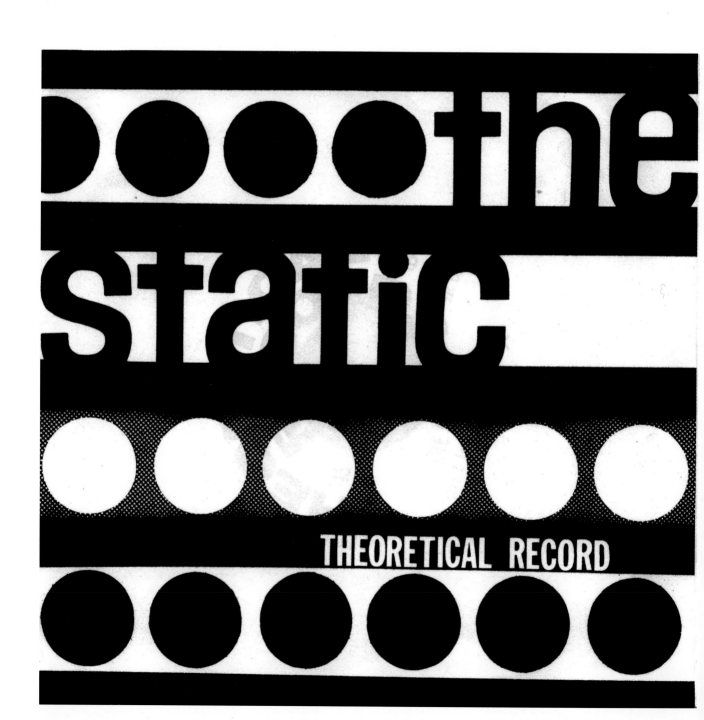

THE CLASH

I Fought The Law b/w (White Man) In
Hammersmith Palais **EPIC** JAPAN 1979

Joe Strummer Vocals, Guitar
 Paul Simonon Bass
Mick Jones Guitar
Nicky 'Topper' Headon Drums

Japanese-only release.

DEAD KENNEDYS

California Über Alles b/w The Man With The Dogs

OPTIONAL MUSIC Berkeley, California USA

June 1979

Jello Biafra Vocals

Klaus Flouride Bass, Vocals

Ray Valium Guitars

Ted Drums

Produced by Jim Keylor and Dead Kennedys

Cover Artwork by Bruce Slesinger

Formed in San Francisco in 1978. This is their debut single, which was also released on Fast Product and Alternative Tentacles in the UK. The band released five albums before disbanding in 1986.

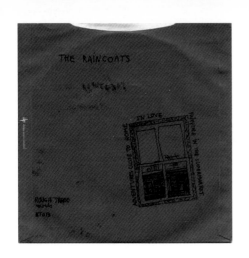

THE RAINCOATS

Fairytale In The Supermarket/In Love /
Adventure Close To Home
ROUGH TRADE UK April 1979

Gina Birch Bass
Ana Da Silva Guitar
Vicky Aspinall Guitar/Violin
Palmolive Drums

Produced by Geoff Travis and Mayo Thompson.

*Post-punk band formed in London in 1977 whilst at Hornsey College of Art.
Palmolive was previously in The Slits. This is their debut single. Band split-up
in 1984, reformed ten years later.*

THE PACK

Brave New Soldiers b/w Heathen

SS *UK* 1979

Kirk Brandon Vocals, Guitar
Simon Werner Guitar
Jon Werner Bass
Rab Fae Beith Drums

Produced by Bazza Sterneberg

The first group of Kirk Brandon, who went on to Theatre of Hate and Spear of Destiny.

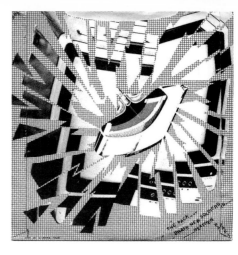

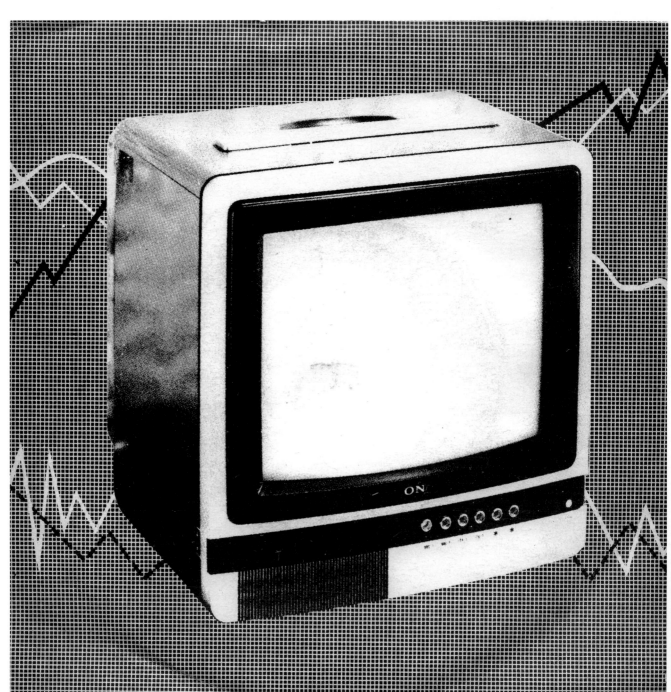

THE RUTS
Babylon's Burning B/w Society

VIRGIN RECORDS UK 1979

Malcolm Owen Vocals
Dave Drums
Vince Segs Bass
Paul Fox Guitar

Produced by Mick Glossop
Design by C. Graves

Formed in London in 1978. Singer Owen died of overdose in 1980. Band carried on as Ruts DC until 1983.

ECHO AND THE BUNNYMEN

The Pictures On My Wall b/w I've Read It In Books

ZOO! UK May 1979

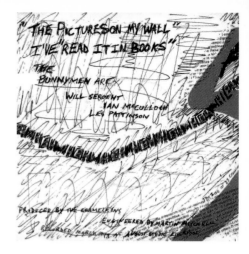

Ian McCulloch Vocals

Will Sergent Guitar

Les Pattinson Bass

A Chameleons Production

Formed in Liverpool in 1978. In 1977 McCullough was in the group The Crucial Three alongside Julian Cope (later Teardrop Explodes) and Pete Wylie (later Wah! Heat). Zoo Records was run by Bill Drummond and David Balfe.

CABARET VOLTAIRE

Nag Nag Nag b/w Is That Me Finding
Someone At The Door Again?
ROUGH TRADE London UK 1979

Richard H. Kirk
Stephen Mallinder
Chris Watson

Produced by Geoff Travis, Mayo Thompson & Cabaret Voltaire

Cover photos taken at Gibus Club, Paris, April 1979 by
Richard Waters **Design by** C.V.

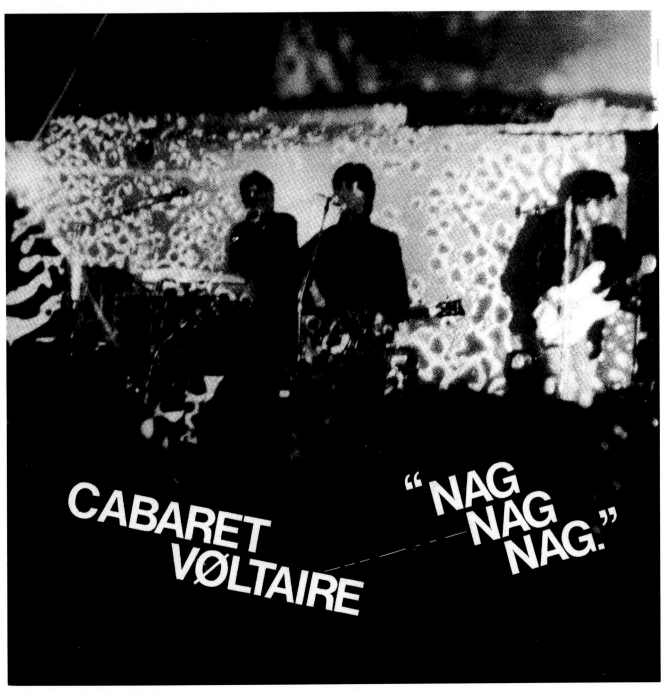

MO-DETTES

White Mice b/w Masochistic Opposite
MODE RECORDS UK Dec 1979

Kate Korus Guitar
Jane Crockford Bass
Ramona Carlier Vocals
June Miles-Kingston Drums

Recorded at Foel Studios, Wales and Berry Studios
Modifications by Bob Black

Female punk band formed in 1979, originally called The Bomberettes. Kate Korus had earlier been in The Slits and briefly The Raincoats. Self-released first single. Band split-up in 1982.

THE URINALS

Another EP
Black Hole/I'm White And Middle Class/
I'm A Bug/Ack Ack Ack
HAPPY SQUID USA 1979

John Jones Vocals, Bass
Kjehl Johansen Guitar
Kevin Barrett Drums, Vocals
Produced by Vitus Matare
Fotos by Barbara **Grafix by** Fetus

Formed in Los Angeles in 1978. Self-released single produced by Vitus Matare
from The Last. Released three singles then became 100 Flowers in the early
1980s.

VKTMS

Midget/Hard-Case/Roma-Rocket/Too Bad!!

EMERGENCY ROOM RECORDS San Francisco, California USA 1979

Nyna 'Napalm' Crawford Vocals
Steve Ricablanca Bass
Louis Gwerder Drums
John Binkov Guitar, Keyboards

Layout photo by Rãñdôm Chåñcé **Photography by** Jon Micheal **Produced by** VKTMS

Formed in San Francisco in 1978. As well as this EP, they made the somewhat controversial 100% White Girl. After recording an album in 1980 and not being able to find a deal, the band split-up. This album was eventually released in 1994 when the band reformed.

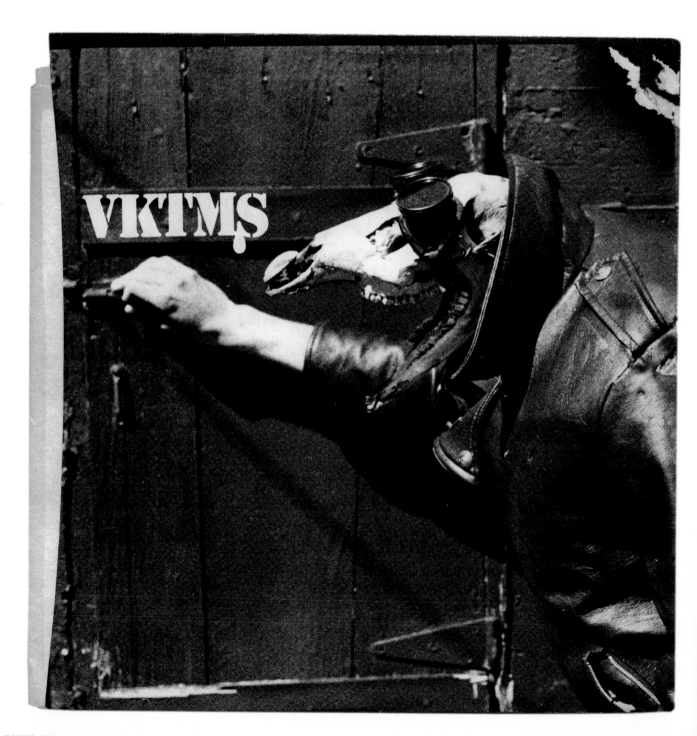

SPIZZOIL

Cold City: 4 EP
Cold City/Red & Black/Solarisation (Shun)
/Platform 3

ROUGH TRADE UK Feb 1979

Spizz (Kenneth Spiers) Vocals, Kazoo
Pete Petroleum (Pete O'Dowd) Vocals, Guitar

Recorded at Berry Street Studio **Produced by** Woods, Spizzoil
Artwork by Byron Lizard**x Sleeve by** Spizz

The many-named group (Spizzoil, Athletico Spizz 80 and The Spizzles). After the band split-up (at this point known as Spizzenergi 2), Spizz went on to solo projects as Spizzorwell, and Spizz and the Astronauties.

BEYOND THE IMPLODE

The Last Thoughts EP
This Atmosphere/Midnight Adventures/
Lassitude/Escape Thru Levitation/Steel Car

DIVERSE RECORD LABEL Runcorn, Cheshire UK 1979

Eddie Cameron Vocals, Guitar

Mike Gardler Lead Guitar

Ian Gardler Bass

Frank Hughes Bass

Design by Eddie Cameron

*Formed by Cameron in Runcorn in 1979. This is their self-released first single.
Imploded in 1981 after one further single.*

THE LINES

On The Air b/w Not Through Windows/
Dance for A Drop Of Blood
RED RECORDS UK 1979

Richard Conning Vocal, Guitar
Joe Forty Bass
Nicholas Cash Drums

Recorded at Soundsuite, Camden, Sep 2nd 1979 **Produced by** The Lines. **Cover Photo** Martin Mossop

Post-punk band formed in London in 1978. This was their second single after White Night which they self-released. Red Record was set up by Steve Brown and also released music by Material and Alex Ferguson. Band split-up in 1983 after two albums.

TONY SINDEN, ALAN BAKER & THE INSECTS

Magnificent Cactus Trees b/w Cast Shadows
PIANO RECORDS UK July 1979

Produced by David Cunningham

Piano Records was started by David Cunningham in 1976 to release his own experimental music (including Flying Lizards) as well as that of Michael Nyman, This Heat, General Strike and others. Tony Sindon was an early pioneer of British video art.

DELTA 5
Mind Your Own Business b/w Now That You've Gone
Rough Trade *UK* Sep 1979

Bethan Peter Bass, Vocals
Ros Allen Bass Vocals
Kelvin Knight Drums
Alan Riggs Guitar
Julz Sale Guitar, Vocals
Jon Langford Extra Guitar

Recorded at The Workhouse Studios, London
Producer by D5 and Rob Warr **Cover Art by** Jon Langford

UK post-punk formed in Leeds in 1979, split two years later after releasing one album and six singles.

BOBBY BERKOWITZ/BEIRUT SLUMP
Try Me b/w Staircase
MIGRAINE RECORDS New York USA 1979

Bobby Swope Vocals
Liz Swope Bass
Jim Sclavunos Drums
Lydia Lunch Guitar
Vivienne Dick Organ

Recorded at Hothouse Studio, New York **Produced by** Woody Payne
Sleeve J. Gorton

New York no wave. Migraine Records was owned by producer Charles Ball who also ran Lust/Unlust. The label released three other singles by Lydia Lunch's other project Teenage Jesus and The Jerks. Other members of Beirut Slump include underground filmmaker Vivienne Dick, artists Jim Sclavunos, Liz and Bobby Swope.

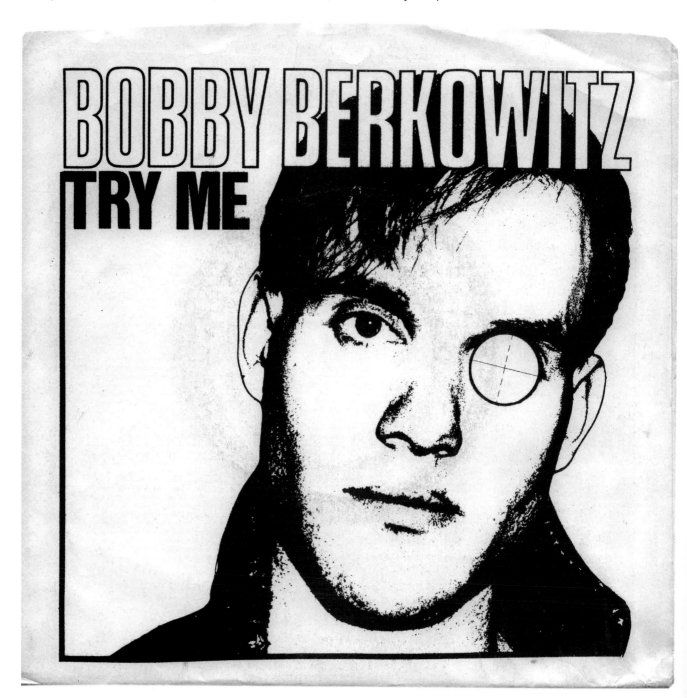

THE MONOCHROME SET

He's Frank b/w Alphaville

ROUGH TRADE London UK 1979

Bid Guitar, Vocals
Jeremy Harrington Bass, Percussion
J.D. Haney Drums
Lester Square Lead Guitar, Backing Vocals

Produced by Geoff Travis and Mayo Thompson **Artwork by** Bo Zartes

Debut single from Monochrome Set, formed in Hornsey, London 1978. Originally came out of a group called The B-Sides, which also included Stuart Goddard (Adam Ant). Split-up in 1985, reformed in 2011.

X - X
1980 b/w You're Full Of Shit
DROME RECORDS Cleveland, Ohio USA 1979

John D Morton Guitar, Vocals
Andrew Klimek Guitar
James Ellis Bass
Tony Fier Drums

Produced by John D Morton/J. Thompson **Front Cover Photography**
John D Morton **Rear Cover Photography** G. Gilchrist

Formed in Cleveland in 1979 by John Morton who had earlier been in the electric eels. "You could put anything between the X's, like 'Appearing tonight, 'X 'Charles Manson and the Family' X.'" X – X released two singles on Johnny Dromette's local Drome Records.

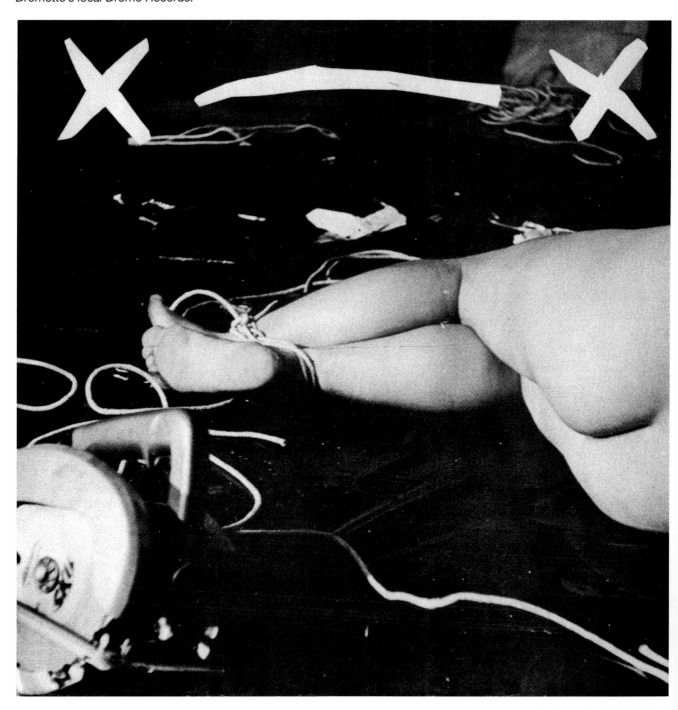

THE SLITS
Typical Girls b/w I Heard It Through The Grapevine

ISLAND RECORDS UK 21 Sep 1979

Ari Up Vocals
Tessa Pollitt Bass
Viv Albertine Guitar
Budgie Drums

Recorded at Basing Street and Ridge Farm Studios
Produced by Dennis Bovell **Photography by** Pennie Smith
Design by Bloomfield/Travis

Formed in London, 1976. Debut single.

THE LEWD

Kill Yourself b/w Pay or Die/Trash Can Baby
SCRATCHED RECORDS
Seattle,Washington USA 1979

Olga De Volga Bass, Vocals
Jon Nay Drums
Brad Ramels Guitar, Vocals
Bobbo Bass

Produced by Clem Fisher

Formed in Seattle in 1978, later moved to San Francisco. Existed 1978-82.

POLICEBAND

Stereo/Mono EP

VACUUM RECORDS New York, USA 1979

Boris Policeband Violin, Electronics, Vocal

Produced by Dike Blair
Front photo by Jonathan Becker
Back photo by Roberto Masotti
Sleeve design by Dike Blair

Boris Policeband's real name was Boris Pearlman.

THE POP GROUP

We Are All Prostitutes b/w Amnesty International Report

ROUGH TRADE UK 9 Nov 1979

Mark Stewart Vocals
Dan Katsis Bass
Tristan Honsinger Cello
John Waddington Guitar
Gareth Sager Guitar, Saxophone
Bruce Smith Percussion

Produced by Dennis Bovell **Artwork by** Rich Beal

The B-side lyrics are taken from a report on British Army torture of Irish prisoners.

```
WE ARE ALL PROSTITUTES


EVERYONE HAS THEIR PRICE
AND YOU TOO WILL LEARN
    TO LIVE THE LIE
AGGRESSION
COMPETITION
AMBITION        CONSUMER FASCISM



CAPITALISM IS THE MOST BARBARIC OF ALL RELIGIONS


DEPARTMENT STORES ARE OUR NEW CATHEDRALS
OUR CARS ARE MARTYRS TO THE CAUSE

WE ARE ALL PROSTITUTES
OUR CHILDREN SHALL RISE UP AGAINST US
BECAUSE WE ARE THE ONES TO BLAME
    WE ARE THE ONES THEY'LL BLAME
THEY WILL GIVE US A NEW NAME
WE SHALL BE


HYPOCRITES    HYPOCRITES    HYPOCRITES



at this moment despair ends and tactics begin.
```

THE LAST GANG
Spirit of Youth b/w Waste It All
GRADUATE RECORDS
Dudley, West Midlands UK Nov 1979

John Ricketts Drums
Rob Shaw Guitar
Mick Homer Bass

Recorded at Rook Studios, Stourport
Produced by David Virr **Photograph by** Dennis

Originally called Stuff Movies. Graduate Records soon after signed another local group UB40, which would sell substantial records. Various members of Last Gang formed Swansway and In Movement after the band split-up.

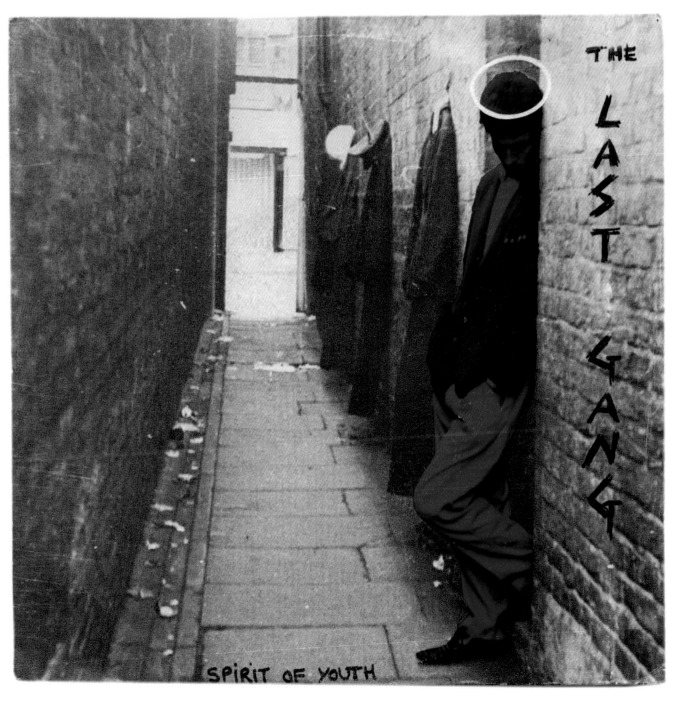

LEGIONAIRES DISEASE BAND

Rather See You Dead (Than With Wool On Your Head b/w Downtown

DISEASE UNLIMITED RECORDS Texas, USA 1979

Jerry Anomie Vocals
David Tolbert Guitar
Gwen Duke Guitar
Norm Cooper Bass
Craig Haynes Drums

Recorded at Magic Rat Studios in 1979

Punk band from Houston, Texas, formed in 1978 by Anomie after returning from the Navy followed by a spell in prison for drug possession. This is the only single released (on their own label) while the group was active. Publicity for the single included Anomie pretending to be dead and lying in a coffin. The single was released again shortly afterwards on the Lunar Lab label.

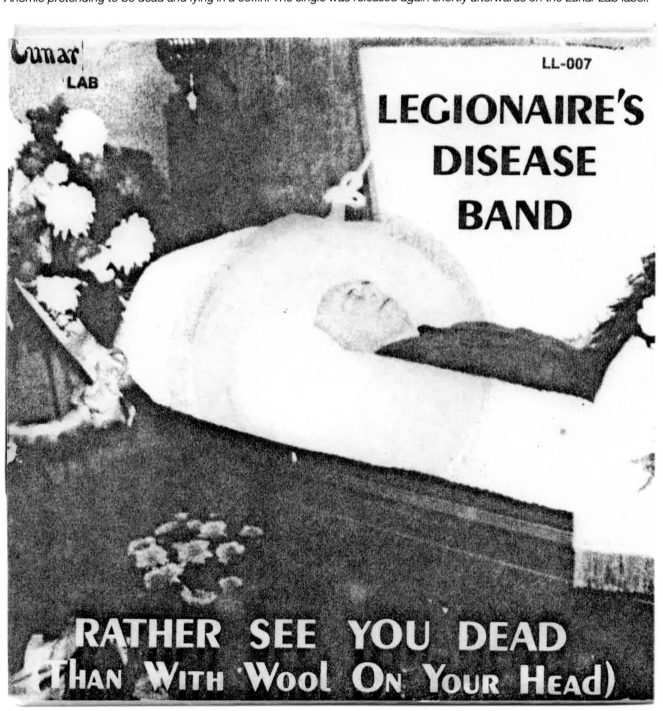

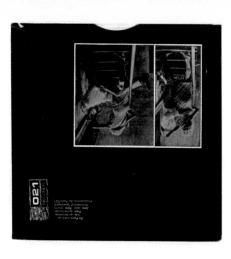

AU PAIRS
You/Domestic Departure/Kerb Crawler
021 RECORDS Birmingham, UK Nov 1979

Lesley Woods Vocals, Guitar
Jane Munro Bass
Pete Hammond Drums
Paul Foad Guitar, Backing Vocals

Recorded at Spaceward Studios, 1979.

Produced by The Au Pairs

Debut single from post-punk group formed in Birmingham, 1978. 021 released material from other Birmingham bands (including Musical Youth's first single!). Also released US group The Bloods' groovy Button Up in the UK.

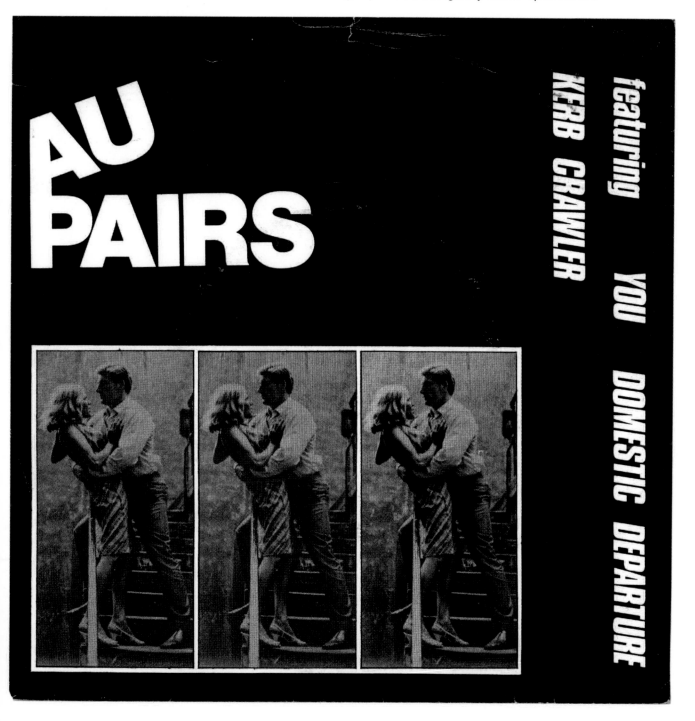

ESSENTIAL LOGIC

Popcorn Boy Waddle Ya Do? b/w Flora Force
ROUGH TRADE/LOGIC RECORDS London UK 1979

Lora Logic Saxophone, Lead Vocals
Mark Turner/Base Bass
Rich Tea Drums
Ashley Buff (Philip Legg) Guitar, Backing Vocals
Dave Wright Saxophone, Backing Vocals

Recorded & mixed at Foel Studios **Produced by** Hugh Jones & Lora Logic
Photography by Paul Tozer **Artwork by** Zut **Graphics**

Band formed in early 1978 by saxophonist Lora Logic, after she left X-Ray Spex. Released one album in 1979. Band split in 1981, reformed 2001. Rich Tea on drums!

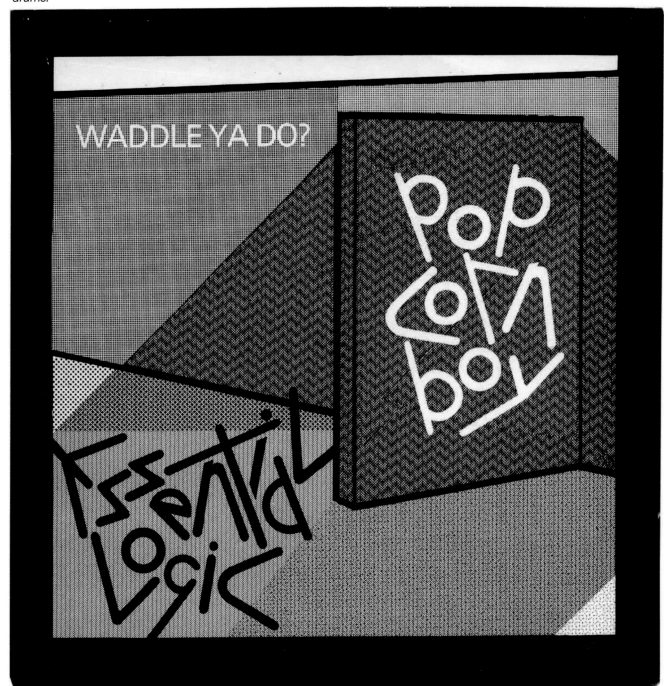

THE FLYING LIZARDS
Money b/w Summertime Blues
VIRGIN RECORDS London UK 13 July 1979

Deborah Evans-Stickland Vocals
David Cunningham Guitar, Piano

Produced by David Cunningham **Photography by** Richard Rayner-Canham

Loose collective of avant-garde musicians under the guidance of David Cunningham remaking pop tunes.

VS276

The Flying Lizards

Money

WAH! HEAT
Better Scream b/w Joe
INEVITABLE MUSIC Liverpool UK 1979

Pete Wylie Guitar, Vocals
Rob Jones Drums
Pete Younger Bass
Colin Redmond Guitar
J.J. Tyler Synthesizer

Artwork by Bob Wakelin and Vic Gelezins

Debut single from Pete Wylie's Wah! Heat released on Pete Fullwell's local Inevitable Music label. The band formed in Liverpool in 1979.

FAD GADGET
Back To Nature b/w The Box
MUTE RECORDS London UK 01 Sep 1979

Fad Gadget All instruments and Voice
Recorded at RMS Studios, London.

Photography by BJ Frost **Design by** Simone Grant

Second ever release on Mute Records following on from Daniel Miller's (as The Normal) own single Warm Leatherette. Fad Gadget was Francis John 'Frank' Tovey.

THE PASSAGE
About Time EP
Taking My Time/Clock Paradox/16 Hours/Time Delay
OBJECT MUSIC Manchester, UK Oct 1979

Dick Witts Percussion
Tony Friel Bass, Guitar, Vocals
Lorraine Hilton Keyboards Vocals, Cello, Drums

Produced by David Cunningham and The Passage
Photography by Kevin Cummins

Manchester post-punk band active between 1978 and 1983. Second single on local label, Object Music, founded by Steve Solamar.

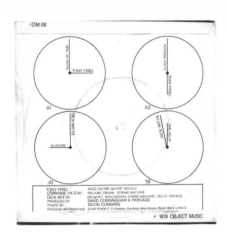

THE FAKES
Production EP
Production/Look-Out/Tony Blackburn/Sylvia Clarke
DEEP CUTS RECORDS Stirling, Scotland 28 Sep 1979

Johnny Vocals
Jamzy Bass
Brian Drums
Mairi Guitar

Recorded at Cargo Studios, Rochdale 1 July 1979
Produced by Deep Cuts and The Fakes **Design by** Laurie Evans

One-off release from group from Sterling, Scotland, formed in late 1977.

Gee Vaucher is the creator of the highly distinctive artwork for Crass, the political group formed in 1977 whose autonomy and do-it-yourself approach became a template that many young bands adopted, avoiding the mainstream music industry.

How was designing record sleeves different from your previous illustrating/ design experience? Not different as far as my personal approach was concerned - I tried to do the best job I could. But illustrating for commercial work, especially in England, was usually both restrictive and unimaginative in terms of what would be acceptable. It was often a balancing trick for me to get work accepted, unless it was a technical illustration of something like the life-cycle of an oyster. That's the sort of job I preferred in the end.

Working in New York was very different. They had much more respect for the illustrator and gave me much more reign, so consequently doing a commercial job was much more fun. Even so, after a couple of years working in New York and trying to push the boundaries, I had to give up, as my work was getting less and less acceptable. Obviously, when you have full control of a situation as I did with Crass, you can do what you like, which was perfect and challenging in every way.

Was there a conscious attempt to pack the sleeve with information in the case of say, Crass's 'You're Already Dead'? Yes, very much so. Image, presentation, word and sound were all of equal importance.

What sort of political ideas were you trying to get across?
I personally - and I think this is true of everyone in the band - wasn't trying to get any political ideas across in terms of follow this, follow that. Our main objective as time went on was to try to get people thinking, asking questions. I include myself in that.

For me, what was important was to be able to share - with young people especially - the understanding that there were other ways of pursuing life to what was being offered by family, school, state, blah de blah, and to realise their own potential.

Was feminism and representing a female point of view also important to you? No, not specifically. What was important to me was that all people have the opportunity to be represented.

I happen to be a woman and I will make myself heard as a woman, but I don't consider myself a feminist. If I have to be an '-ist' of any kind I'd rather be known as a humanist - though even that includes all animals and the earth we inhabit.

How important was the Crass label identity? The grid, the stencilled band name and title, the variations on the flag ...
I liked the idea of a basic foundation that each new cover was built on.

I suppose it was important, as we wanted people to be able to find us easily, to recognise and understand what they would be getting if they bought Crass. A Pandora's box of possibilities.

What is your favourite design?
My hand.

Your Crass sleeves are so successful and unique in the creation of a strong identity for the band. Were there any other bands or designers who you admired or thought also managed to do this? I never really saw other peoples work unless it was put in front of me. As I wasn't an avid collector of pop or punk music I didn't get to see much. The few sleeves I did see seemed well thought out and seemed to compliment word, image and music, but to be honest I can't remember many of them, maybe just the obvious Sex Pistols, Clash and Dead Kennedys.

Do you think the compositional beauty of the sleeves in any way contradicted the anarchism of Crass? i.e. a Crass record is a very well formed 'package' or 'product'. Did any kind of contradictions with consumerism arise from this situation? What a very odd question. Where's the contradiction? Why would you think the idea of a 'well formed 'package' or 'product' lay purely in the domain of commercialism and their methods? Are you saying that anarchism can't produce a well thought out piece of work of great beauty?

What we tried to do as a band was make the most beautiful, informative, inspiring and honest 'product' we could each time. That was also reflected in how we approached each gig. You could say that putting so much into a 'product' in that way was certainly a 'contradiction' to the approach of normal 'products' for the 'consumer'.

Crass has a start and finish date (1984). Does punk also have a start and finish point?
Everything has a start and finish point. Like any movement, punk went in waves. What started off as a business has ended up being a strong worldwide political movement. It takes many shapes - from big politics to small domestic politics, and it takes the widest visual form. These days it feels like the old punk look of mohicans is for the tourists or comes out on special occasions. Fine, but I'm also aware that there are many who have carried the ethos of punk into a much wider arena and have been known to wear suits and uniforms. I like that. We have met so many people that have made their way into the belly of the beast with their punk philosophy and sensitivity intact, and into the most unlikely institutions from the police to midwifery. Great.

CRASS

Nagasaki Nightmare b/w Big A Little A

Crass Records *UK*

Released 1980

Eve Libertine Vocals

Steve Ignorant Vocals

Joy De Vivre Backing Vocals

Pete Wright Bass

Penny Rimbaud Drums, Percussion and Saucepan

Phil Free Guitar

G. Sus Flute

N.A. Palmer Rhythm Guitar and Backing Vocals

Aki Hayashi Voice on Nagasaki Nightmare

Art and design by Crass
*Fold-out poster sleeve containing lyrics,
images and political information.
The first pressing came with a black and
white 'Anti-War' sew-on patch.
Cover article Mike Holderness*

TEENAGE HEAD

Picture My Face b/w Tearin' Me Apart
EPIC Ontario, Canada 1979

Frankie Venom Vocals
Gord Lewis Guitar
Steve Mahon Bass
Nick Stipanitz Drums
Dave Rave Guitar

Back Photos by Rob Sikora **Produced by** Jack Morrow, John Brower.

Group formed in Hamilton, Ontario, 1975. This is their first single. Have gone on to release eight albums.

TEENAGE HEAD

Tearin' Me Apart

Picture My Face

BF 18620 ℗

IC 1421 9/78

bellaphon

SPIZZENERGI

Where's Captain Kirk b/w Amnesia

ROUGH TRADE London UK 15 Dec 1979

Spizz Vocals
Jim Solar Bass
Hero Shima Drums
Scott Guitar
Mark Coalfield Keyboards

Produced by Dave Woods & Spizzenergi **Photography by** Tony Mottram

Formed in 1979 by Kenneth 'Spizz' Spiers, changed their name to Athletico Spizz 80 in January 1980. Then split in 1980 when Spizz, Solar and C.P. Snare signed a major deal under the name The Spizzle. Reformed briefly in 1982 as Spizzenergi2.

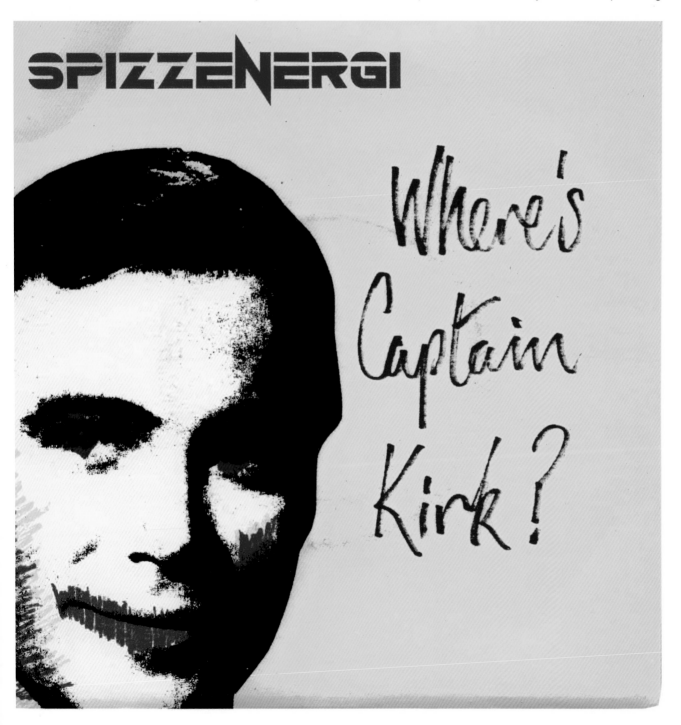

TEENAGE JESUS

Baby Doll b/w The Box

MIGRAINE RECORDS New York, USA 1979

Lydia Lunch Guitars, Vocals
Jim Sclavunos Bass
Bradly Field Drums

Produced by Robert Quine **Sleeve by** J. Gorton

*The no wave/avant-garde Migraine label founded in
New York by Charles Bell.*

TEENAGE JESUS + THE JERKS
LYDIA LUNCH
GUITAR & VOCALS
BRADLY FIELD
DRUM & CYMBAL
JIM SCLAVUNOS
BASS

**FREUD IN FLOP
RACE MIXING**

PRODUCED BY ROBERT QUINE
LUST/UNLUST MUSIC
SLEEVE: J. GORTON

TEENAGE JESUS/BABY DOLL

THE DIALS
All I Hear b/w Running
SCENE RECORDS London UK 1979

Matt Stokes Vocals
Neil Howes Guitar, Vocals
Neil Clarke Sax, Vocals
Jamie Bolster Bass
Jeff Hemsley Drums

Photography and sleeve design by Steve Thrower
Produced by Ranking Tesco and J.M. Carroll

Band from Staines, West London released one single. Band split-up after death of vocalist Stokes. Howes and Helmsley formed Thirteen at Midnight (which my friend Dean Brannagan later joined)..

SCISSOR FITS

Soon After Dark EP
The Government Knows About UFO's/Who Wants To
Live Forever?/Aniseed Trail
TORTCH RECORDS London UK 1979

Nik East Vocals
Vic Watson Guitar, Vocals
Colin Roxborough Guitar
Simon Ives Bass
Pete Garrard Drums

Post-punk from Hounslow, West London, in existence 1978-1979, released
two EPs. Occasional guitarist Mike Always later became head of A&R at
Cherry Red Records.

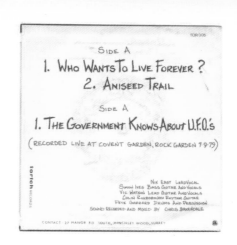

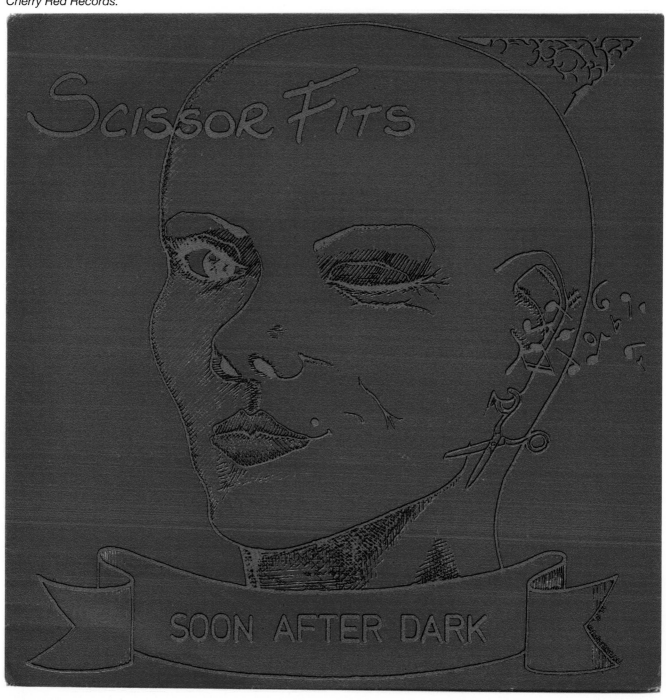

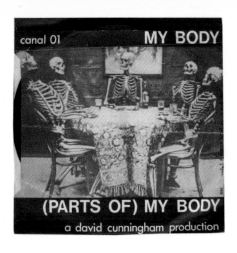

GENERAL STRIKE
My Body b/w (Parts Of) My Body
CANAL RECORDS UK Dec 1979

Steve Beresford Bass, Piano, Horns, Drums
David Toop Tapes, Rhythm tracks, Guitar, Bass
Dawn Roberts Vocals

Produced by David Cunningham

*Experimental group released one single on Canal label and
one cassette album on Touch.*

THE SCABS

The Scabs EP

Amory Building/Leave Me Alone/Don't Just Sit There/U.R.E

CLUBLAND RECORDS Hayes, Middlesex UK 1979

James Young Vocals
John Salmons Guitar, Organ
Steve Pardoe Bass
Simon 'Marcus' Grant Saxophone
Patrick Cunningham Drums

Recorded at Fair Deal Studios, London **Produced by** The Scabs
Artwork by Patrick Cunningham **Pictures by** Nick Harman

One-off EP from band formed in Exeter in 1979. Clubland was the house label of Fair Deal Studios in Hayes, Middlesex.

SCRITTI POLITTI

Work In Progress 2nd Peel Session
Messthetics/Hegemony/Scritlocks Door/OPEC-Immac

ST. PANCRAS/ROUGH TRADE UK 1979

Niall Jinks Bass

Tom Morley Drums

Green Gartside Guitar, Vocals

Produced by John Sparrow and Scritti Politti

Band formed in Leeds in 1977 by Cardiff-born Green Gartside. Third and last release on their own St Pancras label before switching to Rough Trade, four-tracks recorded for John Peel session.

THE RENTALS

I Got A Crush On You B/w New York

RENTAL RECORDS Boston, Massachusetts USA 1979

Jeff Hudson Drums, Guitar
Jane Hudson Bass, Vocals
Pseudo Carol Angel Guitar, Drums, Vocals

Produced by Oedipus **Design by** Babylon Graphics

Formed in 1977 in Boston, The Rentals released their first single 'Gertrude Stein' in 1978 and this single on Rental Records a year later. After moving to New York, they signed to Beggars Banquet Records who reissued this single. The group split in 1980. Jeff and Jane went on to The Manhattan Project, later Jeff and Jane, signing to Lust/Unlust.

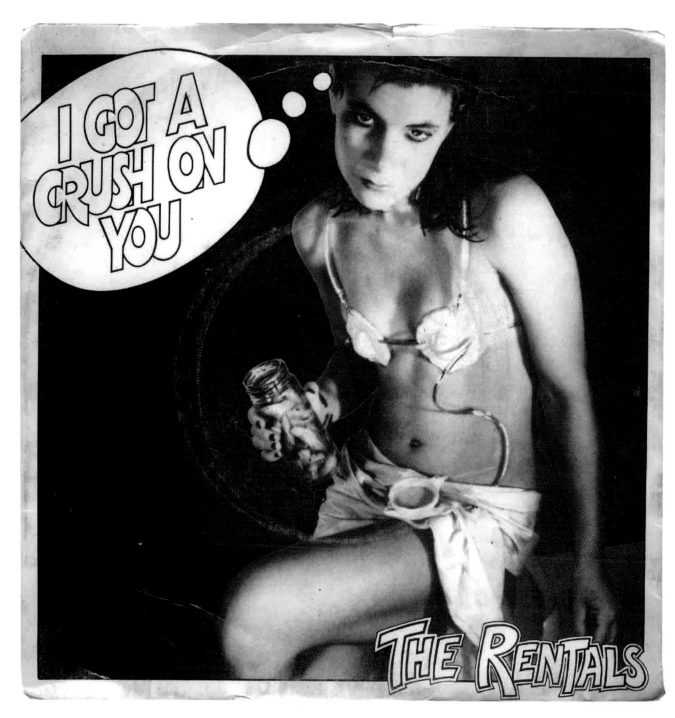

FATAL MICROBES
Violence Grows/Beautiful Pictures/Cry Baby
SMALL WONDER RECORDS London UK May 1979

Honey Bane Vocals
Danny Trickett Guitar
Dave Maltbey Guitar
Derek Hadley Drums

Produced by Richard Famous

Band from Essex, London featuring Honey Bane who recorded two singles on Small Wonder. The original line-up included Pete Fender and Gem Stone who were the children of Vi Subversa, of The Poison Girls – and the two bands shared a first single.

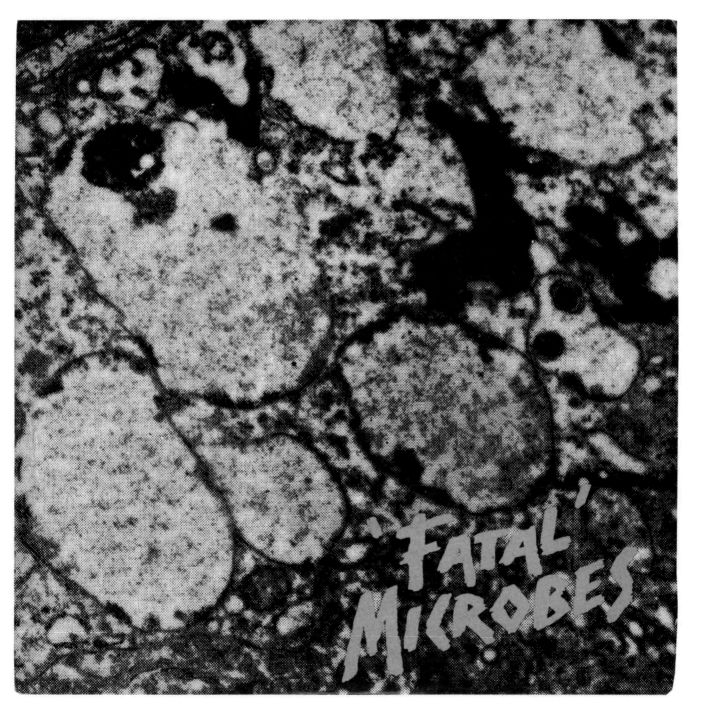

THE TEARDROP EXPLODES

Sleeping Gas b/w Camera Camera /
Kirkby Workers Dream Fades

ZOO RECORDS Liverpool, UK Feb 1979

Michael Finkler Guitar
Paul Simpson Organ
Julian Cope Voice, Bass
Gary Dwyer Drums

Recorded at MCVU 4 track studio 1/12/78
A Chameleons Production

Debut single from the Teardrop Explodes, formed in Liverpool in 1978 by Julian Cope.

THE SPITFIRE BOYS

Funtime B/w Transcendal Changing
IMPECCABLE RECORDS Liverpool, UK 1979

Maggot (Paul Rutherford) Vocals
Blister (Peter Clarke AKA Budgie) Drums
Jones (David Littler) Guitar
Zero (Peter Griffiths) Bass

Formed in Liverpool in 1977, released two singles. Blister better known as Budgie, later joined Slits & The Banshees, and Maggot (Paul Rutherford) became part of Frankie Goes To Hollywood.

CRASH COURSE IN SCIENCE
Cakes In The Home/Kitchen Motors/Mechanical Breakdown
GO GO RECRDS Philadelphia, Pennsylvania USA 1979

Dale Feliciello Vocals
Mallory Yago Keyboards and electronics
Michael Zodorozny Keyboards and electronics

Recorded at Third Story Recording, Philadephia.
Photography by Dale Feliciello **Artwork by** Mallory Yago, Michael Zodorozny

Experimental synthetic post-punk formed in Philadelphia in 1979. Instrumentation included toys and kitchen appliances.

GL*XO BABIES

Christine Keeler b/w Nova Bossanova

HEARTBEAT RECORDS Bristol UK Sep 1979

Rob Chapman Vocals
Melancholy Baby Guitar, Synth Guitar
Tony Wrafter Tenor Saxophone
Slow Death Bass
Charles Llewelyn Drums

Recorded at Crescent Studios, Bath
Produced by Gl*xo Babies & Tim Aylett

*Post-punk band formed in Bristol late 1977. Glaxo Babies are called Gl*xo Babies on this release to avoid legal issues with Glaxo pharmaceutical company.*

PSYKIK VOLTS

Totally Useless b/w Horror Stories No. 5

ELLIE JAY RECORDS London, UK 1979

Nathan Teen Bass
Victor Vendetta Guitar & Vocals
M/J Reed Drums

Design by Nathan Teen

DIY single from band from Dewbury, West Yorkshire formed in 1978. Ellie Jay
was a label run by Lyntone pressing plant that offered facilities to any band
wishing to make a record (you could choose the release to be on Ellie Jay

THE PAGANS
Dead End America b/w Little Black Egg
DROME RECORDS Cleveland, Ohio USA 1979

Michael Hudson Vocals
Tim Allee Bass
Brian Morgan Drums
Tommy Gunn Guitar

Recorded at Styrene Money Studio **Produced by** Johnny Dromette
Photography by Chris Carr **Design by** Dromette

Second single

SEMA 4

Up Down Around EP
Capital City/Talking/Dynamite/Up Down Around
POLLEN RECORDS York, Yorkshire UK Dec 1979

Jock Bass, Lead Vocals
Jeff Drums
Steve Guitar, Vocals

*Punk/neo-mod band from York, made up of members of earlier groups
Cyanide and Stratford Canning. Released two self-made EPs in wraparound
paper sleeves.*

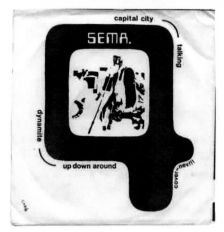

THE TEA SET
Parry Thomas b/w Tri-X Pan
WALDO'S RECORDS Watford UK 1979

Nic Egan Vocals
Ron West Bass
Cally Drums
Nick Haeffner Guitar
Mark Wilkins Keyboards

Post-punk band formed at Watford School of Art, released on Phil Smee's local Waldo Records. Cally also recorded a solo single for the label as Nigel Simpkins. The Tea Set released four singles in total.

KLEENEX

Ü b/w You

ROUGH TRADE London UK 12 May 1979

Regula Sing Vocals
Marlene Marder Guitar
Klaudia Schiff Bass, Vocals
Lislot Ha Drums

Recorded by Kingsway Recorders **Produced by** Kleenex
Design by Peter Fischli

Second single before they became LiliPUT.

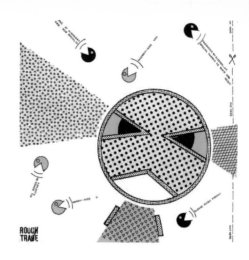

TV PRODUCT/THE PRAMS

Nowhere's Safe/Jumping Off Walls B/w Me/Modern Man
LIMITED EDITION RECORDS Sheffield UK Nov 1979

TV Product Line-Up:
Tony Perrin Bass, Vocals
Jess Jespersen Drums
Simon Hinkler Guitar, Vocals
Recorded at Western Works,
Sheffield **Produced by**
Cabaret Voltaire

The Prams Line-Up:
Caroline Boaden Drums, Percussion
Brian Pearson Guitar, Backing Vocals
John Flanagan Vocals
Simon Ellis Bass, Backing Vocals
Recorded at Cargo Studios, Rochdale
Produced by The Prams

Split-single in folded poster sleeve from two Sheffield groups on Marcus Featherby's Limited Edition Records, a local independent label that released four singles including one by Artery.

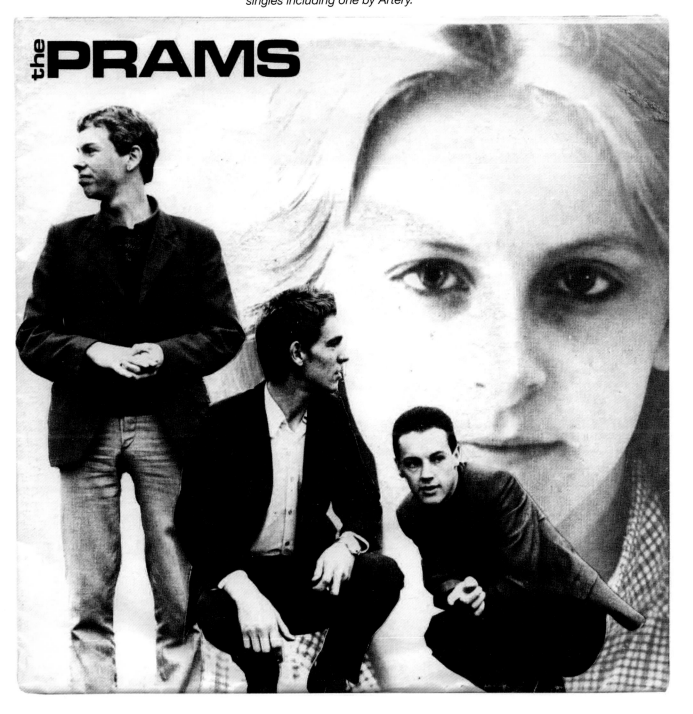

THOSE NAUGHTY LUMPS

Iggy Pop's Jacket B/w Pure and Innocent
ZOO RECORDS Liverpool, UK 1979

P.M. Hart Vocals
Kev Wilkinson Drums
Martin Armadillo (Martin Cooper) Bass, Vocals
Peter 'Kid' Younger Bass
Tony Mitchell Guitar
Gerry Culligan Saxophone

Recorded at MCVU Studio, Dec 1978 **Produced by** Noddy Knowler
Sleeve design by Bill Drummond and Dave Balfe

Formed in Liverpool, summer of 1977.
Released two singles before splitting up in 1980.

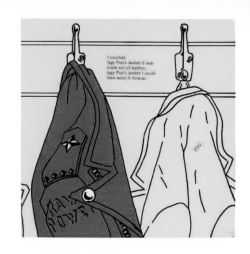

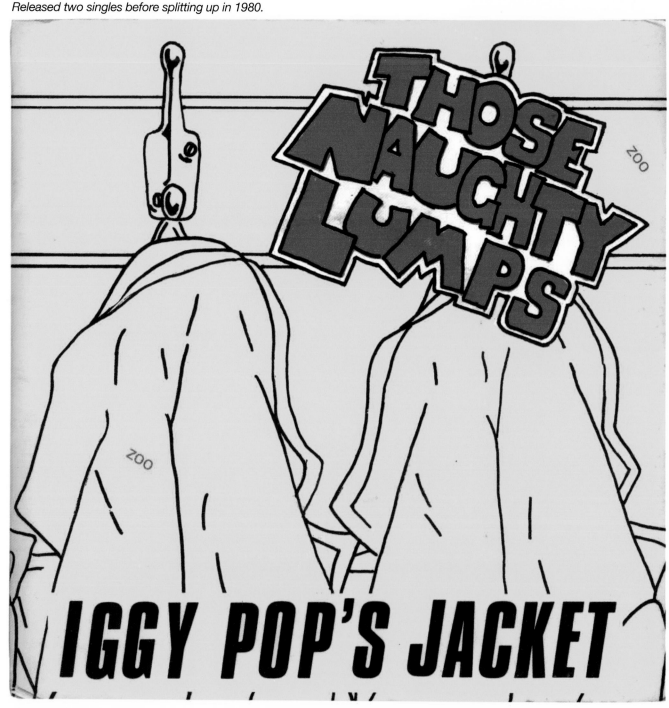

THE SHAPES

Wot's For Lunch Mum? (Not B***s Again!)/College Girls/(I Saw) Batman (In The Launderette)/Chatterboks

SOFA RECORDS Leamington Spa UK 1979

Seymour Bybuss Vocals
Brian Helicopter Bass
Dave Gee Drums
Steve Richards Guitar
Tim Jee Guitar

Produced by John A. Rivers **Artwork by** Chandler and Monsieur Bybuss

Formed in Leamington Spa in early 1977. Started their own Sofa label after briefly and unsuccessfully signing to EMI. Released one further single on Good Vibrations.

THE SHAPES

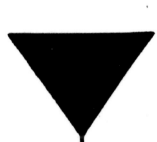

PRODUCED BY · JOHN A RIVERS

SEYMOUR BYBUSS · VOCALS · TIM JEE · GUITAR · STEVE RICHARDS · GUITAR · BRIAN HELICOPTER · BASS · DAVE GEE · DRUMS · INSERT CONCEPT BY MONSIEUR BYBUSS · ART BY CHANDLER · RECORDED AT WMRS LEAMINGTON SPA · ENGINEERED BY J A RIVERS · THE SHAPES ARE A BOOKABLE BAND · PHONE LEAM 25108 · THANKS TO EVERYONE WE LIKE · PRODUCT OF ROYAL LEAMINGTON SPA ·

R.L. CRUTCHFIELD'S DARK DAY
Hands In The Dark b/w Invisible Man
STRIKE IT FROM THE RECORDS
New York USA 1979

Robin Crutchfield Vocals, Piano
Nina Canal Guitar
Nancy Arlen Drums
Produced by Charles Ball
Design by R.L. Crutchfield **Photography by** Jack Zalonga

Dark synthwave formed in New York in 1978 by Robin Crutchfield after he had left the no wave group DNA alongside Nina Canal (Ut) and Nancy Arlen

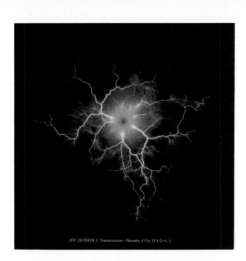

JOY DIVISION
Transmission b/w Novelty
FACTORY RECORDS Manchester, UK October 1979

Ian Curtis Vocals
Bernard Sumner Guitar
Peter Hook Bass
Steve Morris Drums

Produced by Martin Hannett
Design by Peter Saville

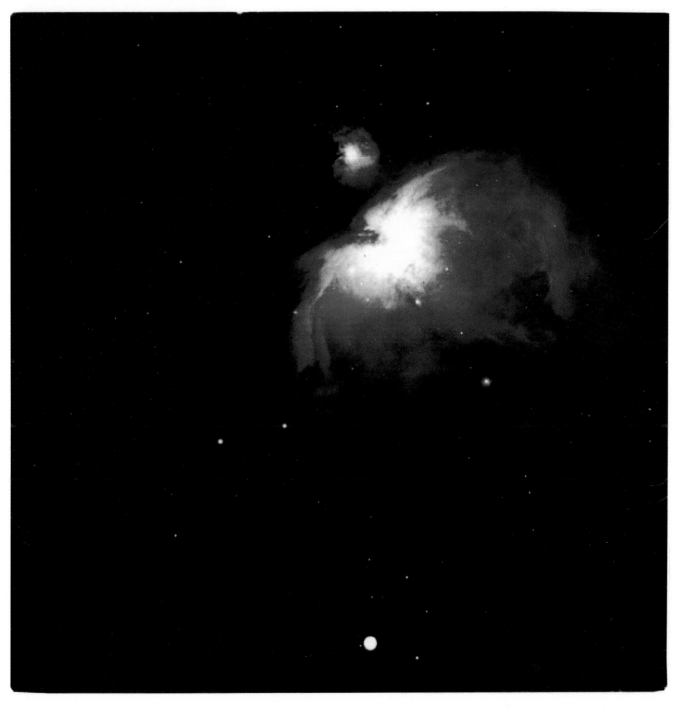

The designs of Peter Saville, graphic designer, art director and partner in Factory Records – and in particular the work he did for Joy Division and New Order – shaped a generation's visual aesthetics.

Jamie Reid's ransom note typography and safety pins defined the most iconic visual identity of punk after the New York drag of The Dolls and the jeans and leather of The Ramones - but Saville's graphic work symbolised everything that came after punk. While both graphic artists share an anarchic attitude to re-appropriation of imagery, Saville subverted industrial and corporate design, and was inspired by early modernist typographers – notably Herbert Bayer and Jan Tschichold – rather than Reid's newspaper headline cut-outs and visual rebellion. Saville explored parallels he found between Herbert Spencer's book Pioneers of Modern Typography and the emerging post-punk/new wave identity of a number of emerging bands, and also his home city.

Peter Saville was born in Hale, a suburb of Manchester, in 1955. At age 19, he began studying graphic design at Manchester Polytechnic alongside fellow designers Malcolm Garrett and Linder Sterling (the latter also founded the post-punk group Ludus). Inspired by both the spirit and energy of punk and a love of visual art, all three set about changing history.

Peter Saville: 'We were filled with the "anyone can do it" attitude of punk, to pick an instrument - whether it was a guitar, or a pen for Paul Morley or Jon Savage, or myself and Malcolm with design. We realised we could be a part of popular culture rather than merely observers.'

Garrett became friends with members of the Buzzcocks while still at college and (after the group's own DIY- designed Spiral Scratch EP) began designing their record sleeves. These began with Orgasm Addict, which featured a memorable feminist illustration by Sterling of a woman with an iron in place of her head. In the hope of finding work for himself, Saville, through a network of acquaintances, began hanging out with the group. On the advice of Richard Boon, the Buzzcocks' manager, he was told to 'go and see Tony Wilson', who was about to start a new music night in the city.

Tony Wilson was known to everyone in Manchester as a presenter on Granada Television. Wilson was from an earlier generation than punk, but felt a connection with the idealist politics of his student days at Cambridge in the late 1960s. Wilson had done much to promote punk on his own Granada music show, So It Goes, which brought bands up to Manchester to play live. These included the Sex Pistols (their first television appearance), Patti Smith, The Clash, The Buzzcocks, The Stranglers and Iggy Pop.

Peter Saville: 'I didn't know Tony before, but this did not bother me. Everyone in Manchester sort of knew Tony from the television. He couldn't walk along the street without people coming up to him constantly and going, "Hello Tony!" So I went to meet him at Granada studios. He told me he was going to put some gigs on, and the night was going to be called Factory. I showed him some design references, principally the Jan Tschichold book I liked, and he agreed to let me design the poster for the opening night.'

The Manchester live music scene had erupted with the arrival of the Sex Pistols to the city. They'd been invited by the Buzzcocks to play at the Lesser Free Trade Hall in June 1976. Nearly everyone who attended the gig subsequently formed a band – including Joy Division, The Fall and The Smiths. But after the media backlash against punk following the Sex Pistols' appearance with Bill Grundy on the Today programme in December 1976, Manchester police clamped down on local music venues that promoted punk music, such as The Electric Circus. This had left a gap in the city's nightlife that Wilson intended to fill with his new night at the Russell Club in Moss Side. Its success led to a series of nights put on by Wilson and co-promoter Alan Erasmus.

Saville graduated in spring of 1978, intending to head down to London. But he prevaricated for six months – an uncertainty which proved decisive to his career, as it was during this time that he designed a series of posters for the Factory nights.

One evening, while Saville was at Erasmus's flat, Wilson noted that none of the bands they were putting on at the Factory nights had record deals. He suggested, 'Why don't we make a record?' Wilson and Erasmus were already managing Durutti Column. Their idea was that any records they made could act as a stepping stone for bands to get future 'proper' record deals.

Wilson had little time to offer in order to start the label due to his television work, but offered to invest £5,000 he had got from his parents. Wilson also offered Saville, in lieu of any payment, a partnership in this new record label. Significantly for Saville, this financial non-reward was sweetened by complete artistic and creative freedom, and he was left free to explore his ideas of graphic experimentation unhindered by consumerist restraints.

A number of other key figures would later also become partners alongside Wilson, Erasmus and Saville: Rob Gretton, Joy Divison/New Order's manager, and Martin Hannett, producer of Joy Division and many other Factory bands. Says Saville: 'Factory was in essence an autonomous collective of non-business heads who didn't really know what being partners meant.'

And thus was born Factory Records. Released on 24 December 1978, A

Factory Sample featured the music of Joy Division, Durutti Column, Cabaret Voltaire and John Dowie. The product was a luxurious package designed by Saville – a double- pack seven-inch single with a sleeve made from rice paper printed silver and sealed inside a thin plastic bag. The package also came complete with a five-sticker set insert.

Saville's stunningly stark and fresh modernist design and typography displayed an interest in European art and design history, and instantly made all other record sleeves look out of date. The template for post-punk had arrived with a mixture of punk spirit and art-school ambition.

As a partner in Factory Records, Saville designed all the first record sleeves for the new venture. The label benefited from the newly established Rough Trade distribution network for independent labels, but Saville's work for Factory was not enough financially for him to live on. He had no expectations that it ever would be. Eventually he felt compelled to leave Manchester in 1979 and headed for London to get a full-time job.

In London, Saville became art director at Dindisc, an offshoot label of Virgin Records, while still designing for Factory. At Dindisc Saville designed sleeves for pop/new wave bands such as Orchestral Manoeuvres in the Dark (whom he had already worked with at Factory) and Martha and the Muffins, and also created freelance designs for Ultravox, Roxy Music and even Wham!.

Saville's work became highly in demand in the industry, but it is the sleeves of Joy Division and New Order which were most influential.

Saville recalls making the cover for Joy Division's Unknown Pleasures: 'I had laid out the sleeve for the album before the record was cut. The band had given me a wave image from the Cambridge Encyclopedia of Astronomy and I had done the design. I knew that I did not want the name of the band on the front, believing that anyone who wanted this record would find it. I felt as soon as you put a band's name on the front it made it seem like any other record.' This uncommercial freedom for Saville only existed at Factory Records.

'When I told Rob Gretton [Joy Division's manager] I had finished, he said, "Peter, I've just got test pressings of the album back. Do you want to come and hear it?" And I remember thinking, Oh, God. Do I really want to go and listen to a whole album of their music?

'But within 30 seconds I was transfixed. I knew this was one of the great records of the new wave. The record was extraordinary, and what Martin Hannett had done was also extraordinary - I realised that in those 40 minutes. And I knew I had been given the opportunity to work on a truly great record.'

By the time of Joy Division's second album, Closer, Saville had moved to London. The band were recording nearby at Britannia Row Studios in Islington, and they came to see him. The group asked Saville if he had any ideas for their new album and so Saville showed them some photographs

he had recently seen and liked in Zoom, a photography magazine.

The band flicked through the magazine and together chose one picture that they liked - a photograph by Bernard Pierre Wolff of the Appiani family tomb in the Cimitero Monumentale di Staglieno in Genoa, Italy.

Barely a month later, singer Ian Curtis had taken his own life. Saville had already completed his design, and the album was released the following month.

As the essentially leaderless New Order rose from of Joy Division's ashes, Saville continued to design the group's sleeves. He was free to continue pushing the limits of design, disregarding traditional boundaries of high art and popular art and exploring new technologies alongside art history. Saville created a body of work that was to influence a generation.

The design agency Peter Saville Associates –was essentially just the name for Saville's studio in the 1980s. Saville became conscious that his style was being appropriated by major record companies to sell sometimes inferior product. A similar tactic was being employed by big business, which led many people to distrust design. Saville notes with bitter humour the influence of his work on the modernist design of Midland Bank's telephone-based retail bank, First Direct, launched in 1989.

By the 1990s a new generation had grown up inspired by Saville's early work for Factory Records, and he began working with bands such as Suede and Pulp. Saville also consulted for companies such as Selfridges, EMI and Pringle and took on commissions and collaborations within the world of fashion. These included John Galliano at Dior, Yohji Yamamoto and Alexander McQueen.

In 2003, the Design Museum in London assembled The Peter Saville Show. A 'Peter Saville Show Soundtrack.'A CD recorded by New Order was made available to early visitors to the exhibition.

The following year Saville also became (and remains) creative director of the City of Manchester, responsible for the municipal identity of the city, a role he cherishes both in terms of bringing design into the everyday and in shaping the identity of Manchester in a way that Factory Records did a generation earlier. Tony Wilson would have been proud.

1980 PUNK 45s

THE URINALS

Sex b/w Go Away Girl

HAPPY SQUID Los Angeles, California USA 1980

Kevin Barrett Toy drums
Kjehl Johansen Guitar
John Jones Bass

Produced by Vitus Matare
Illustration Carey Southall

Both songs are on Side A. Side B consists of a series of five reference tones.

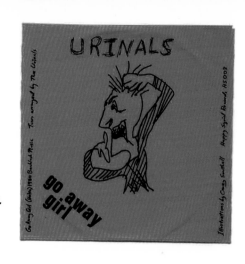

BAD BRAINS

Pay to Come b/w Stay Close to Me
BAD BRAINS RECORDS
Oxon Hill, Maryland USA June 1980

Darryl Jenifer Bass
Earl Hudson Drums
Dr. Know Guitar
H.R. Lead Vocals

Recorded December 1979 At Dots Studio, New York.
Produced by Jimmi Quidd **Photography by** Charles Davis and Paul Bishow

Hardcore punk band formed in Washington, D.C., in 1977.

X

White Girl b/w Your Phone's Off The Hook (But You're Not)
SLASH RECORDS

Los Angeles, California USA 1980

John Doe Bass, Vocals
D.J. Bonebrake Drums
Billy Zoom Guitar
Exene Vocals

Produced by Ray Manzarek
Front Cover by Tim Norman **Back Cover by** Michael Hyatt

First single after the group switched to Slash Records, produced by The Doors' Ray Manzarek.

SNAKEFINGER

The Model b/w Talkin' In The Town

RALPH RECORDS

San Francisco, California USA March 1980

Philip Charles Lithman (Snakefinger) All instruments

Produced by The Residents and Snakefinger

Art direction by Porno Graphics **Cover Illustration** Craig Gockley

Long term Residents collaborator does Kraftwerk, released on The Residents' label.

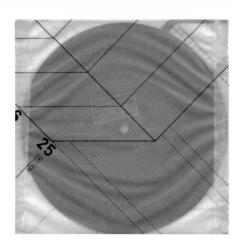

SECTION 25

Girls Don't Count b/w Knew Noise b/w Up To You
FACTORY RECORDS Manchester, UK July 1980

Larry Cassidy Bass, Vocals
Vince Cassidy Drums
Paul Wiggin Guitar

A Fractured Production (Ian Curtis and Rob Gretton)
Design by Saville Associates (Peter Saville) and Ben Kelly

Their first single from group formed in Blackpool, Lancashire in 1978.
Sleeve is printed on tracing paper.

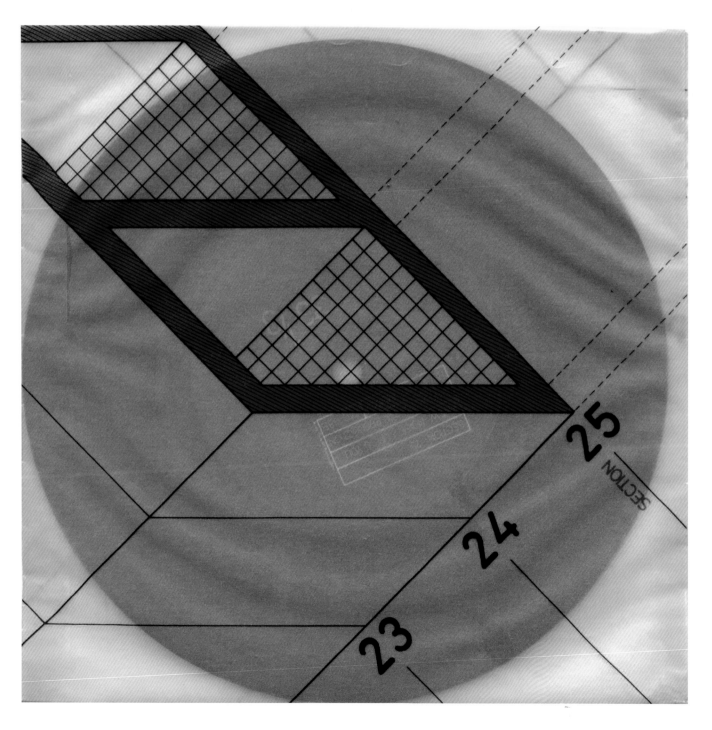

X - X

No Nonsense b/w
Approaching The Minimal With Spray Guns
DROME Cleveland, Ohio USA 1980

John D Morton Guitar, Vocals
Andrew Klimek Guitar
James Ellis Bass
Tony Fier Drums

Produced by John D Morton and Johnny Dromette
Artwork John D Morton **Photo** C. Gilchrist

CABARET VOLTAIRE
Seconds Too Late b/w Control Addict
ROUGH TRADE London, UK 1980

Richard H. Kirk Guitar, Voice
Chris Watson Electronics, Tape, Voice
Stephen Mallinder Bass, Voice

Produced by CV and Geoff Travis

AGENT ORANGE

Bloodstains b/w America/Bored of You

AGENT ORANGE RECORDS California, USA 1980

James Levesque Bass, Vocals

Mike Palm Guitar, Vocals

Scott Miller Drums

Produced by Daniel Van Patten

Debut single from Orange County, California surf punk band formed in 1979.

THE PRATS
Disco Pope/Nothing/TV Set/Nobody Noticed
ROUGH TRADE London, UK 1980

Greg Maguire Guitar, vocals
Jeff Maguire Bass, vocals
Dave Maguire Drums
Recorded at Mike's Studio Complex, Edinburgh.
Produced by Nobby Clarke and The Prats.

Formed in late 1977 in Edinburgh by two brothers Dave and Greg and later joined by their older brother Jeff. They were between the ages of 12 and 15 when they started the group.

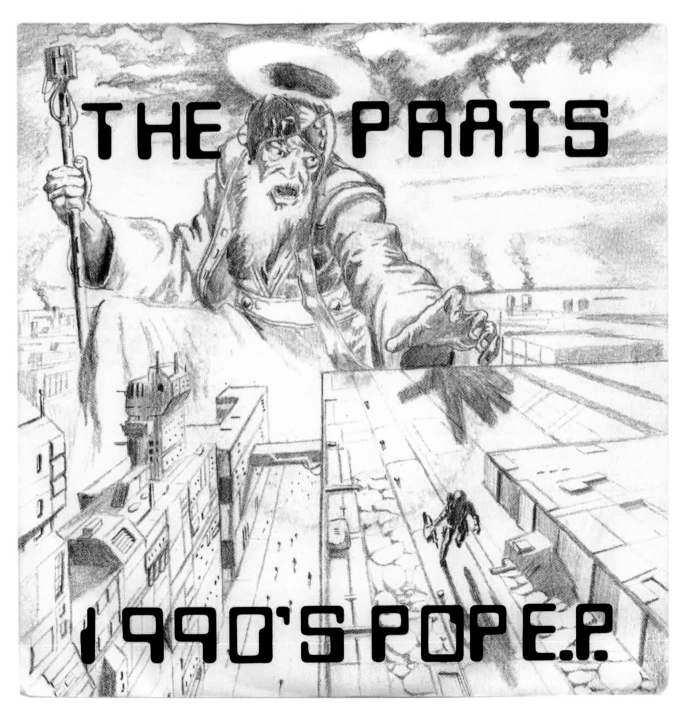

JOSEF K

Radio Drill Time b/w Crazy To Exist (Live)

POSTCARD RECORDS *Glasgow, Scotland* August 1980

Paul Haig Guitar and Vocals
Malcolm Ross Guitar, Violin
David Weddell Bass
Ronnie Torrance Drums

Produced by Josef K **Design by** Barbara Hale

Scottish post-punk band formed in 1979, originally called TV Art. Postcard Records was founded by Alan Horne and Steven Daly the same year with Josef K, Orange Juice and Aztec Camera all signed to the label. Closed in 1981 after the departure of Orange Juice and Aztec Camera to majors. Josef K split-up in 1982 after two albums when Paul Haig began solo career.

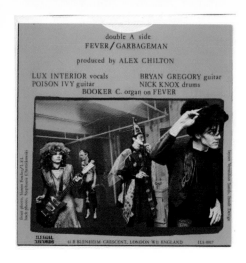

THE CRAMPS
Fever b/w Garbageman
ILLEGAL RECORDS UK 1980

Lux Interior Vocals
Poison Ivy Guitar
Bryan Gregory Guitar
Nick Knox Drums
Booker C Organ

Layout by Vermillion Sands **Photography by** Stephanie Chernikowski,
L.F.I. and Simon Fowler **Produced by** Alex Chilton

A CERTAIN RATIO

Shack Up b/w And Then Again

FACTORY BENELUX/LES DISQUES DU CREPUSCLE Belgium Aug 1980

Simon Topping Vocals, Trumpet
Jez Kerr Bass
Martin Moscrop Guitar, Trumpet
Peter Terrel Guitar, Effects
Donald Johnson Drums

Design by Benoît Hennebert

This is their second seven-inch single – a Belgium-only release from the Factory-connected Les Disques du Crepuscle. Cover of Banbarra funk rock track.

THE VAINS
School Jerks/The Loser/The Fake
NO THREES RECORDS
Seattle, Washington USA 1980

Chris Crass Utting Guitar, Vocals
Duff McKagen (Nico Teen) Bass, Vocals
Andy Freeze (Andy Fortier) Drums

15-year old bassist McKagan (as Nico Teen) formed the punk band the Vains in Seattle in 1979, releasing this one single. In 1985 McKagan joined Guns 'n' Roses. Seattle-based No Three Records also released music by The Accident, The Cheaters, The Fast Bucks, Pure Joy and the Silly Killers.

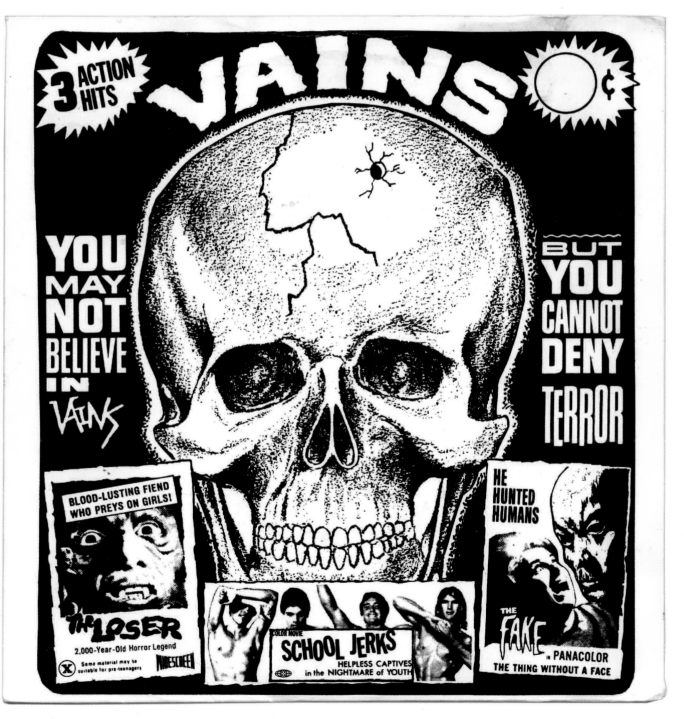

THE POP GROUP
Where There's A Will
Y/ROUGH TRADE London, UK 1980

Mark Stewart Vocals
Gareth Sager Guitar
Simon Underwood Bass
John Waddington Guitar
Bruce Smith Drums

Recorded at Foel Studios **Produced by** Dave Anderson and The Pop Group

Shared single with The Slits (who also shared label, drummer and manager with The Pop Group at the time). First release on Dick O'Dell's Y Records which would later release Pigbag, Maximum Joy, Shriekback, Pulsallama and other post-punk/dance artists.

THE SLITS

In The Beginning There Was Rhythm

Y/ROUGH TRADE London, UK 1980

Ari Up Vocals
Tessa Pollitt Bass
Viv Albertine Guitar
Bruce Smith Drums

Recorded at Foel Studios **Produced by** Dennis Bovell and The Slits

REALLY RED

Modern Needs b/w White Lies

CIA RECORDS Houston, Texas USA 1980

Ronald U-Ron Bond Vocals
John Paul Williams Bass
Robert N.M.N. Weber Drums
Kelly Younger Guitar

Recorded at MRS, Houston. **Produced by** Really Red
Photography by Doug Mattice

*First generation punk/hardcore bands from Houston, Texas, existed
from 1978-85. Made two albums and four singles on CIA Records,
their own label.*

WHITE LIES

WRITTEN, PERFORMED AND PRODUCED	REALLY RED
RECORDED AT	M.R.S. HOUSTON
ENGINEER	BOBBY GINSBURG
PHOTOGRAPHY	DOUG MATTICE
GRAPHICS AND PRINTING	RANDOM STUDIO U.S.A.
HAIR	WAVELENGTH
CLOTHES	SALVATION ARMY

We would like to thank everyone else who helped us with this record but we couldn't think of anyone.

CIA002

REALLY RED

MODERN NEEDS

ORANGE JUICE
Simply Thrilled Honey b/w Breakfast Time
POSTCARD RECORDS
Glasgow, SCOTLAND Nov 1980

Edwyn Collins Guitar, Vocals
David McClymount Bass, Backing Vocals
Steven Daly Drums, Backing Vocals
James Kirk Guitar

Produced by Malcolm Ross and Orange Juice

Scottish post-punk band formed in Glasgow as the Nu-Sonics in 1976. First releases on Alan Horne's Postcard Records, switched to Polydor in 1981. Split-up in 1984.

THROBBING GRISTLE
Adrenalin b/w Distant Dreams (Part Two)
INDUSTRIAL RECORDS London, UK *23 Oct* 1980

Genesis P-Orridge Vocals
Peter 'Sleazy' Christopherson Synthesizer
Cosey Fanni Tutti Guitar
Chris Carter Synthesizer

Issued in polythene camouflage bag. Formed in 1975 Throbbing Gristle came out of performance art group COUM Transmissions. The confrontational, industrial and avant-garde group debuted in 1976. Industrial Records was set up by the group to release their own and related music.

THE MANIC DEPRESSIVES

Going Out With The In-Crowd/Silence On The Radio/
You Know Where You're Gonna Go

VINYL SOLUTION RECORDS New Orleans, Louisiana, USA 1980

Mandeville Mike Vocals
L The P Bass
Charlie Bouis Drums
Mike C Guitar

Recorded at B.B. Studio, Belle Chasse, LA **Photography by** Fish **Producer by** L The P

New Orleans punk band that existed1979-81, started by Larry Holmes (L The P) who also ran the Vinyl Solution Records label. Beginning in 1979, Vinyl Solution released singles by early New Orleans punk bands Red Rockers, Shell Shock, Toxin III as well as The Manic Depressives sole single.

GIRLS AT OUR BEST

Getting Nowhere Fast b/w Warm Girls
RECORD RECORDS Leeds, UK 1980

Judy Evans Vocals
Chris Oldroyd Drums
Gerard Swift Bass
James Alan Guitar

Post-punk band formed in Leeds in 1979. Originally known as The Butterflies. Released one album and four singles, split 1982.

NUCLEAR SOCKETTS
Honour Before Glory EP
SUBVERSIVE RECORDS Norfolk, UK 1980

Kes Vocals
Mark Guitar, Backing Vocals, Synthesizer
Brett Bass
Phil Drums

Recorded at UMK Studios

Formed in King's Lynn, Norfolk in 1979. Released just two singles, split in 1983. 'West Norfolk's Finest'!

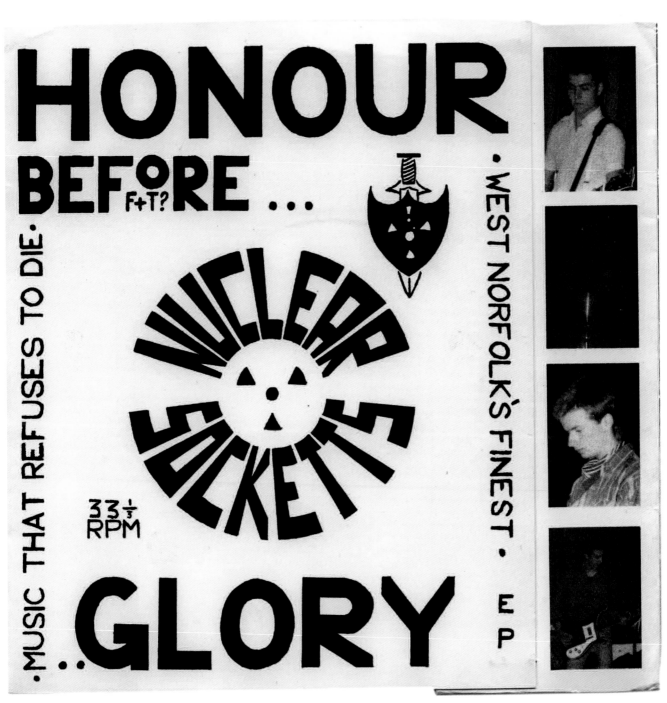

THE FLATBACKERS

Pumping Iron b/w Kid From Kidbrooke

RED SHADOW RECORDS London, UK 1980

Lucy Dray Bass, Vocals
Julie Usher Guitar, Vocals
Lyn Monk Drums

Produced by Andy Arthurs

All-female group formed in South London, 1978, released three singles.
Split-up in 1981.

RECORD ONE

A.Unbalanced
1.The Slide

produced by Steve Hopkins
recorded at Graveyard Studio, Manchester

RECORD TWO

1.Perhaps
2.Turtle
3.Toytown
4.Heinz

recorded live at Rotherham Arts Centre by INPUT-February '80

ARTERY info: 107 Whitham Road, Sheffield S10 2SL

STEEL 3

ARTERY

Unbalanced/The Slide EP

AARDVARCK RECORDS Sheffield, UK 1980

Mark Gouldthorpe Vocals, Harmonica, Guitar
Neil McKenzie Bass
Garry Wilson Drums, Vocals
Simon Hinkler Keyboards, Backing Vocals
Michael Fidler Saxophone, Guitar, Vocals

Produced by Artery/Steve Hopkins **Photography by** Marcus Featherby, Peter Bargh

Two-pack seven-inch single release with gatefold sleeve. Post-punk/art punk band formed in Sheffield in 1978 (originally known as just The) and went on to release three studio albums. Split in 1985, since reformed.

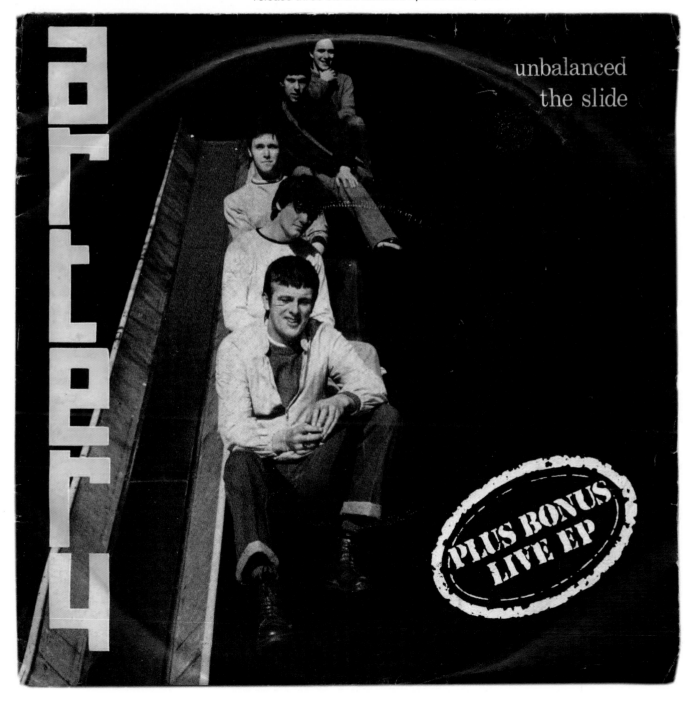

unbalanced
the slide

PLUS BONUS LIVE EP

DISCHARGE

Realities Of War/They Declare It/But After The Gig/Society's Victim

CLAY RECORDS Stoke-on-Trent, Staffordshire UK 1980

Kelvin 'Cal' Morris Vocals
Tony 'Bones' Roberts Guitar
Terry 'Tezz' Roberts Drums
Roy 'Rainy' Wainright Bass

Recorded at Redball Studios. **Produced by** Mike Stone
Sleeve Design by Martin H.

*Hardcore band formed in Stoke-on-Trent in 1977. Mike Stone founded Clay Records in 1980 out of a local record shop.
The label signed other hardcore bands such as GBH and released music by Sex Gang Children, Demon and The Lurkers.*

JILL KROESEN
I Really Want To Bomb You b/w Jesus Song
INFIDELITY Records New York, USA 1980

J. Kroesen Vocals, Piano, Organ
Fred Smith Bass
Arthur Russell Cello
Tony Machine Drums
Peter Gordon Keyboards, Reeds

Recorded at Sundragon & Right Track, NYC. **Producer by** Jay Burnett and Peter Gordon **Photography by** Gary Green, Gerrit Van Der Meer, Nathaniel Tileston **Design by** Jill Kroesen

No wave performance artist Kroesen with Arthur Russell on cello.

YOUNG MARBLE GIANTS

Final Day EP
Final Day/Radio Silents/Cakewalking/Untitled
ROUGH TRADE London, UK 1980

Alison Statton Vocals
Philip Moxham Bass
Stuart Moxham Guitar, Organ

Recorded at Foel Studio

*Debut single from post-punk group formed in Cardiff, Wales in 1978.
Statton later went on to form Weekend.*

FIRE ENGINES

Get Up And Use Me b/w Everything's Roses
CODEX COMMUNICATIONS
Edinburgh, Scotland 1980

David Henderson Vocals, Guitar
Murray Slade Guitar
Graham Main Bass
Russell Burn Drums

Produced by Wilf Smarties

Post-punk band from Edinburgh formed in 1979. This is their debut single recorded for £46. Shortly afterwards signed to Fast Products off-shoot label Pop Aural for one album and two singles. Split-up at the end of 1981.

THE NEWTOWN NEUROTICS

When The Oil Runs Out b/w Oh No

NO WONDER RECORDS Harlow, Essex UK 1980

Colin Masters Bass, Backing Vocals
Tig Barber Drums, Backing Vocals
Steve Drewett Guitar, Vocals

Recorded at Village Way Studio
Photography and artwork by Tony Mottram

Formed in Harlow, London 1979. Became the Neurotics after 1986, split-up in 1988 after five albums.

GLAXO BABIES

Limited Entertainment/Dahij b/w There'll Be No Room
For You In The Shelter/Permission To Be Wrong
Y RECORDS London, UK 20 June 1980

Tom Nichols Bass
Charlie Llewelyn Drums
Dan Catsis Guitar
Tim Aylett
Produced by Glaxo Babies and John Etchells

*By the time of this release the band had already split-up. Tony Wrafter, Dan
Catsis and Charlie Llewellin found Maximum Joy with Janine Rainforth. Tracks
from a John Peel Session recorded on 19th February 1980*

THE BUSH TETRAS

Too Many Creeps b/w
Snakes Crawl/You Taste Like The Tropics
99 RECORDS *New York, USA* 1980

Cynthia Sley Vocals
Laura Kennedy Bass
Dee Pop Drums
Pat Place Guitar

Co-produced by Donny Christensen and Ed Bahlman **Photography by** Brian Randall and Pat Place **Artwork by** Judy Steccone and Laura Kennedy

Ed Bahlman's 99 Records remains perhaps the definitive New York no wave/post-punk/dance label, with releases including Bush Tetras, ESG and Liquid Liquid.

THOSE INTRINSIC INTELLECTUALS
Radio Iceland b/w Do The Executive
FAULT LINE RECORDS *Inverness, Scotland* 1980

Rory Black Vocals
Gregor Morgan Bass
John Godsman Drums
Njal MacDonald Guitar
Recorded at Noel Eadie Sound Services, Tong Studio, Isle Of Lewis, Scotland. **Produced in** the Western Isles. **Photography by** Lex MacVanish

Scottish post-punk band from Inverness, released this one single on their own Fault Line label.

THOSE HELICOPTERS

Shark b/w Eskimo

STATE OF THE ART RECORDS UK 1980

Alan Robinson Vocals
Harlan Cockburn Guitar, Saxophone
Vince Whitlock Keyboards, Vocals
Steve Maughan Bass, Vocals
Andy Barnden Drums, Vocals

Recorded at Underhill Studios, New Cross
Produced by Harlan Cockburn **Design by** Andy McInnes

Post-punk group formed in Maidstone, Kent, released three independent singles.

shark/eskimo

Those Helicopters are:—

Harlan Cockburn....guitar, sax.
Steve Maughan......bass, vocals.
Alan Robinson......vocals.
Vince Whitlock.....keyboards, vocals
Andy Barnden......drums, vocals

produced by Harlan Cockburn
recorded and mixed at Underhill Studios, New Cross
sleeve design and artwork...Andy McInnes
thanks to Terry Medhurst and Nigel Barker
State of the Art Records, 2/45 Earls Court Sq. London S.W.5
enquiries : 0483 76853

State 000001

LILIPUT
Eisiger Wind b/w
When The Cat's Away Then The Mice Will Play
OFF COURSE RECORDS Switzerland 1980

Klau Schiff Bass, Accordion, Vocals
Chrigel Freund Drums, Vocals
Marlene Marder Guitar, Vocals

Produced by Liliput Photos Katja Becker **Design** Fischli/Wittwer

The renamed Kleenex.

REC, SUNRISE STUDIO KIRCHBERG, FOTOS: KATJA BECKER, COVER: FISCHLI/WITTWER, RT 062 ROUGH TRADE RECORDS, 137 BLENHEIM CRESCENT, LONDON W 11

JOY DIVISION

Love Will Tear Us Apart b/w
These Days/Love Will Tear Us Apart
FACTORY RECORDS *Manchester, UK* June 1980

Ian Curtis Vocals
Bernard Sumner Guitar
Peter Hook Bass
Stephen Morris Drums

Produced by Joy Division and Martin Hannett
Photography by Trevor Key **Design by** Peter Saville and Ben Kelly

This single came out one month after the suicide of Ian Curtis.

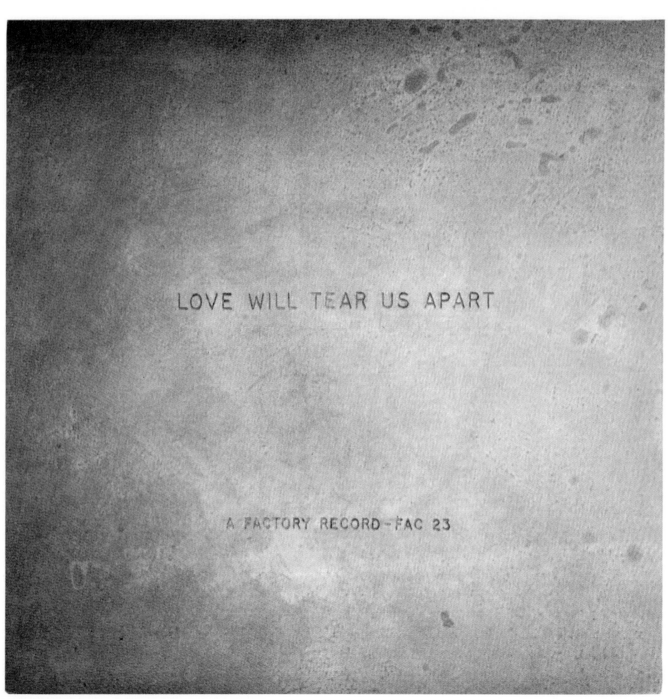

LOVE WILL TEAR US APART

A FACTORY RECORD - FAC 23

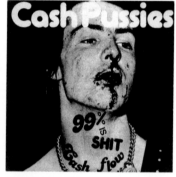

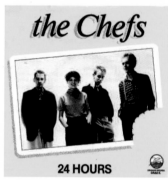
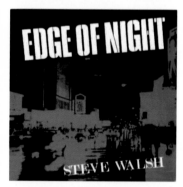

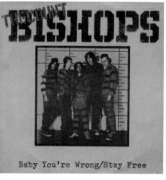

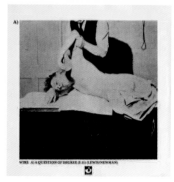

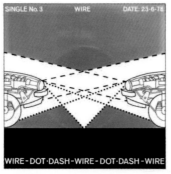

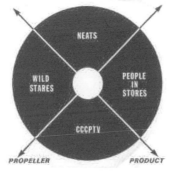

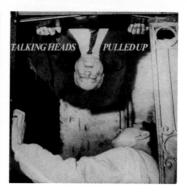

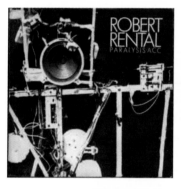

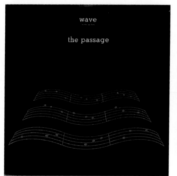

INFLATABLE BOY CLAMS

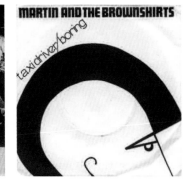

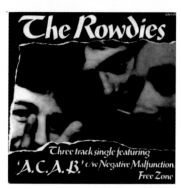

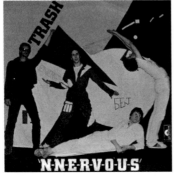

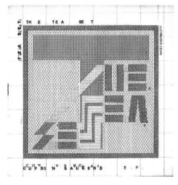

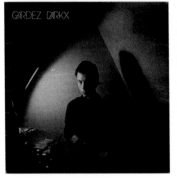
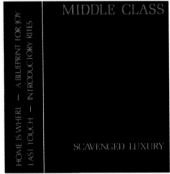

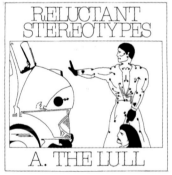
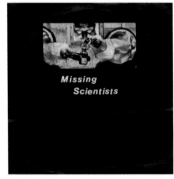

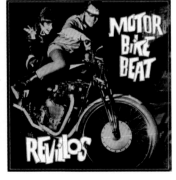

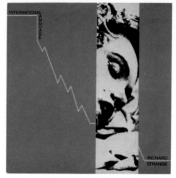